THE MULTILINGUAL MIND

Issues Discussed by, for, and about People Living with Many Languages

Edited by
Tracey Tokuhama-Espinosa

PRAEGER

Library of Congress Cataloging-in-Publication Data

The multilingual mind : issues discussed by, for, and about people living with many languages / edited by Tracey Tokuhama-Espinosa.
    p. cm.
  Includes bibliographical references and index.
    ISBN 0-89789-918-0 (alk. paper) — ISBN 0-89789-919-9 (pbk. : alk. paper)
    1. Multilingualism. 2. Bilingualism. 3. Language and education. 4. Language and languages—Study and teaching. 5. Sociolinguistics. I. Tokuhama-Espinosa, Tracey, 1963–

P115.M85 2003
404'.2—dc21   2002070874

British Library Cataloguing in Publication Data is available.

Library of Congress Catalog Card Number: 2002070874
ISBN: 0-89789-918-0
    0-89789-919-9 (pbk.)

First published in 2003

Praeger Publishers, 88 Post Road West, Westport, CT 06881
An imprint of Greenwood Publishing Group, Inc.
www.praeger.com

Printed in the United States of America

∞™

The paper used in this book complies with the Permanent Paper Standard issued by the National Information Standards Organization (Z39.48-1984).

10 9 8 7 6 5 4 3 2 1

Copyright Acknowledgment

The editor and publisher gratefully acknowledge permission to use excerpts reprinted from Asher et al ed, *The Encyclopedia of Language and Linguistics*, Vol. 1, François Grosjean, "Individual Bilingualism," pp. 1656–1660, copyright 1994, with permission of Elsevier Science.

Contents

Tables and Figures

Preface
Individual Bilingualism

I first read François Grosjean's *Life With Two Languages: An Introduction to Bilingualism* (1982) as a university student, and I have followed his research ever since. This book, one of the very first accounts by an individual presenting his own perceptions as a speaker of more than one language, opened the door of research into individual bilingualism and has been a catalyst of new insights into the multilingual mind. It is with the greatest humility and respect that I include this passage from his work here, with his permission.

François Grosjean is currently a professor of psycholinguistics and director of the Language and Speech Processing Laboratory at Neuchâtel University in Switzerland. In addition to his teaching and research activities, he is coeditor of *Bilingualism: Language and Cognition* (Cambridge University Press).

The following extracts are from his entry titled "Individual Bilingualism," which appeared in *The Encyclopedia of Language and Linguistics* (Oxford: Pergamon Press, 1994) and in B. Spolsky (ed.), *Concise Encyclopedia of Educational Linguistics* (Oxford: Elsevier, 1999).

Few areas of linguistics are surrounded by as many misconceptions as is bilingualism. Most people think that bilingualism is a rare phenomenon found only in such countries as Canada, Switzerland and Belgium and that bilinguals have equal speaking and writing fluency in their languages, have accentless speech and can interpret and translate without any prior training. The reality is in fact quite different: bilingualism is present in practically every country of the world, in all classes of society and in all age groups; in fact, it has been estimated that half the world's population is bilingual. As for bilinguals themselves, the majority acquired their languages at various times during their lives and are rarely equally fluent in them; many speak one of their languages less well than the other (and often with an accent) and many can only read or write one of the languages they speak. . . . (1994: 1656–1660)

As François Grosjean points out, it is estimated that at least half of the world is bilingual, indicating that this is not a strange or rare phenomenon, but rather much more common than many of us would have suspected. However, while speaking more than one language may be the norm in the world, Grosjean emphasizes that multiliteracy skills are an exception; indeed, as Andrew Ellis points out in *Reading, Writing and Dyslexia: A Cognitive Analysis* (Hillsdale, NJ: Lawrence Erlbaum Associates, 1993), literacy skills in even one language are not yet the norm.

Although a few researchers have defined bilinguals as those who have native-like control of two or more languages, most others agree that this position is not realistic. If one were to count as bilingual only those people who pass as monolinguals in each of their languages, one would be left with no label for the vast majority of people who use two or more languages regularly but who do not have native-like fluency in each. This has led researchers to propose other definitions of bilingualism, such as: the ability to produce meaningful utterances in two (or more) languages, the command of at least one language skill (reading, writing, speaking, listening) in another language, the alternate use of several languages, etc. For our purposes, we will call bilingual those people who use two (or more) languages (or dialects) in their everyday lives. Thus, our definition includes people ranging from the migrant worker who speaks with some difficulty the host country's language with (and who cannot read and write it) all the way to the professional interpreter who is totally fluent in two languages. In between we find the foreign spouse who interacts with friends in his first language, the scientist who reads and writes articles in a second language (but who rarely speaks it), the member of a linguistic minority who uses the minority language only at home and the majority language in all other domains of life, the deaf person who uses sign language with her friends but a signed form of the spoken language with a hearing person, etc. Despite the great diversity that exists between these people, all share a common feature: they lead their lives with two (or more) languages. . . .

Bilingualism, then, is not only a matter of degrees or levels of fluency, but rather a question of frequency. Grosjean defines the majority of the world's bilingual population as those people who use more than one language in their daily life, not only those who do so in perfectly equivalent ability levels. Additionally, Grosjean's key point here is that such frequency occurs at all economic levels, from the poorly educated migrant farmer to the sophisticated cosmopolitan.

The reasons that bring languages into contact and hence foster bilingualism are many: migrations of various kinds (economic, educational, political, religious), nationalism and federalism, education and culture, trade and commerce, intermarriage, etc. These factors create various linguistic needs in people who are in contact with two or more languages and who develop competencies in their languages to the extent required by these needs. In contact situations it is rare that all facets of life require the same language (people would not be bilingual if that were so) or that they always demand two languages (language A *and* B at work, at home, with friends, etc.). In fact, bilinguals acquire and use their languages for different purposes, in different domains of life, with different people. It is precisely because the needs and uses of the languages are usually quite different that bilinguals rarely develop equal fluency in their languages. The level of fluency attained in a language . . . will depend on the need for that language and will be domain specific. It is thus perfectly normal to find bilinguals who can only read and write one of their languages, who have reduced speaking fluency in a language they only use with a limited number of people, or who can only speak about a particular subject in one of their languages. . . .

Grosjean clarifies here that people learn languages based on their needs and depending on the demands of their life situations. This also accounts for why so few bilinguals become equally fluent in all of the languages; there is not usually an equal "need" for each language in the person's life.

Researchers are now starting to view the bilingual not so much as the sum of two (or more) complete or incomplete monolinguals but rather as a specific and fully competent speaker-hearer who has developed a communicative competence that is equal, but different in nature, to that of the monolingual. This competence makes use of one language, of the other, or of the two together (in the form of mixed speech), depending on the situation, the topic, the interlocutor, etc. This in turn has led to a re-definition of the procedure used to evaluate the bilingual's competencies. Bilinguals are now being studied in terms of their total language repertoire, and the domains of use and the functions of the bilingual's various languages are being taken into account.

That is, a "successful bilingual" has become a largely relative term, and competencies in one's languages are also being seen on a comparative, rather than subjective, scale.

In summary, Francois Grosjean's definitions of the phenomena of individual bilingualism highlight the following points. (1) At least half of the world is bilingual, but only in oral skills, as (2) multiliteracy skills are an exception, not the rule. (3) Bilingualism is not only a matter of degrees or levels of fluency but rather a question of frequency. (4) Bilingualism occurs at all economic levels. (5) People's fluency depends on their needs and life situations, and (6) successful bilingualism is more relative than ever. *The Multilingual Mind* brings attention to each of these six aspects of bilingualism and multilingualism. It is hoped that this investigation of individual experiences with languages will emphasize Francois Grosjean's final message, that being the relative nature of people's experiences with their linguistic identity and the need to view each person's experiences in relation to their personal needs and the needs of the societies they live in.

Acknowledgments

I would like to thank my husband, Cristian, for his never-ending encouragement to create, and for helping raise our beautiful children, Natalie, Gabriel, and Mateo.

I would also like to thank Marie Ludewigs and Lisa Cirieco, who devoted many careful hours reviewing the manuscript offering many insightful comments, and to Jane Garry for her guidance.

Finally, a deep amount of gratitude to my co-authors of this book: Sara Ackerman Aoyama, Jennifer Frengel, Marie Petratis, Andrea Bader-Rusch, Manuela González Bueno, Suzanne Barron-Hauwaert, Nicola Küpekilinç, Cristina Allemann-Ghionda, Maria Johnson, Konrad Gunesch, and Raymond Federman. I have learned so much from their insights, and gained so much from their friendships.

Introduction

In the spring of 1999, I began giving workshops and lectures based on *Raising Multilingual Children: Foreign Language Acquisition and Children*, which I was writing at the time as a practical guide for parents, teachers, and researchers in the field of bilingualism and multilingualism. I began working with members of the Swiss and international communities residing in the Geneva area, and eventually expanded to groups and schools in other parts of Switzerland and the rest of Europe and to exchanges throughout Asia and the Americas. Within the workshops I conduct, I enjoy spending time on individual questions and comments about particular family situations. Both the workshops for families and those for teachers and educational professionals yielded some very intriguing questions to which answers were not readily available. This book is a response to some of the most intriguing questions and fascinating comments that emerged from those encounters about multilinguals.

Is there a correlation between musical ability and foreign language ability? What language do bilinguals do math in? Is there such a thing as a "superior" language? What is the best way to cultivate multiliteracy skills? Why do I feel like a different person when I use Spanish than when I speak in English? How is trilingualism different from bilingualism? Can children with other language challenges, such as Down's syndrome, deafness, or dyslexia, become successful bilinguals? Of the hundreds of questions that came up, I have chosen twenty-one of the most intriguing to share with you here. This book is divided into questions about multilinguals and their schooling, about bilingualism and certain subject matters (such as math and music), how individuals differ in their degrees or abilities, how they are perceived by society, and individual differences between multilinguals.

I do not claim to be an expert in all of these areas, and have sought to find those "more in the know" to share their insights with us. There are eleven contributing authors with whom I am flattered to share these pages. Their expertise and research shed light on the intrigue of the multilingual mind. Sara

Ackerman Aoyama, formerly of the School for International Training in Brattleboro, Vermont, shares her research on multisensory applications to foreign language learning ("The Role of the Sense of Smell in Language Learning"). Dr. Cristina Allemann-Ghionda, professor of education at the University of Cologne in Germany ("The Yellow Streetcar") relates her experiences as one of the original Third Culture Kids and the language baggage and benefits that come with such an upbringing. Andrea Bader-Rusch ("Languages and the Womb"), founder of a parents and early childhood development organization in Zurich, writes of the very special case of prenatal language learning. Jennifer Frengel, a graduate of the University of California at Berkeley in interdisciplinary studies with a focus on English as a second language and linguistics, brings us new research on joining the disparate groups of language education under the umbrella of "Two-Way Immersion Programs." Spanish native Manuela González-Bueno, assistant professor of foreign language education, University of Kansas, writes of her own struggle as a parent attempting to raise a bilingual daughter and shares her many insights in "Bilingualism from Birth." French-born Raymond Federman is a novelist, poet, essayist, and translator who answers questions about linguistic identity, or "the other half," in "Federman Translating/Translating Federman." Suzanne Barron-Hauwaert has taught English as a foreign language in Japan, Poland, and Hungary, and is on the editorial board of the *Bilingual Family Newsletter* (Multilingual Matters, Ltd.). She shares part of her master's thesis with us in "Trilingualism: A Study of Children Growing Up with Three Languages." Dr. Nicola Küpelikilinç is a psychologist who works with multilingual children and youth in Germany, and specializes in "Foreign Adoption and Bilingualism." She has also contributed a case study of her own trilingual family in "What, You Speak Only One Language!?" Maria Johnson ("Bringing Up Bilingual Children in Scarce Language Environments: How the Internet Can Help!") is the founder of the website www.multilingualmunchkins.com, an Internet service center for people wishing to bring their children up bilingually. Marie Petraitis is a linguist with a background in Japanese who tackles the question of "Multilingual Mathematics." Konrad Gunesch, a lawyer with a master's degree in European studies, is currently a doctoral candidate in education at the University of Bath. He has contributed, in one of his ten languages, part of his dissertation in "Multilingualism and Cosmopolitanism." My own expertise is grounded in work as a teacher in international schools in Ecuador, Japan, and France, my extensive research into these areas of linguistic intrigue and the firsthand information I have documented from thousands of multilingual families. It is most strongly based in raising my own three children in English, Spanish, German, and French.

With answers to these commonly asked questions now available, it is my hope that what multilinguals ask about themselves, and what is often asked about them, will be clearer, and that the benefits of speaking more than one language are even more attractive to view in others and to pursue for ourselves.

1

Myths About Multilingualism

Tracey Tokuhama-Espinosa

There are many myths surrounding bilingualism and multilingualism. While there are undoubtedly benefits to knowing more than one language, what are the drawbacks, and how can we avoid them? In our ever-expanding world, which often shrinks the distance between cultures, it is important to have the right information to make choices about how and when to learn other languages.

Some of the most common statements made about bilingualism are false, and unfortunately some come from well-meaning professionals. Why are the information and new research about bilinguals and multilinguals so poorly disseminated? Perhaps one reason is that most of the technology for studying the working brain has been developed only since the mid-1970s, and observation of healthy, normal, multilingual brains has become commonplace even more recently. Or perhaps it is because the phenomenon of thousands of new multilinguals each year is a relatively new one, and the research has a hard time reflecting reality. Another reason could be that "bilingual education" still sounds suspicious to many, especially with the backtracking that has taken place in the field. A fourth reason could be the relatively few opportunities for multilinguals to discuss their traits in a critical light. After all, even those who a generation ago grew up in "international families" and traveled quite a bit as youngsters were probably not given the opportunity to reflect on their situations (see Pollock and Van Reken 1999). What is clear is that multilinguals now account for a majority of the world's population, and that their numbers grow each year. Information about them needs to keep pace.

Some information about bilingualism and multilingualism is counterintuitive. How do you measure up on the questions below?

True or False?

1. By learning more than one language, children can suffer "brain overload."
2. Some languages are easier to learn than others.

3. Multilingualism can cause language problems such as stuttering or dyslexia.

4. It is impossible for an adult to learn a new language as fast as a child.

5. Adults cannot learn to speak a foreign language without an accent.

6. The ability to speak many languages is a type of intelligence.

7. All people use the same area of their brain to speak languages.

8. A nine-year-old has the same size brain as an adult; therefore the two learn languages in the same way.

9. Most of the world is monolingual.

10. The more languages you know, the easier it gets to learn an additional one.

1. BY LEARNING MORE THAN ONE LANGUAGE, CHILDREN CAN SUFFER "BRAIN OVERLOAD"

I have heard more than a few dozen well-meaning, thoughtful, intelligent parents, as well as teachers and even some doctors, make this statement. However, it is false. Why would so many people believe it is true? There are at least four categories of answers.

First, some adults feel that too many languages can cause "brain overload," or undue stress on a child because they themselves find foreign languages stressful. Often monolingual parents cannot understand what their bilingual or multilingual child is going through when he or she enters a new school system in a new language, or undertakes a foreign language in a monolingual school system. Why can't they understand? Because the closest thing that parents have for reference is their own reactions, and their own feelings about undertaking a foreign language (which may be rooted no where else but in a high school French class that was taken in order to get enough units to graduate). Because of their age and motivation, parents approach the language learning experience on a completely different level than the child. This is due to social, psychological, and neurological reasons. Psychologically, as adults we are baffled by things children approach on the level of a game. As I wrote in *Raising Multilingual Children*:

I guess you could say that this is very similar to board games. When my husband and my daughter pull out a new board game (*Candyland, Chutes and Ladders, Monopoly*, etc.), my husband will carefully and methodologically read every rule before doing anything else. My daughter will open the packages of cards and playing pieces and, if my husband takes too long, will make up her own game according to the materials she has to work with. . . . Parents "think" a language, young children "sense" it. (Tokuhama-Espinosa 2001: 30–31)

Socially, Judith Rich Harris (1998) points out that people of different ages have different peer groups, and therefore different pressures to pursue activities. One's group can influence motivational levels drastically. An infant, a five-year-old, a teenager, and their parent will each approach the task of foreign language learning on a very different level, with different pressures and, inevitably, different levels of success. Neurologically, the infant, the five-year-old, the teenager, and the parent have brains of different sizes, and different experiences to rely on when learning a new language.

Second, some adults see children with "too many" languages as being slower than their peers when it comes to academics. Bilingualism is an easy target when problems arise at school. It is true that multilinguals begin speaking slightly later than their monolingual counterparts. It is also true that a number of multilinguals tend to hesitate before answering a question, and may appear to be grasping for an answer when in reality they may know the answer but lack the vocabulary to express it. This is a matter of learning words, not a question of comprehending the subject matter. On measures of creativity and innovation in problem solving, multilinguals have been shown to be superior to monolinguals (Ricciardelli 1992), perhaps due to the necessity to approach problems from many angles and their tendency to view situations on various levels for full comprehension as a result of the tools a second language provides them with. Multilingualism, as we shall see, is actually categorized by many educators as a type of intelligence, and those individuals with many languages are increasingly admired for such a skill.

Third, children often mix their languages during a certain stage in their proficiency development, leading adults to view them as "confused." For children brought up bilingual from birth, there is a perfectly normal stage of mixing. Linguists Jules Ronjat (1915) and Werner Leopold (1949) both described this thoroughly in their copious notes on their respective children's upbringing, as did François Grosjean in his autobiographical sketch (1982). Children initially see their languages as a single unit, and they use them as such, drawing from all of their languages where they see fit. Somewhere between ages two and a half and three and a half, children can separate their languages and label them ("Mommy speaks Italian and Daddy speaks Chinese"). With this cognitive separation, they understand the concept of "translation." Occasionally, proficient bilinguals "borrow" vocabulary from their stronger language when they do not know the word in their weaker language; this is a question of learning words, not of mental distraction or confusion.

Fourth, parents have offered examples of children with poor verbal expression who happen to be bilinguals, and they take this as evidence bilinguals can never reach their full potential in their *native* language because their "brain space" is divided. This is the argument that it is preferable to be "excellent in one language than to be mediocre in several," as if there were a single pie for language and it would have to be divided if more than one language were present. While at first glance this seems like a fair challenge, it is false because, first, we now know that bilinguals actually store their languages in different (though sometimes overlapping) areas of the brain. Second, a bilingual with poor verbal expression would have probably been a monolingual with poor verbal expression; some individuals just have poorer verbal skills than others (Gardner 1983; Hagège 1996).

Most of the world's population has the primary language area in the left frontal and parietal lobes of the brain. This is true for 95 percent of right-handed people and 70 percent of left-handed people (the rest have their primary language area either spread bilaterally—over the left and right hemispheres—or are right-hemisphere dominant for languages). Research in the late 1970s and early 1980s (Genesee et al. 1979; Albert and Obler 1979; Ojemann and Whitaker 1978; Paradis 1983) shows that languages learned at different times in one's life are stored in different areas of the brain. The right hemisphere plays a much larger role in language processing in multilinguals than in mono-linguals, according to studies being conducted at the University of Basel in Switzerland (www.unibas.ch/themultilingualbrain). So, physically speaking, second languages do not encroach on the first language's brain space nor on one's overall potential for fluency.

2. SOME LANGUAGES ARE EASIER TO LEARN THAN OTHERS

One's immediate reaction to this question would tend to be "yes." But let us rephrase the question to read "Some languages are easier to learn than others *for children*." It may seem obvious, as adults, to say that there are "difficult" languages and "easy" languages. Didn't many of us opt for Spanish in high school? Not because it is a beautiful language spoken by millions around the world, and particularly useful in the United States, but rather because it was "easier" than German? Don't we cringe at the idea of being sent overseas by our employer to a far eastern country because we think Malay, Japanese, or Korean is impossibly difficult to learn? As adults, we see a clear division between languages that are easy (often the Latin or Romance languages of Spanish, French, Italian, or Portuguese) versus languages that are difficult (those with unrecognizable sounds and a different writing system, such as Arabic, Chinese, and Thai). However, to an infant bilingual, there is no such distinction. No language is easier or harder for an infant to learn. If this were not the case, then in a kind of Darwinian response, all the "hard" languages would die out because no one would bother to learn them (Pinker 1994). Children learn all parts of speech of all languages around the world with an uncanny universal timetable, generally mastering all points of grammar by four, and reading well by eight years old (Slobin 1992). To a child, no particular language is harder than any other.

3. MULTILINGUALISM CAN CAUSE LANGUAGE PROBLEMS SUCH AS STUTTERING OR DYSLEXIA

In the 1950s it was commonplace in the United States to blame multiple languages for problems such as stuttering and dyslexia. Many intelligence tests

showed that immigrants not only had lower rates of intelligence, but also suf-
fered from far higher rates of stuttering. As recently as the 1980s, questions
were raised about deepening dyslexia problems if many languages were "layered" on a child. The social origins of the speaker have given rise to new debate
(Bernstein and Brannan 1996) in which the links between the speaker's social
background and her speech (whether "restricted" or "elaborate") comes into
question. Since we are faced with so many cases in which a person's social roots
correlate with their language abilities, both positively and negatively, this question is ripe for discussion. Linguistically speaking, abilities (education) in one's
first language have a great bearing on subsequent success. That is, if a child
comes from a poor social background with little education in her first language,
chances for success with a second language are also poor, at least on the level
of literacy skills (though the child may become orally proficient). Like the
intelligence test administrators of the 1950s it is easy to jump to conclusions:
There must be a link between bilingualism and language problems, such as
stuttering and dyslexia, right? Wrong.

The tests of the 1950s were given in English to newly arrived immigrants,
mainly from Europe, who rarely had the English-language ability to respond
correctly, and even if they did have the English (in the case of Irish immigrants,
for example), their responses were often misunderstood and taken for incorrect
answers. There was often a repetition of the question or word, allowing the
testers to believe the respondent was stuttering. Wendell Johnson's research
on stuttering (1967) does not even entertain the idea that bilingualism causes
stuttering. Harding and Riley (1996) note that countries with high levels of
bilingualism do not have high levels of stuttering. And since the majority of
the world is bilingual, stuttering would be the norm worldwide, not the exception, if such a correlation existed.

While it may be true that a child who suffers from dyslexia can find reading
in any language a trial as well as stressful, the fact that the child is bilingual
does not cause the dyslexia. The child is, however, confronted with the dilemma
of reading in multiple languages, and so is faced with additional challenge of
more reading and writing. Bilingualism does not make dyslexia worse, but
acquiring biliteracy skills means more time at the challenging tasks that may
be an overwhelming burden in just one language, let alone in two or more.
Since dyslexia is caused by "measurable brain differences in processing the
sounds represented by written language . . . intense and highly detailed instruction in phonics" (matching the letters to their corresponding sounds) begun early and using subject matter of interest to the children is the key to
overcoming the pitfalls of dyslexia, say University of Washington researchers
(Kantrowitz and Underwood 1999: 72–78). New studies reveal that by working
with children on a strong phonemic system, it is actually possible to "re-train
the brain" in language processing, easing the path toward good and even great
literacy skills in monolinguals as well as bilinguals. The key is repetition and

practice with the phonic alphabet(s), again emphasizing that the bilingual dyslexic child will be faced with the challenge of additional reading practice.

4. IT IS IMPOSSIBLE FOR AN ADULT TO LEARN A NEW LANGUAGE AS FAST AS A CHILD

I have met many parents who arrived as immigrants in California and who
are in awe at the speed with which their children learn the new country's
language. Similarly, I know many parents sent abroad on assignment by their
companies or as members of their country's diplomatic corps who often compare their language progress with that of their children: "It's amazing how fast
children learn languages!" "I wish I was as good at languages as my daughter.
We've been here just six months, and she's nearly fluent. Look at me, can't
even make the cashier at the grocery understand me!" Is it true that children
learn languages faster than adults?

Actually, research shows that adults can learn languages just as fast as children, when and if they invest the same amount of time in the process (Harley
1986). In fact, adults have an edge over children because they have developed
cognitive skills that enable them to "decode" a language with greater success
and speed than a child.

Let us take one of these expatriate overseas family's "average" daily routine.
Presumably the child is in school anywhere between three and eight hours of
the day; if the school is conducted in the target language, it is almost unavoid-
able that the child gains fluency by such consistent exposure. When he comes
home, he plays with the neighbors' children, who often speak the target language. If he relaxes in front of the television, in all likelihood he will have to
do so in the target language. If he has after-school activities (judo, ballet, soccer,
theater, etc.), these may also be in the target language, and many of the other
participants may speak the target language as well. In short, the child spends
the greater part of his day in the target language. Now let us look at Mom.
Mom goes to her target language class twice a week, for an hour and a half
each time. She makes friends in the general "ex-pat" community and gains a
passing acquaintance with the target language. Mom got a cable extension
installed so that she does not miss the news or her favorite TV show in her
native language from back home. In short, Mom does not have nearly as much
chance to practice her foreign language skills as her child does.

Though it might seem obvious, it deserves repetition: Compared to children,
adults are actually more adept at learning the rules of grammar in a foreign
language, and have a firmer base to which they can compare new languages
(many years of practice in their native language) than children. Aside from
frequency and exposure to the language, where else do we differ from children
in relation to learning a new language? In security. Adults do not feel secure
jumping into a language the way a child does, and are handicapped by believing
they will look foolish babbling in another tongue (which, unfortunately, often

happens as a self-fulfilling prophecy). An adult is sure he will look silly speaking another language, and so makes mistakes, thus fulfilling his own worst dream of looking ridiculous and reducing the chances that he will try again.

So, in a word, adults can learn to speak a foreign language as fast as a child, but they have to overcome the barriers of frequency and security to do so.

5. ADULTS CANNOT LEARN TO SPEAK A FOREIGN LANGUAGE WITHOUT AN ACCENT

Children who learn a second language in the first window of opportunity (bilingual from birth) generally have perfect accents in both of their languages, because they have treated both languages as a single unit since birth. After about two years of age, a human's auditory cortex narrows quite drastically; he is thus unable to distinguish different sounds, and is therefore hard pressed to reproduce them. Recent studies show that children are universal receivers of sounds; that is, they can distinguish all sounds of all languages at birth, but they lose this ability within the first nine months of life (Werker 1997). This means all children are able to pronounce all languages fluently if exposed from birth, in consistent manner, and presumably with input from a native speaker.

A very small percentage of the world's population is auditorily inclined, that is, they have "a good ear." It approximates the number of people who possess gifts in other realms, such as a gift for music, a gift for ballet, or a gift for mathematical skills, which I estimate to be around 10 percent of the world's population. Auditorily inclined or gifted individuals are able to use the exposure to a foreign language as infants to later reproduce sounds for which they have no acknowledged reference point. That is, if an auditorily inclined person was exposed to Czech from birth through the first two years of life, in a consistent manner and from a native speaker (though he never consciously "learned" the language), he stands a great chance of being able to pronounce Czech at a good or even fluent level at the age of twenty (or thirty or forty) when he studies the language. That is, this small percentage of people who have exceptional auditory memory can call on this gift to speak a foreign language without an accent if given the exposure to the language within the first two years of life

However, there is an argument which indicates that adults can learn foreign languages without accents, if they choose to. This is based on the fact that your tongue is an organ that can be treated like a muscle. You can train your tongue to pronounce sounds that it has never produced before, so long as your ear is first trained to recognize the normally unintelligible sounds. Tomatis's music therapy involves this learning task, and adults have learned to perfect accents in foreign languages (1960). Why doesn't everyone strive to learn his or her languages without accents, then? Because other studies show that adults actually like their accents (Harley, Allen, Cummins, and Swain 1990). Foreign accents let the listener know that something non-native, unnatural, even difficult, is being undertaken. While many adults strive to lose their accents, a large number enjoy them. My husband speaks five languages, grammatically fluently, but with an accent. I dare say he does this because he thinks his Latin accent is charming, and I must confess, to my Anglophone ear, he is right!

6. THE ABILITY TO SPEAK MANY LANGUAGES IS A TYPE OF INTELLIGENCE

In the Western world, and particularly in the United States, we are emerging from a trend of categorization that excluded most of our population from the "intellectual elite." As a high school counselor in both Japan and Ecuador, I watched many bright and deserving students fail to score high enough on U.S. standardized exams (which primarily tested verbal and math skills), and thus be denied entrance to good institutions of higher learning. This has changed quite a bit since the 1990s, and much of the credit, I believe, is due to thinkers such as Howard Gardner. Gardner, a professor at Harvard University, says there are seven types of intelligence, not our traditional two of verbal and math skills (Gardner 1983). The seven are linguistic intelligence; logical-mathematical intelligence; spatial intelligence (as with sailors, engineers, surgeons and sculptors, who can form a mental vision of the physical world); musical intelligence; bodily-kinesthetic intelligence (abilities in balance, as in the dancer who choreographs a new piece or the outfielder who can catch a pop fly with his back to the ball); interpersonal intelligence, which is the ability to understand others and interpret others' signals (as in a good psychiatrist or counselor); and intrapersonal intelligence (such as a philosopher or psychologist might possess). The answer to our question lies in the definition of "intelligence."

Gardener believes that each of the seven areas is a separate type of intelligence because they are located in different areas of the brain and they can be developed. That is, linguistic ability is located in an area of the brain that can be increased in size and connections with rehearsal. Inversely, if this area of the brain is removed, the individual loses this type of intelligence. Under this definition, foreign language ability, as a subheading under linguistic intelligence, is indeed a type of intelligence.

7. ALL PEOPLE USE THE SAME AREA OF THEIR BRAIN TO SPEAK DIFFERENT LANGUAGES

Before we can deal with this statement, we must ask whether all people use the same area of the brain to speak the *same* language? Ninety-five percent of right-handed people in the world have the left frontal and parietal lobes as the main language area. These incorporate Wernicke's area and Broca's area, which are connected by the arcuate fasciculus. Seventy percent of left-handed people also have the left frontal and parietal lobes as the main language area—meaning

5 percent of right-handed people and 30 percent of left-handed people *do not.* Thus most of the world has the main language area in the same place.

What about foreign languages? If someone learns two languages from birth, he effectively has his main language area in the same place as a monolingual (the left frontal and parietal lobes) because all languages are treated as the "first" language. If a person learns a foreign language after nine months of age, however, there is a greater cross-lateralization of language abilities; that is, there is more use of the right hemisphere by bilinguals who learn their languages after the age of nine months. Additionally, people who learn more than one foreign language (they have learned three, four, five, six, or more) have those languages in different (though often overlapping) areas of the brain (see Paradis's dual system hypothesis 1983; Albert and Obler 1979; Whitaker, Bub, and Leventer 1981).

Depending on the age at which a person learns a language, and in which hemisphere he or she is dominant for languages, first, second, and subsequent languages are housed in different places. So, do all people use the same parts of their brain to learn foreign languages? No, though most normal, right-handed bilinguals will use more of their right hemisphere in language processing than a normal right-handed monolingual. Exciting new studies being done with MRI (magnetic resonance imaging) scans clearly illustrate how second languages learned after the first window (birth to nine months) are in different parts of the brain (University of Basel studies 2002; www.unibas.ch/themultilingualbrain).

8. A NINE-YEAR-OLD HAS THE SAME SIZE BRAIN AS AN ADULT; THEREFORE THE TWO LEARN LANGUAGES IN THE SAME WAY

First, it is true that a nine-year-old and an adult have roughly the same size brain (Mai et al. 1998). What differs drastically, however, is the number of connections between neurons in their brains. Do the nine-year-old and the adult learn languages in the same way because their neurological development is similar? Absolutely not. Language learning in this case is due not to neurological reasons but rather to social ones.

A nine-year-old and an adult learn languages differently because they have different motivations to do so, and they have very different peer groups influencing their learning process. Whether or not a nine-year-old finds learning the new language socially acceptable or not will influence his motivation to undertake the task. If learning the new language means he will be able to join the local soccer team or play with the neighbor next door, it is very likely he will pursue the language and learn it quickly. If the adult, on the other hand, has a peer group consisting of other monolingual parents who do not see an inherent benefit to learning the new language, he will in many cases not be so successful in learning a new language.

Add a teenager to the picture and it becomes even clearer. The influence peer groups have on an individual's learning process is high. There is a great difference between the teenager who falls in love with the speaker of a foreign language and learns it quickly, and the teenager who has been taken out of her home country due to her dad's two-year move abroad, and hates both family and the new language. The teenager will probably seek out peers who share her disgruntled attitude and probably will not make the most of the opportunity to learn a new language.

9. MOST OF THE WORLD IS MONOLINGUAL

Most of the world is bilingual, but this needs clarification. Most of the world is bilingual but not biliterate; that is, most people around the world speak at least two, and often more, languages but can write in only one, if that. This is mathematically logical if one looks at the number of languages that exist in the world. There are between 2,500 and 6,000 languages, depending on whether one counts dialects, creoles, and pidgin languages. There were roughly 200 countries at the turn of the century, meaning that many people have to speak more than one language, if not several! In India, for example, there are twelve major languages, including Hindi, Urdu, Bengali, and English. Many people from India have been educated in three languages because of the way the school system is designed. Indonesia has 250 distinct languages, and most people speak Indonesian plus at least one dialect (Britannica 2001). The United States is no exception. While there is no official national language, it is assumed that education is conducted in English, though millions of families speak something other than English at home.

10. THE MORE LANGUAGES YOU KNOW, THE EASIER IT GETS TO LEARN AN ADDITIONAL ONE

One might argue that if the languages being learned have completely different linguistic roots, no benefits will be found. This was disproved by McLaughlin and Nation (1986), however, who conducted a study showing how monolinguals, bilinguals, and multilinguals differed in their approach to an unknown language. They found that bilinguals were better than monolinguals, and multilinguals better than bilinguals in identifying grammatical structures in languages. They made assumptions about strings of an unknown written language that later proved to be correct. I would guess the internal monologue of the multilingual participants went something like "This must be a verb because it has the same stem here and here, but with a change; so this other thing must be the subject. . . ." McLaughlin and Nation concluded that knowing more than one language gave individuals an edge in learning additional languages because they could make certain educated guesses about language structure.

An additional idea contributing to this argument might come from the mind of a child. If I can roller-skate, and I can ski, then why shouldn't I be able to roller-blade or use a scooter, which is very similar? While it may be an entirely different sport (or an entirely different language), if I could learn the first two, why shouldn't I be able to learn a third (or a fourth or a fifth)? The use of prior knowledge to learn new, related information is evident in foreign language development.

CONCLUSIONS

These ten myths of multilingualism have existed for many years, though it is only recently that definite refutations can be offered. In the coming years, further evidence will come forward to clarify the abbreviated responses found in the essay. In summary, can learning more than one language cause brain overload? No. Are some languages easier for children to learn than others? No. Can multilingualism cause language problems such as stuttering or dyslexia? No, but it can aggravate it. Is it impossible for an adult to learn a foreign language as fast as a child? No, not when the adult invests as much time in the task as the child does. Is it true that adults cannot learn to speak a foreign language without an accent? Generally this is true, though a certain percentage of the population has a gift for foreign languages and can indeed do so. Is this ability to speak foreign languages a type of intelligence? According to some modern theorists in education and psychology, such as Howard Gardner, yes, because it resides in a clearly defined area of the brain, can be developed with stimulation, is destroyed if removed, and is given value by many cultures. Do all people use the same area of the brain to speak languages? Not all, though most do. Five percent of right-handed individuals and 30 percent of left-handed individuals are different. Do a nine-year-old, a teenager, and an adult learn a foreign language in the same way? No, but primarily due to sociological reasons as opposed to neurological ones. Is most of the world monolingual? No, most of the work speaks more than one language, but may not write even in one. Is it true that the more languages you learn, the easier it gets to learn a new one? Yes, MacLaughlin and Nation's work showed precisely this to be true.

On balance, the myths about multilinguals that are being dispelled put a very positive face on polyglots in the twenty-first century.

REFERENCES

Albert, M.L., and L. Obler (1979). *The Bilingual Brain: Neuropsychological and Neurolinguistic Aspects of Bilingualism.* New York: Academic Press.

Bernstein, B., and J. Brannen (eds.) (1996). *Children, Research and Policy.* UK: Taylor and Francis.

Gardner, H. (1983). *Frames of Mind: The Theory of Multiple Intelligences.* New York: Basic Books.

Genesee, F., W.E. Lambert, L. Mononen, M. Seitz, and R. Starch (1979). "Language Processing in Bilinguals." *Brain and Language* 5, no. 5: 1–12.

Grosjean, F. (1982). *Life with Two Languages: An Introduction to Bilingualism.* Cambridge, MA: Harvard University Press.

Hagège, C. *L'Enfant aux deux langues.* (1996). Paris: Editions Odile Jacob.

Harding, E., and P. Riley (1996). *The Bilingual Family: A Handbook for Parents.* 9th printing. Cambridge: Cambridge University Press.

Harley, B. (1986). *Age in Second Language Acquisition.* England: Multilingual Matters.

Harley, B., P. Allen, J. Cummins, and M. Swain (eds.) (1990). *The Development of Second Language Proficiency.* Cambridge Applied Linguistic Series. Eds. Michael H. Long and Jack C. Richards. Cambridge: Cambridge University Press.

Harris, J.R. (1998).*The Nurture Assumption.* New York: The Free Press.

Johnson, W., with R. Leutenegger (1967). *Stuttering in Children and Adults: Thirty Years of Research at the University of Iowa.* Minneapolis: University of Minnesota Press.

Kantrowitz, B., and A. Underwood (1999). "Dyslexia and the New Science of Reading" *Newsweek,* Nov. 23, 1999, pp. 72–78.

Leopold, W. (1949). "Speech Development of a Bilingual Child, a Linguist's Record." In *Vocabulary Growth in the First Two Years.* New York: AMS Press.

Mai, J.K., J.K. Assheuer, and G. Paxinos (1998). *Atlas of the Human Brain.* New York: Academic Press.

McLaughlin, B., and R. Nation (1986). "Experts and Novices: An Information-processing Approach to the 'Good Language Learner' Problem." *Applied Psycholinguistics* 7: 41–56.

Ojemann, G.A., and H.A. Whitaker (1978). "The Bilingual Brain." *Archives of Neurology* 35: 409–412.

Paradis, M. (ed.) (1983). *Readings on Aphasia in Bilinguals and Polyglots.* Montreal, Canada: Didier.

Pinker, S. (1994). *The Language Instinct: How the Mind Creates Language.* New York: William Morrow.

Pollock, D., and R. Van Reken (1999). *The Third Culture Kid Experience: Growing Up Among Worlds.* Yarmouth, ME: Intercultural Press.

Ricciardelli, L.A. "Creativity and Bilingualism." *Journal of Creative Behaviour* 26 no. 4 (1992): 242–254.

Ronjat, J. (1913). *Le development du langage observe chez un enfant bilingüe.* Paris: Librarie Ancienne H. Champion.

Slobin, D.I. (ed.) (1985–1992). *The Crosslinguistic Study of Language Acquisition.* 3 vols. Hillsdale, NJ: Lawrence Erlbaum.

Tokuhama-Espinosa, T. (2001). *Raising Multilingual Children: Foreign Language Acquisition and Children.* Westport, CT: Bergin & Garvey.

Tomatis, A.A. (1960). "Conditionnement Audio-Vocal." *Bulletin de l'Academie National de Medicine,* 144, no. 11 et 12: 197–200.

Werker, J.F. (1997) "Exploring Developmental Changes in Cross-language Speech Perception." (1997). In D. Osherson (ed.), *An Invitation to Cognitive Science.* vol. 1, *Language,* 2nd ed. Vol. ed. L.R. Gleitman and M. Liberman. Cambridge, MA: MIT Press.

Whitaker, H.A., D. Bub, and S. Leventer (1981). "Neurolinguistic Aspects of Language Acquisition and Bilingualism." In H. Winitz (ed.), *Native Language and Foreign Language Acquisition.* New York: New York Academy of Sciences.

Part I

Schooling and Foreign Languages

2

Teaching Languages Using the Multiple Intelligences and the Senses

Tracey Tokuhama-Espinosa

If you think there is a grammatical problem with the title, you share a type of intelligence with my computer, which has underlined the word in red. How can there be multiple *intelligences*? Aren't you either smart or, well, not so smart?

In 1983 Howard Gardner wrote his groundbreaking book *Frames of Mind*, which allowed many of us nontraditionally intelligent people to let out a great sigh of collective relief. His book has been followed by a rich flow of new teachers' aids, including *The Best of Multiple Intelligence Activities* (1999), *So Each May Learn: Integrating Learning Styles and Multiple Intelligences* (2000), and *Multiple Intelligences in the Classroom* (2000), to name a few. It seems that there is not just smart, there are smarties; not just one kind of intelligence, but various intelligences. Gardner labeled seven different areas of the brain that correlate to different human capacities which can be enhanced and can grow, and which are valued in one or more cultural settings. These smarties can be cultivated, if you will, in the garden between our ears.

Why does this release us from the traditional stranglehold definition of intelligence? Because it means that entrance into the exclusive club of Brains is not just for the kind of person who can make a good SAT (Scholastic Assessment Test) score in high school. The SAT is divided into math and verbal sections, both of which are included in Gardner's paradigm. According to Gardner, however, you could also be the type of person who is intelligent in another field: musical intelligence, spatial intelligence, bodily-kinesthetic intelligence, interpersonal intelligence, or intrapersonal intelligence.

So aside from its being good news for the newly labeled modern intellectuals, what can we do with this information? Well, as a teacher, I felt like I was being pleasantly tickled under the chin by the novel possibilities for the classroom. Take foreign language learning. Did you like high school French? Or Spanish? Or German? Did you ever get the chance to learn Chinese, the most widely spoken native language in the world? Wouldn't it have been wonderful to have lived those languages, rather than have had points of grammar shoveled down your throat? I was lucky, and had a very creative Spanish teacher (who was really an actor in disguise), and the halls would echo with his booming voice and *Don Quijote de la Mancha*. But it wasn't until college, when I fell in love with a native Spanish speaker that I really began to use the language, and not until years later, when I lived in a Spanish-speaking country, that I became fluent. What we want to do is take advantage of the windows of opportunity for foreign language learning in children and help them fall in love with such a language early in life. Little kids can do it. And they do it best when each of the intelligences is savored with the tongue (of a new language), and when all of their senses are stimulated.

Teaching a new language through the multiple intelligences means that you touch all seven areas, as well as all five senses, with the language. How?

Let's make a checklist of the intelligences cross-referenced with the senses.

Modern learning theory has proved over and over again, with children and adults alike, that the best way to remember anything is to get it into your head in a variety of ways. The challenge is to find activities that can be taught in as many ways as possible, cross-referencing as many of the intelligences with as many of the senses as is reasonable. The overall problem with any type of new learning is in retrieval, not input. That means that the more ways we put it in, the easier it will be for us to pull it out when we need it. If we learn the colors in Arabic by seeing them, painting them, talking about them, hearing a poem about them, experiencing them in nature, tasting them in foods, talking about different fruits and tastes that are different colors, then we will find it infinitely easier to find the word *red* in Arabic when we need it than if we had simply memorized it in a vocabulary list of words.

What formula, then, can even little children follow in learning a new language? The goal is love. If they love the language, if they see it has use for them, they will learn, and learn far more permanently than our seventeen-year-olds in high school who remember exactly enough to pass their exams

Table 2.1
The Seven Intelligences and Five Senses

	Smell	Taste	Touch	Sight	Hearing
Music					
Spatial					
Bodily/Kinesthetic					
Interpersonal					
Intrapersonal					
Math/Logic					
Linguistic					

but cannot repeat a word, one year later, when faced with a Mexican immigrant in real life. The formula does not mean abandoning all established curricula. It means modifying Grandma's wonderful cake recipe to today's taste buds.

Take a pinch of music, equal parts of spatial, body/kinesthetic, and inter- and intrapersonal intelligences. Add a smidgen of linguistic and mathematical-logical intelligences, and bake for an academic year. A spoonful each of sight, sound, taste, touch, and smell, and we have the frosting on the cake. Now what does each of the ingredients consist of?

1. *Music.* Sing songs. Listen to music composed in the country. Talk about the composers in that language. I have found that music opens a fascinating set of connections in the brain which allow information to get stored in places where it may not normally have landed. Use music as background to all other activities. There is nothing like a good song, a catchy rhythm to keep a language in a child's mind all day long, long after the school's doors close. Most children will not come home and say, "Hey, Mom, guess what? I learned what the definite and indefinite articles are in German," but they may come home and sing a song about it. (See chapter 6 of this book, on musical ability and foreign language.)

2. *Spatial.* It has been shown that bilingual and multilingual children have a far greater ability to envision spatial puzzles and to "see" images within images, such as viewing a three-dimensional cube within a flat two-dimensional drawing. This should work in the opposite direction as well. By enhancing language skills, children will probably improve in the ability to do spatial problems. Treat children to a variety of such games. (All ages from four-years to adults love to see if they can see what others say they see.) Two examples are the picture of the old woman who is also a young woman in a long coat, and the picture of a pair of vases which is also two faces. These games are amusing, and cause the brain to perform the kind of mental gymnastics that aids in second language learning. Why is this so? Brain research shows that people who learn their foreign languages after the first window of opportunity (birth to nine months) have their second (and third and fourth) languages stored over a greater area of the brain, including large areas of the right hemisphere that usually do not play a role in monolingual language abilities. Spatial ability is also located in the right hemisphere of the brain. Stimulation of one area (foreign language) could enhance stimulation of the other area (spatial intelligence).

3. *Body/kinesthetic* intelligence can be used to encourage foreign language learning by acting out a short play in the language, or just by moving. There is nothing more boring than sitting in the same place, at the same desk, for forty-five minutes while someone talks at you. Unfortunately, that is what occurs in many of our foreign language classrooms. Get those kids out of their chairs, not just to stand up in front of the class to watch them sweat and stutter, but in pairs or groups, to act out a survival scene at the local mall or at a soccer match, or to dance. This helps forge connections to the language in a completely

different realm. Have students physically manipulate letter shapes with Play-Doh or by writing words in the air. A great stimulation is to have students write on each other's backs and have them guess what word was traced there. This is the same realm as writing, for example, so the act of taking notes is also important for children who know how to write. (A four-year-old would be a poor candidate for such an exercise, but your typical eighth grader should do it well). Writing notes puts information into your brain in a way that is different from hearing, which is different from speaking, and so on (as we will see in chapter 4).

4. *Interpersonal.* The child with a well-developed sense of interpersonal intelligence is one who can "read" others. This is the kid who empathizes with the new guy in class and shares his lunch with him. This is the type of youngster who is able to interpret signals from others and feel their joy and pain. If your child doesn't know how to do this, maybe it's a good time to learn. And if she is already good at it, maybe she can use this intelligence to learn a foreign language. How? By "getting into" a character from the novel being read in French. By guessing the feelings of people in magazine photos and expressing that in the new language, which can be a great vocabulary builder. Through charades, seeing the world through another's eyes. By imaging a trip to Switzerland and being Heidi for a day. What does she do during her day? How does she feel when she wakes up in the morning in the Alps with a bunch of goats? Is she happy, sad, disillusioned, naive? And how do you say all that in German? Would you like to be Heidi in real life? Such exercises use the interpersonal intelligence in a particularly targeted way, and lead to excellent language development in real-life situations.

5. *Intrapersonal.* Children with a well-developed sense of intrapersonal intelligence are very in touch with their own feelings. They are the little philosophers around us who question and reflect on the world. These are the little ones who keep great diaries or write notes to themselves, who write poetry and feel every word of it. Maybe, just maybe, another language would be the key to identifying their emotions. What is the Portuguese *saudade*, anyway? It is a sense of melancholy and longing, but not exactly. Is it something one can express only in Portuguese? Then maybe Portuguese is the language we want to know. There is a beautiful attraction between intrapersonally intelligent children and their desire to know more words, because more words means they are able to identify, label, give a name to more of what is going on inside of themselves.

6. *Mathematical-logical,* scientifically intelligent youngsters love numbers, love order in their world, love to know what comes next in the sequence. These are kids who do very well learning foreign languages in the traditional fashion. They enjoy the regular verbs (and relish having the "in" on which ones are irregular). They like to do the exercises in the workbook and to have their papers corrected by the teacher (because they have already done it themselves in the back of the book, and know they are right). These children do well by

stimulating all of the senses, as we will see in the next paragraph, but they like doing it all in an orderly way.

7. *Linguistically* intelligent children have a naturally high aptitude for foreign languages and will benefit even more than other children from stimulation in the other intelligences. These are children with a good ear who enjoy sound and who generally show a great deal of fluency in their native languages as well as foreign languages.

We turn now to the senses. The five senses of smell, taste, touch, sight, and hearing should also be stimulated in the best of all foreign language learning worlds. Why stimulate taste if you're learning Chinese? Because one of the great treasures of China is its food. Wouldn't it be wonderful to learn colors by serving up a plate of chow mein and labeling all the colors of the vegetables? And what about sight? Can you imagine a room full of six-year-olds looking at the Great Wall of China in a slide projected onto their normally alphabet-strewn, clock- and flag-covered chalkboard? And then learning how to say the words for Great Wall, emperor, walk, run, and dance in Chinese? What did they observe in the picture? How do you say that in Chinese? That's a lesson they'll never forget.

Then there is smell. How many Chinese herbs, teas, and typical flowers can you find in your kitchen? Bring in the one you find the most attractive to smell and be ready to tell the class *why* you like it so much.

Touch. Who has a Chinese coat they can bring to class, or something made of Chinese silk? And what is the word for silk? And what about coat, or jacket, or hat, or shoes? And of course sound. What does Chinese music sound like? How is the rhythm different from your favorite music? Describe what sounds you hear. What kind of instrument can make that noise? How many different ways can we say *wa* in Chinese just by changing our intonation? And what is *intonation* itself? By teaching children foreign languages through all five senses, they will retain the information in at least four more ways than they normally would.

By capitalizing on the different intelligences that our children have, we are able to address which child learns best in which ways and to augment intelligences that may otherwise go unrecognized. Most important, we may give children who do not fit into our traditional category of "smart" a chance to be brilliant.

REFERENCES

Armstrong, T. (2000). *Multiple Intelligences in the Classroom*, 2nd ed. Alexandria, VA: Association for Supervision and Curriculum Development.

Gardner, H. (1983). *Frames of Mind: The Theory of Multiple Intelligences*. New York: Basic Books.

Gardner, H. (1993). *Multiple Intelligences: The Theory in Practice*. New York: Basic Books.

Lambret, N.M., and B.L. McCombs (eds.) (1997). *How Students Learn: Reforming Schools Through Learner-Centered Education*. Washington, DC: American Psychological Association.

Silver, H.F., R.W. Strong, and M.J. Perini (2000). *So Each May Learn: Integrating Learning Styles and Multiple Intelligences*. Alexandria, VA: Association for Supervision and Curriculum Development.

Wild, R. (2000). *Raising Curious, Creative, Confident Kids: The Pestalozzi Experiment in Child-based Education*. Boston: Shambhala.

3

The Role of the Sense of Smell in Language Learning

Sara Ackerman Aoyama

Perhaps due to the constant high humidity and the condensed nature of the cities, Japan has always been an olfactory treat for me; the ginkgo leaves on the summer nights, fragrant olive trees in the autumn, plum blossoms in the winter, and sweet daphne in the spring. The smell of fresh tatami mats, broiled fish, the fishmonger, laundry detergent, roasted sweet potatoes, and curry instantly bring back memories of Japan. Humidity is particularly high in June due to the onset of the rainy season, and as I walked through the streets, I breathed deeply and enjoyed all the different smells.

There I attended a JALT (Japanese Association of Language Teachers) meeting on the topic of neurolinguistic programming (NLP). In the NLP model, all human behavior is believed to result from combined and sequenced nervous-system representations (sights, sounds, sensations, and smells), and people think in preferred systems: visual, auditory, or kinesthetic (Cockett 1988). In order to know how a particular person thinks, you have to read the visual clues that they unconsciously exhibit. One way to do this is to listen for verbal clues, such as an answer of "Yes, I see what you mean" (visual), "I don't feel that way" (kinesthetic), or "That sounds right" (auditory). Another way to do this is by following the person's eye movements. In general, people who are visually inclined will look upward when asked a question (to the right for visual recall, and to the left for visual construct, as in imagining something). Those who are auditorily inclined will shift their eyes parallel to the level of their ears. Those kinesthetically inclined will look down.

During the lecture, we broke into groups of three. One person asked questions, a second person answered them, and a third kept track of eye movements. In the process of doing this, I noticed that eye movements for each individual came faster for some groups of questions than for others. The questions were divided into six categories: visual, auditory, kinesthetic, gustatory, olfactory, and unspecified. In my case, group members noted that eye movements came the fastest for the olfactory questions. I asked the speaker if a faster response might indicate a preference for a particular cognitive style, and she agreed that it might be so. Having always had a keen sense of smell, I was not surprised by my results, but was puzzled about how I could apply what I had learned to my teaching.

Later that year I enrolled my son at a karate dojo. From the very beginning my children and I felt an affinity for the dojo. As we walked into the room, my daughter noted that it "smelled like Japan," and my son said that he liked the smell. For me, it brought back memories of my visits to temples, since the incense that the teacher had lit was identical to that burned at Japanese temples and shrines. We went to the dojo five days a week, and my children always commented on the smell. I noticed that no matter how I felt when entering the dojo, I always felt relaxed and refreshed upon leaving. There was an altar, like those seen in Japan, and Japanese art decorated the walls. Quite often, Japanese music was played, and the language of the dojo was Japanese. These visual and auditory factors were obviously important, but I wondered just how important a role the incense played. I asked the other parents and children (who had no memories of Japan to link to this smell) how they liked it, and they all gave favorable comments. This made me wonder if this was just a pleasant smell that was relaxing for everyone, or if it was my own family's memories of Japan that was affecting us. I could draw no conclusions, but I kept observing and did notice that if the incense was not burning when we arrived, it was always my son who asked to light it. My son, who was in Japan for only nine months when he was three years old, could have had a subconscious memory of this smell. The day-care center that he attended was located near a number of shrines, and the teachers often brought the children to play on the grounds of the shrines. We passed temples daily, and I have some memory of his commenting on the smell, although he has no conscious memory of this. My daughter, who was in Japan from birth to age three, and then again at age six, was able to make a connection between the smell and the temples near our house.

My experience with NLP and the karate dojo were the impetus for my exploration of smell and learning.

BACKGROUND

Looking back in history, we can see the sense of smell being used in almost every culture and in different religions. The Greek Orthodox Church has a philosophy of incorporating all five senses into its service. Incense is burned to appeal to the sense of smell. In Judaism, a spice box is used in the Havdalah service, which is held at the end of the Sabbath, to start the new week afresh. Pungent and pleasant spices such as cinnamon, cloves, and cardamom are used.

Aromatherapy was perhaps first practiced by the ancient Egyptians. In their temples, priests used different scents to raise the spirits of their congregation or to relax them. Aromatic substances such as crushed cedar bark, caraway seeds, and angelica roots were steeped in wine or oil and then burned. *Kyphi*, a mixture of sixteen different essences, including myrrh and juniper, was used to raise spiritual awareness and heighten the senses of the priests. Incense is still used for much the same purpose (Ryman 1993).

Perhaps no other sense is as culture-bound as the sense of smell. This may be because of the clear link between smell and memory, and because smell was the most refined and acute sense of our prehistoric ancestors, who relied on smell more than any other sense for protection against enemies and in the search for food. Most people enjoy floral scents, but to some people such scents are linked to funerals and death. The only universally pleasant smell is cola, which may account for the success of Coke and Pepsi worldwide (Wilke 1995). Sensitivity to the degree of smell varies from culture to culture. The French can eat a whole truffle, which has an aroma that for most other cultures would be overwhelming. Americans are averse to strong smells, which may be due to a taboo on death. When Americans smell a strong odor, it seems to remind them of their animality or mortality. On the other hand, vanilla is known to be comforting to Americans, but has no particular effect on Japanese. This may be because it is an unfamiliar smell and therefore has no link to the granny's kitchen of their childhood. It was reported in the *Boston Globe* that, within the same culture, people of different generations experience nostalgic feelings triggered by different odors. People born in the 1920s, 1930s, and 1940s have these feelings when smelling flowers, sea air, cut grass, and burning leaves, but those born in the 1950s, 1960s, and 1970s became nostalgic when smelling Play-Doh, window cleaner, hair spray, suntan lotion, and felt-tip pens (Klein 1995).

There is a very strong connection between smell and memory. Aroma processing is wired directly into the limbic system, where memory is stored and emotion resides. The limbic system, which is the most primitive brain area, was called the rhinecephalon or "smell brain" by early anatomists, who believed it was primarily olfactory in nature. Odor/nerve messages are first analyzed by the amygdala and hippocampus, which are memory centers, and also play a large role in emotional responses. These are the points where smell may trigger a recent or distant memory.

Before man evolved, the sense of smell might very well have been the most important sense, since it could determine survival. However, with evolution, the sense of smell began to be less and less important. Researchers at the Monell Chemical Center in Philadelphia theorize that the sense of smell now may be most acute immediately after birth, and nursing newborns are able to distinguish their mothers from other lactating women. One researcher hypothesizes that deja-vu is a phenomenon whereby a smell too faint to be perceived registers in the subconscious mind and then triggers a memory, causing a sudden and inexplicable sense of familiarity (Roach 1992).

THE ROLE OF SMELL IN RELAXATION, REFRESHMENT, AND CONCENTRATION

Today many scientists are trying to find out more about the power of the sense of smell. Studies have shown that certain smells can be helpful in enhancing relaxation. One of the best-known studies was done at Sloan-Kettering Memorial Hospital, on patients undergoing MRI, where the patient must lie motionless in a capsule while their internal organs are scanned. When the vanilla-like aroma of heliotrope was introduced into the tube, 63 percent of the patients showed reduced anxiety. In a different kind of study, Robert Baron, psychologist and chairman of the department of management at Rensselaer Polytechnic Clinic, found that scenting a room with spiced apple or "powder fresh" Glade markedly improved performance on a high-stress task. No conclusion was reached on whether the effects of the fragrance were physical, or just due to cognitive distraction—the fragrance could elicit pleasant memories or moods that distract one from the source of anxiety.

It is now possible to chemically produce almost any kind of smell and then diffuse it through "environmental fragrancing." The Walt Disney World Magic House at Epcot Center in Florida has a room scented with the smell of fresh-baked chocolate chip cookies. The intention is to induce feelings of relaxation and comfort. In Japan, the Shimizu construction company has invented something called "aromatherapeutic environmental fragrancing." About every six minutes, air-conditioning ducts hidden in the ceiling tiles release a mixture of eight therapeutic "aroma chemicals." As of October 1992, eighty companies were using this system. Different fragrances are used to improve alertness and concentration, to alleviate stress, and to relax workers at the end of the day. Psychologists at the Russian Academy of Sciences found that saturating the air with smells of fruit and flowers can ease the load of computer operators, who spend long hours in front of displays each day. Lemon, jasmine, or eucalyptus boosted productivity and helped to prevent drowsiness. When the smell of jasmine was diffused in the room, keyboard errors were reduced by almost 30 percent, and the smell of lemon reduced keyboard errors by almost 50 percent. A keypunching study done in Japan by Shimizu showed similar results with the use of a lemon scent.

IN THE CLASSROOM

After having read a number of these studies, I began to wonder about potential applications for the foreign language classroom. Since I myself am an English as a second language (ESL) teacher, I was mostly interested in applications in the ESL classroom, where anxiety levels may be particularly high due to exposure to a new culture.

One issue I looked at is the need for relaxation in the classroom. In September 1995, I started a master's program at the School for International Training in Brattleboro, Vermont. During the first week of school, we were required to participate in a "shock language" class, to put us in the role of a student again and remember how it felt. Of course, everyone had a different reaction, but many people, myself included, felt a high degree of anxiety. In fact, there is a type of anxiety labeled "foreign language anxiety" that E.K. Horowitz and others (Horowitz, Young, and Cope 1991: 30) define as having three components:

1. Communication apprehension, arising from learners' inability to adequately express mature thoughts and ideas
2. Fear of negative social evaluation arising from a learner's need to make a positive social impression on others
3. Test anxiety or apprehension over academic evaluation.

In *Language Learning Strategies,* Oxford (1990) suggests that effective strategies for lowering anxiety could include using progressive relaxation, deep breathing, meditation, music, or laughter. The use of a smell to lower anxiety seems to be appropriate here as well.

Another issue I explored is what smell can do to increase alertness and attention. The Shiseido Company in Japan markets environmental fragrancers and suggests the use of a combination of lemon, jasmine, and mint to improve alertness and concentration. I used to teach a late afternoon class on Friday, made up of sixty students seated in an auditorium, and I sometimes found myself in the awkward position of waking up students. Everyone has periods in the day when they just aren't as alert as they need to be. The application of fragrances seems appropriate here for the classroom.

Different approaches to language teaching may lend some validation to the use of the sense of smell. In Suggestopedia/Accelerated Learning, the relaxation of the student is of the utmost importance and is achieved through the use of music, comfortable chairs, a relaxed environment, and the use of plants and other decorative objects. It would seem that the use of smell would be a logical extension here.

Krismonde Gaudinier (personal conversation, 1995), suggested the following equation:

$$\text{Relaxation} + \text{Alertness} = \text{Learning.}$$

If a certain smell can bring about a state of relaxation and/or alertness, then we could carry the equation a step further and say

$$\text{Smell} \Rightarrow \text{Learning.}$$

SAMPLE LESSON PLAN FOR A SMELL UNIT

In addition to the application of fragrance to reduce anxiety and promote relaxation, smell can be used directly as the content of a language lesson. The following are some very open-ended lesson plans for the introduction of smell into the language classroom.

LESSON 1

Objective: To introduce smell as a vehicle for group discussion and list making.

Materials: Markers, poster paper, tape.

Procedure: Teacher introduces the topic of smell by discussing teacher's own favorite and least favorite smells, or talks about what teacher and class could smell today, or what they can smell in that particular season. Then students are divided into pairs or small groups and asked to brainstorm their five most liked and least liked smells, and make a poster listing them. Posters are then hung on the wall and time is allotted to read them. The class then makes some observations by comparing and contrasting each group's list.

Follow-up: Students write about why they like or dislike a certain smell.

LESSON 2

Objective: To practice using the past tense for narrative and the use of the phrase "it reminds me of . . ."

Materials: Posters from previous class.

Procedure: Teacher picks one of the smells from the posters and makes a sentence using "it reminds me of . . .", and explains how a smell can remind us of events in our past. Teacher demonstrates with a memory of his/her own, using the past tense. Students then each write down a smell-linked memory of their own and read them to a partner. Each person asks his or her partner three questions about the memory described.

Follow-up: Students pick another smell and write about a memory linked to it.

***Past continuous, modal "would" (=past habit), and periphrastic modal "used to" may be used for more advanced students.

LESSON 3

Objective: To practice using "feeling" words.

Materials: Things that smell, such as spices, cut fruits, perfume, flavored jelly beans, flavored magic markers, etc.

Procedure: Teacher gives some examples of how a certain smell makes him/her feel. Examples: "The smell of gasoline makes me feel dizzy," "The smell of roses makes me feel relaxed." Then the teacher asks students how certain smells make them feel. After some practice and new vocabulary, students break into groups and pass items around. After each item is passed around, students write down how it makes them feel. Answers are then summarized and one representative from each group reports to the class on what they have found.

Follow-up: Students pick a day to be aware of what they smell throughout the day, and record smells and feelings into a journal.

LESSON 4

Objective: To practice using the comparative.

Materials: Posters created in Lesson 1.

Procedure: Teacher uses two scents to express preference in smell. For example, "I prefer cinnamon to lemon because it is more comforting." After teacher gives some examples, students pick two scents of their own and go around asking all others which scent they prefer and why. Each student shares his/her results with the class.

Follow-up: Students write a report summarizing the results they have obtained.

***A similar exercise may be done using the superlative form.

LESSON 5

Objective: To practice descriptive writing.

Materials: Different kinds of incense, matches, and music.

Procedure: Teacher gives some examples of descriptive writing evoked by smells. (If teacher has access to the Internet, many examples of this kind of descriptive writing can be found by doing a search using "smell" or "smell and memory.") Next, teacher lights a stick of incense without telling the class what scent it is. Music is played, and the students are told to relax and let their imaginations lead them into a page of descriptive writing.

Follow-up: Students exchange writings and practice error correction. They may also write their reaction to their partner's writing. If class time allows for a few types of writing, students may choose to expand one of their pieces at home for homework.

In addition to using smell as the focus of the lesson, a certain smell may be diffused for relaxation or refreshment during a normal classroom lesson. Table 3.1 offers some suggestions for what scents could be used. This list is by no means definitive; there are many other possibilities. The most important criterion for the use of smell is that the smell being diffused is pleasant to everyone. If the whole class is in agreement that they enjoy the scent of dandelions, then that scent will be the one that is effective.

Table 3.1
Suggested Scents and Their Functions

FUNCTION	SUGGESTED SCENTS
Reduces errors	lemon, peppermint
Boosts productivity	lily-of-the-valley, lavender, jasmine, mint, eucalyptus
Reduces stress	spiced apple, jasmine, rose, chamomile
Reduces anxiety	vanilla, neroli, lavender
Relaxes	basil, cinnamon, citrus flavors
Energizes	peppermint, thyme, rosemary
Relieves tiredness	woodsy scents, cedar, cypress

APPLICATION

A scent can be diffused in a number of ways. One way is simply burning a stick of incense. Incense used in the karate dojo does not seem to cause much smoke, perhaps because the dojo is a very large room. Smoke could be a problem in a small classroom. Another way is through the use of oils, which must be used very sparingly because their strength can be overwhelming. Some of the oils are prohibitively expensive. A very safe way to start out might be to use a scent or spice box similar to the one used during the Havdalah service, which can be passed around. This has the advantage of allowing persons who are overly sensitive to smell to approach it gingerly.

WARNING

There are some pitfalls that teachers must be aware of in the use of any smell in the classroom. Just as some people have an aversion to a certain kind of music, an individual may have an aversion to a particular smell. Having to listen to music that is unpleasant is merely disagreeable, but exposure to an irritating smell can cause an allergic reaction. It is essential that a teacher ask students about any odor sensitivities before introducing an odor into the classroom. About 15 percent of the American population suffers from "increased allergic sensitivity" to chemicals. Even low levels of the stimuli may trigger reactions in people with multiple chemical sensitivity/environmental illness. Symptoms may include fatigue, migraine, headache, rashes, difficulty breathing, and dizziness.

CONCLUSIONS

In conclusion, there is no doubt that smell will play an important role in our future. The Japanese already spritz fragrances in factories and offices to keep workers alert and to boost productivity. Annette Green, president of the Fragrance Foundation says, "In the twentieth century fragrance will be used as much for its behavioral effects as for adornment" (Green and Warren 1995: 24). "Fragrance-evoked mood changes are small, but beneficial to our well-being," says Craig Warren (1995: 24), director of fragrance science at International Flavors and Fragrances, the world's largest manufacturer of flavors and fragrances. If we are able to find a scent that relaxes or refreshes our students in the classroom, is beneficial to the classroom environment, increases well-being and awareness, and is conducive to learning in the classroom environment, certainly the role of smell is well worth exploring.

REFERENCES

Classen, C., D. Howes, and A. Synnott (1994). *Aroma: The Cultural History of Smell.* London: Routledge.

Cockett, M. (1988). "Neuro-linguistic What?" *Mainichi Daily News* (Tokyo), 25 November, p. 9.

Disability Services, University of Minnesota. (1995). *Guidelines Regarding Multiple Chemical Sensitivity/Environmental Illness (MCS/EI)*. Minneapolis: University of Minnesota.

Dranov, P. (1995). "Making Sense of Scents (A Surprisingly Scary Update)." *Cosmopolitan*, August, p. 204.

Engen, T. (1991). *Odor Sensation and Memory*. New York: Praeger.

Erb, R.C. (1968). *The Common Scents of Smell: How the Nose Knows and What it All Shows!* Cleveland, OH: World Publishing Co.

Gaudinier, K. (1995). Personal conversation.

Green, A. and C. Warren (1995). *Perfume*. Advertising Supplement. *New York Times*, October, p. 24.

Griffin, K. (1992). "A Whiff of Things to Come." *Health*, November/December, pp. 34–36.

Horowitz, E.K., D.J. Young, and J.A. Cope (1991). "Foreign Language Classroom Anxiety." In E.K. Horowitz and D.J. Young (eds.), *Language Anxiety: From Theory and Research to Classroom Implications*. Englewood Cliffs, NJ: Prentice Hall.

Hunter, B.T. (1995). "The Sales Appeal of Scents." *Consumer's Research*, October 1995, pp. 8–9.

Klein, R. (1995). "Get a Whiff of This: Breaking the Smell Barrier." *The New Republic*, February, pp. 18–23.

Le Guerer, A. (1992). *Scent: The Mysterious and Essential Powers of Smell*. New York: Turtle Bay Books.

Neumann, P.G. (1992). "Russian Computer Productivity in Ascent in de Scent Exposure." *The Risks Digest* 13, no. 4. Available: http://catless.ncl.ac.uk/Risks/13.04.html

Oxford, R.L. (1990). *Language Learning Strategies: What Every Teacher Should Know*. New York: Newbury House.

Roach, M. (1992). "Scents and Science." *Vogue*, November, p. 208.

Ryman, D. (1993). *Aromatherapy: The Complete Guide to Plant and Flower Essences for Health and Beauty*. New York: Bantam Books.

Wilke, M. (1995). *Scent of a Market*. Riverton, NJ: American Demographics.

4

Multiliteracy Skills

Tracey Tokuhama-Espinosa

In *Raising Multilingual Children* (2001) I wrote about multiliteracy skills and offered basic suggestions on how families could go about fostering such skills in light of information provided by international and bilingual schooling systems around the world. In this essay I would like to address parents' questions that often arise when their children are going through the process of obtaining multiliteracy skills. For clarification purposes, I will first summarize what is said in *Raising Multilingual Children*, and then address specific parent questions.

THE LINGUISTIC BASE OF THE TARGET LANGUAGES AND THE BASIC STEPS

In a nutshell, families should first evaluate their language goals. When it is determined that learning to read and write in more than one language is part of the family language goal—and this is by no means true in every family's case—they should look at the languages in which they wish their child to gain literacy skills. Second, if the target languages' alphabets are the same—as in the Phoenician alphabet, which is shared by English, Spanish, French, and German, among others—then the following four steps are important.

1. Understand the use of the written word. If the child is young enough that she is not yet learning to read in school, and she shows a natural curiosity about learning letters, parents should encourage basic prereading skills in the home language, or her native language, before she undertakes literacy in the school language (assuming the family or home language is different from the school's). This involves an understanding of the function of print, how a page is laid out from top to bottom and left to right, how writing is used in society to keep lists, to label, to relate information, and so on.

2. Learn the phonemic alphabet. As Adams (1996) pointed out so clearly in *Beginning to Read*, the most important of prereading skills is recognition of the phonemic alphabet, or the sounds that go with the symbols. That is, A is *ahh*, B is *buh*, C is

kuh, and so on. The child and parent should work together to make the connection between the physical symbol of the letter and that letter's sound.

3. Acknowledge exceptions in sound-to-letter relationships. After learning the basic phonemic alphabet, children should learn the "exceptions," which typically consist of the vowels and a few consonants (such as the letter *e* in English, which sometimes sounds like *eh* as in "egg" but also can sound like *ee* as in "me"). In total, this means the child should learn twenty-six symbols (A, B, C) and forty-four sounds (Ziegler 1986: viii–ix) if learning the English alphabet.

4. Acknowledge differences between languages. The child should then learn that the two alphabets of her two languages have the same symbols (A, B, C, etc.) but sometimes have different sounds, just as some of the letters have exceptional sounds in her first language, as she learned with the vowels. The exceptions are not limited to the vowels, however; some consonants may also have exceptions, such as with the *w* in German and the *w* in English, which look the same, but are pronounced differently.

5. Practice. Familiarity, repetition, and frequency are shown to be the best factors in maintaining literacy skills (Ellis 1994). Good readers read a lot, whatever their language(s).

While this may sound technical, it actually boils down to the child learning what the letters are, what sounds correspond to them, and how words are used in society. If the target languages have different writing systems (for example, Chinese pictographs, Japanese kanji, Russian, Hebrew, or Korean symbols, which are different from the English alphabet), the process is slightly different.

1. Understanding the use of the written word. Again, if the child is not yet learning to read in school and shows a natural curiosity about learning letters, families should encourage basic prereading skills in the home language before this occurs in the school language. This involves an understanding of the function of print and how a page is laid out (which may vary drastically, depending on the writing system involved). Japanese is from right to left, top to bottom, for example.

2. Sound to symbol: The most important of prereading skills is recognition of the sound(s) that go with each symbol. Depending on the symbol system being considered, this could mean the "name" of the symbol or the "meaning(s)" of the symbol, or both. Whereas the Phoenician alphabet has just twenty-six symbols to memorize, other writing systems can have thousands of characters to consider. The most basic symbols should be the focus of this stage of "prereading," along with the child's own name and symbols that the child shows an interest in learning.

3. Differences between languages. The parents should help the child acknowledge the differences between the two writing systems. "In Korean we write 'house' like this . . . but in Russian we write it like this . . ." or "In Japanese, 'moon' looks like this . . . but in German we write 'moon' like this. . . ." This is something children come to realize on their own and will be curious about, and parents can aid their children by being as clear and as simple as possible in their explanations.

4. Practice. Similarly, the three guides of familiarity, repetition, and frequency are the best factors in maintaining literacy skills (Ellis 1994). Good readers read a lot, whatever their language(s).

PARENTS' QUESTIONS

Parents often ask a variety of questions related to literacy skills: When should I begin? Which language should be taught first? What materials should I use to teach letters? If my child has already learned to read in the school language, when can I introduce literacy in the second language? Should I read to my child in a language I don't speak fluently? What if my daughter's teacher has told us we shouldn't teach reading at home before she does so at school?

To answer these questions, I would like to look at them in the setting of six categories. These are questions about

1. Family goals
2. The role of the home vs. the role of the school
3. The age factor in literacy skills
4. Strategy
5. Target language similarities and differences
6. Materials

Questions About Family Goals

What are your own family language goals? Are they clear?

I usually begin discussing multiliteracy by asking parents to reflect on their family language goals. Do they want their child to speak a foreign language well enough to play with the kids next door? Do they want their child to pass second grade in a foreign language? To graduate with a bilingual diploma? To be able to attend university in any of her languages? To be completely fluent? All of these goals are legitimate ones; each family must decide its own. But decide they must, for each of these goals requires a very different level of engagement and preparation on the part of the entire family.

If the family wants their child to acquire basic communication skills in order to play with neighbor's children, multiliteracy skills will not even come into the picture. If they want their child to be able to pass a university entrance exam in several languages, a far greater level of skills is required to so do.

Deciding the exact goal is a first-step question parents must ask themselves. This must be done individually with each child. A set of goals for one child may be completely different from those for a sibling because of aptitude, opportunity, and other factors.

"Is reading to preserve culture a legitimate goal of literacy?"
(Mara, a Hungarian mother of a two-year-old living in Geneva)

Almost all goals and their attached motivations can be justified as the basis for wanting to encourage multiliteracy skills. Are all of the motivations always practical, and are they all legitimate? These are other questions altogether, and

each family will have to respond individually. I personally believe that one of
the strongest motivating factors when pursuing multiliteracy skills for our
children is preserving their cultural links. In my own case, not only do I want
my children to read and write English, but I also want them to know they are
half American. I want them to know George Washington and Thanksgiving
and Big Bird. I want them to know the Declaration of Independence and how
the country was founded and who Pocahontas is—as Hirsch (1988) puts it, to
be *culturally literate* in the United States. The function of literacy may be to
decode symbols and sounds, but the purpose of literacy is to open doors on
culture.

Other reasons that are often promoted by parents who want their children
to have multiliteracy skills have to do with success in the local school system.
Others are related to needing English in addition to another language because
English is the new "universal language." Others have to do with the desire to
communicate with relatives in the home country. Still others speak of the
attractiveness of another language in relation to the advantages it offers later
in life. All of these reasons can be viewed as legitimate; each family has to
recognize its own reasons for pursuing this skill.

**"What if the parents' goals and the child's goals about language
are different?"** (Jean-Claude, grandfather of four multilingual children
who speak French, German, Swiss German, and English but write
"only" in French)

Parents are often compelled to push language skills on children because "I
know what is best for him." In many cases, parents actually do know what is
best for their children; in other cases, their enthusiasm for pursuing such a
lofty skill as multiliteracy should be tempered with a bit of reality. It is difficult
to learn and then to maintain literacy skills in several languages. If a child is
to learn to be a good reader in more than one language, he will have to read
often in all his target languages. Think of your own child for a moment. Does
he have the interest, ability, and time to do this? What if he just is not a reader,
and does not enjoy reading? Should he be forced to spend time doing it? Different styles of parenting come into play here; I always return to a single rule
of thumb that I use in relation to languages as well as to many other areas of
child upbringing: Can I help my child find a reason to want to do this himself?
That is, my job is not to teach him to read, but to make him want to read.
There are two pairs of motivation: positive and negative, and internal and
external. (See table 4.1.)

If I force my child to learn to read and write in Chinese because I know it's
good for him, and withhold my love and approval until he does so (or spank
him or ignore him when he is not successful), that means I am using *external
negative* motivation to achieve multiliteracy skills. If, on the other hand, I find
ways to make Chinese so attractive that he cannot resist pursuing the language

Table 4.1
Motivation Types

	Internal	External
Positive	(Best way)	
Negative		(Worst way)

and give him the opportunities to feed his curiosity about the language, so that he wants to do it for himself—and not to please Mommy—then I have achieved multiliteracy skills using *internal positive* motivation. This will be with my child for life. Though the skills may be learned in the first scenario, too, in the second case they will also be used. Thus the second approach is, overall, a much healthier one.

Questions About the Role of the Home vs. the Role of the School

"What do I do if the teacher's advice is to NOT teach the children to read at home before school?" (Elsa, German mother of a five-year-old living in French-speaking Switzerland)

First, it is important to understand the teacher's reasoning and then to understand if your prereading objectives challenge it or not. Though the view is not commonly preached in the United States, some schools in Europe and Asia believe that all education is conducted in the schools; home has no role in education. In other words, the job of the teacher is to educate, and the parents' job is to help the children develop balanced social skills. Strategically, is there a way to achieve both your goal of teaching prereading skills in the home before the child attends school and learns them formally, without upsetting the philosophical boat of the school?

Well, yes: If you are able to achieve the school's goals (producing a socially adept child who fits in well with the class), you presumably can teach prereading skills without disturbing the methodology in the school. How? A child can learn the alphabet at home, but he must also learn that "the way Mommy says/writes this is different from the way your teacher says/writes this."

"Why?"

"Because we learned it differently when we were little. You need to learn both ways." If your son is the happy, socially adjusted child the school hopes you are delivering to them for education, then your child will not make a point of showing off this "insider" knowledge; rather, he will most likely be recognized as "very quick" in picking up the literacy skills being taught in the class.

Though such a tactic does not always work, it generally smoothes over the role limits that some teachers would like to impose on parents. They are, after all, the teacher. Does the teacher always know best? As a teacher myself, I'd like to think so, and so would most people who join this profession, but most of us know better than that. Parents have to be careful not to detract from the authority of the teacher, which can only lead to poor relations and have bad effects on the child's experience in the classroom.

Other, more pedagogic reasons exist for telling parents not to teach reading and writing at home before the school does this. Most school systems have very clear guidelines for how they want their children to read and write, including very specific script types. Parents teaching literacy skills at home before they are learned at school buck the system. The conformist way of teaching ensures that all handwriting looks the same (an experienced eye can see which children were educated in the German school system or the Japanese school system by the form of the letters). Teachers are concerned that children can become confused by how the letter "f" looks different in English printing and in French script, for example. Capital versus lowercase letters, as well as when script writing is taught (in the United States, cursive writing comes after printing is understood; in Europe it is often done before). While these are legitimate school concerns because they can cause a great disturbance to a classroom situation ("But Mrs. Matrice, *you* wrote my name wrong, my mommy writes it different!"), much depends on the individual child. Some children have more tact than others. Some children are able to learn to read and write flawlessly, and then enter school and simply are considered "one of the brightest," while others can be labeled a disturbance. Children with a developed sense of associative labeling (a small red triangle and a large blue triangle are both still triangles) have less trouble realizing that the teacher can write her name in cursive, and Mommy does it in all capitals, but both are still her name (Miller and Dollard 1941). Our job as parents is to help our children learn multiliteracy skills without making them a burden to the school system (but rather a benefit to the class).

Another rebuttal to this taboo of teaching reading and writing in the home is related to curricula. Most schools that teach multiliteracy skills encourage a strong foundation in the mother tongue before the child learns literacy skills in a second or third language. If the child's mother tongue is different from the school language, it makes added sense to teach literacy skills at home in the mother tongue before the child learns the second language in school.

"When does this 'natural curiosity' about letters usually arise? How can I take advantage of this time?" (Nicola, mother of an eight-month-old being brought up bilingually in Russian and English)

Children differ drastically in the development of their cognitive skills, but there is a general guideline. Many children show an interest in the function of writing sometime around the age of three or four years. At this time they also recognize other symbols, like the Coca-Cola wave or the arches of McDonalds, and pretend to "read" them. Some do this earlier, some much later, and some never show an interest in letters at all. Linguistic awareness games that encourage preschoolers and kindergarten children to apply sounds to words and letters to sounds are excellent tools for later reading preparedness (Adams 1996 suggests games such as those developed by Elkonin 1993; Liberman et al. 1980; or Lundber, Frost, and Peterson 1988). Children in this age group (three to six) are generally very receptive to such games, which means this is probably the best time to home in on "natural curiosity" about language. Children may typically begin with "Is this my letter?" meaning the first letter of their name, move on to general questions like "Does snake begin with 's'?" and then pose more sophisticated inquiries comparing letter sounds in questions like "Does 'cookie' start with 'c' or 'k'?"

"When do children normally learn to read around the world?
What is normal?" (Junko, Japanese mother of a four-year-old in a
Swiss school)

Reading and writing curricula around the world are very particular to the individual countries. All formal systems of education tend to introduce literacy skills some time between the ages of three and nine. In Hong Kong, formal reading and writing begin at age three and a half; in Sweden and other Nordic countries these do not occur until seven, eight, or nine. "Equally logical but different" is a dictum I learned on an exchange when I was in high school, and I still apply it today, especially in relation to age standards in differing school systems. Each school system has it own reasons for undertaking the task of literacy at a particular age. Some systems believe that earlier is better, while others feel that children should be children for as long as possible, and thus literacy should be kept at bay until the latest possible time.

The Age Factor in Literacy Skills

"When is the ideal time to teach my child to read and write in
his two languages? And what about a third?" (Jenny, from Israel,
raising a thirteen-month-old daughter in English, French, and Hebrew)

Depending on the child's age when multiliteracy skills are undertaken, and on the age when literacy skills are introduced in the schools, the answer to this question can be found. Let's imagine the "ideal" linguistic life for a moment. A child is brought up bilingually, with each parent speaking a different language. The parents read to her every day for an average of twenty minutes or more. When the child's natural curiosity about languages peaks (at three, four, five, or six), they introduce letter-to-sound recognition at home. This can be done in one or both of the languages, but it is generally recommended that the stronger of the two languages be encouraged first, so that the child develops a firm grounding in it before attempting literacy skills in the second language.

In the best-case scenario, this means that before the child formally learns letters in school, she has learned the native language alphabet and the corresponding sounds. She then should go on to do this formally at school. While the child is learning the letters in school, parents should give the home language a rest, and allow the teacher's philosophy and the school's pedagogic methods to prevail. After the child has a firm grounding in the school's literacy program, the parents can resume further literacy skills in the home language(s).

For example, my daughter Natalie is now eight. From birth she was read to in English and Spanish daily. Between the ages of five and six and a half, she learned the English alphabet and the corresponding phonemic sounds in a pre-reading class. At six and a half she began first grade in a German school, where she began reading and writing in German. We continued to read to her and with her in English and Spanish at home, but we stopped formal English reading classes. At the end of the first grade she had a good grounding in German reading and writing, but we continued not to emphasize reading in English and Spanish because we felt her perfection in German was more important—it was the school language and her third spoken language (native neither to my husband nor to me).

In the middle of second grade everything suddenly clicked. One evening she said, "I can't read in Spanish."

"Why do you think you can't read in Spanish?" I asked her.

"Because I never learned it in a class," she responded.

"I think you can read in Spanish. Would you like to try?" I asked, extremely excited that she had found it within herself to broach the subject. "The sounds are very similar to German, with a few exceptions," I said encouragingly, knowing that she felt completely comfortable in German. She then picked up a simple book in Spanish and read the entire text herself. Excited, she then turned to the English books that her American grandmother had sent over a year earlier and were meant for first grade readers in the United States, and found, with some concentration, that she could read those as well. She has since begun to read in French, the school's second language.

Admittedly, I think Natalie has a very high aptitude for foreign languages, but possessing multiliteracy skills in four languages by the time one is eight years old is an admirable feat nonetheless. We recognize, as well, that she has a long way to go to solidify these skills to a sophisticated level, meaning reading and writing in all four with frequency if she wants to maintain grade level abilities. It should be remembered that her story is meant to illustrate an ideal situation, however. Many families do not have access to the resources that we were lucky enough to encounter, nor is the choice of schooling or timing available to them.

*"It seems that my child's dominant language has become the
school language, whereas it used to be the home language. Is this
normal?"* (Lisa, mother of eight- and eleven-year-old English-speaking
boys attending a French-language school)

Language dominance fluctuation is completely normal, and can be directly
related to the amount of time a person spends in a language situation and the
number of opportunities that person has to use the languages in meaningful
situations. A child who has considered English his native language (it is the
home language) for the first eight years of life may find that his dominant
language becomes French due to living in a French-speaking environment and
attending a school conducted in French. Should parents worry about this?

Depending on family language goals, this phenomenon is taken in stride by
some and is a call for panic to others. Has the child forgotten his roots? His
mother tongue? No, he is just choosing not to use it. And like many other
aspects of child upbringing, forcing them to return to the language probably
will not yield better results than helping him discover the value of his mother
tongue once again. Many a teenager brought up with English as a mother
tongue while living abroad—say in Japan—has found a wonderful tool for
revenge on parents who misunderstand them. They simply stop using English
at home. And when that bothers Mom, all the better. I say this facetiously, of
course, but on a more serious note, I always feel it is better for the parent to
encourage home language skills as opposed to threatening punishment for use
of the school language. Pretending to ignore your child because he does not
speak your language is one method, but rather childish, as the child knows full
well you do understand. If the parents' goal is to maintain the home language
level, then their job is to continue to give as many opportunities for home
language use as possible, and to guide the child into situations where he will
see the usefulness of the language for himself. What can the minority language
parent (one who does not speak the language of the community) do when
children stop using his native language and adopt the dominant one? Help find
ways to make the language attractive in and of itself. "So you want to see that
movie? Ok, but I see it's only available in English . . ." or "Here's that new
Madonna CD you wanted. Those lyrics are really special, aren't they?"

This, of course, has different successes, depending on the languages being
discussed, the options available in the language environment, and the child's
personality. We shall discuss this further in "Questions About Materials."

Questions About Strategy

"Which language should reading and writing be taught in first?"
(Claudia, bringing up a Swiss-German four-year-old with her British
husband in Zurich)

International school systems that foster multiliteracy skills work hard
to ensure a firm base in the mother tongue before launching into a second

language. In *European Models of Bilingual Education*, Baetens-Beardsmore (1993) shows how the European School in Brussels requires three languages for graduation, with an optional fourth. How does it achieve multiliteracy skills? Primary school instruction is in the child's first language (which could be any of the official languages of the European Community), and a second language (usually English, French, or German) is also taught. There is a great emphasis on clarity of thought in the child's first language throughout his school career. The second language is used to teach subjects requiring less verbal skills (physical education, art, music), in the third, fourth, and fifth grades of primary school. Writing in the second language occurs between the sixth and eighth grades.

Beardsmore's survey of schools puts great emphasis on a child's first language skills. It is believed that understanding the function of literacy in one's first language is key to success in learning subsequent languages. Therefore, the standard advice is to teach literacy skills in the child's native language first.

"Can I switch strategies from one parent, one language, and now read to my child in my nonnative language?" (Lisa, American-Swiss mother raising two sons with her Italian husband in French-speaking Geneva)

One of the ten key factors in raising multilingual children is acknowledging a chosen language strategy. Families must decide how they are going to approach multiple languages (whether it be one parent, one language, or one language spoken at home and another spoken elsewhere), and be consistent with that strategy. This does not mean that the strategy must be simple.

Many parents who have been faithful to a one-person, one-language strategy find a dissonance of sorts when thinking of reading to their children in the "other" language. Parents have at least two options. The first is to realize that one parent, one language plus story time in the child's choice of language is also a strategy. It is a more complex strategy but, if it is applied consistently, can be successful. Second, parents can remain completely faithful to their one parent, one language strategy and only play taped stories in the "other" language or have another caregiver read to the child.

If the family strategy has been to keep one language in the home and one language in the community and school, but the child now wants to hear stories in the school language, the family will have to decide whether or not that compromises the success of the family language, or whether or not it simply changes the stated strategy. An option is to allow children to hear school language stories at a different time, say right after dinner, before homework, and keep bedtime stories in the home language. A key factor in switching language strategies is to have the child's consent. Does he understand and accept the change you are proposing? If so, you can build on an existing strategy by creating a more complex one that meets the changing family goals.

Questions About Target Language Similarities
and Differences

"Is it harder for a child to have biliteracy skills when her target languages do not share a symbol system?" (Maureen, raising three girls in English, Arabic, and French in France)

This question asks whether or not a child learning Korean and English (which do not share a symbol system) has a harder time than one learning French and Spanish (which do share a symbol system); or whether a child learning Arabic and French has a harder time than one learning Dutch and German. Such a question can be answered by looking at two factors: the linguistic relationship between the languages being learned, and the difference between the spoken and written word.

As I wrote in *Raising Multilingual Children* (2001), when languages have similar linguistic roots and share a writing system, people find them easier to learn. In the book I offer the example of some of my husband's colleagues when he went to Tokyo to study Japanese. There he found that a friend from Taiwan could pick up the local Japanese newspaper and "read" it. Though he was unable to say the words out loud (he had no clue about the sounds of the specific symbols in Japanese), he was able to decipher the meaning due to the similarities of the Japanese kanji writing and the Chinese characters he had been schooled in. Similarly, many Spanish-speaking friends of mine can follow Italian radio and television, or even the Portuguese soap operas in the native language, because Spanish, Italian, and Portuguese share linguistic roots and sound relatively similar.

The influence of the language's roots is not as important, however, if we are considering verbal skills only, as opposed to literacy skills. Linguistic similarities are more important when we consider literacy skills, because oral language does not consider symbols of the written language. A chart from *Raising Multilingual Children* clarifies the difference between speaking and reading and writing. (See table 4.2.) The difference between the spoken and written word is what makes the concept of "easy" versus "hard" languages clearer. When a child learns to speak two languages from birth, neither language is considered "easier" or "harder" by that child. Slobin (1992) wrote, amazing as it may seem at first, that all children acquire all parts of speech of their languages, all around the world, by the time they are four. When do languages become "hard"? When languages are not acquired from birth, and when one wishes to learn to read and write the languages.

Writing adds a further mental step to language processing compared to speaking. Whereas speaking in conversation entails hearing the word by using the auditory cortex, deciphering its meaning in Wernicke's area, passing through the arcuate fasciculus, and then responding in speech by using Broca's area, to write, one must do all this plus retrace this process, then use the motor cortex and put pen to paper (or fingertips to keyboard). The visual represen-

Table 4.2
The Spoken Versus the Written Word

Spoken	Written
Natural language (utterances)	Formal language (text)
Highly implicit	Highly explicit
Context bound	Context free
Unique	Repeatable
Idiosyncratic	Memory supported
Personal	Impersonal
Intuitive	Logical, rational
Sequential descriptive	Expository content

tation of a word in symbols requires not only vocabulary to understand what is being said but also an understanding of the symbol system used to write the word.

What does this mean in relation to the original question of whether or not multiliteracy skills are complicated by diverse language systems? The answer, in short, is yes, it is harder for a child to acquire biliteracy skills when her two languages do not share a symbol system. This is primarily due to the fact that two separate symbol systems must be learned, as opposed to a single system that has "exceptions." However, on the brighter side, there are no competing sounds for a single symbol when the systems are so different. For example, the Greek epsilon does not compete visually with the Phoenician "e" in the brain, whereas German and French speakers may have difficulty understanding how "e" can be one symbol but be pronounced very differently. So whereas it may at first appear more complex to have two different symbol systems, there may be an advantage in the uniqueness of the visual separation in the brain.

"Are there 'transferable' benefits of literacy from one language to another? Does being a good reader in English transfer to being a good reader in other languages?"

Whereas the benefits of learning two languages verbally have transferable benefits, reading and writing must be developed in each language on their own. While some cross-referencing can occur when the alphabets are the same, as we pointed out earlier, there are far fewer transferable benefits than in speaking. In verbal skills, when a child learns that "dog" is *inu* in Japanese, he generalizes and realizes that all things must have an equivalent in other languages. When a child learns to write, the frequency, repetition, and familiarity (see Ellis 1994) needed to become a good reader must be done language by language. That is, if a child wants to learn to read and write well in Spanish and English, each must be given its own time for practice.

Clearly, the correlation between one's ability to write well in one's native language and one's level of verbal proficiency in the second language has an influence on the ability to be a good writer in the second language. Writing performance in a second language is influenced by mother-tongue writing expertise and by proficiency in the second language (Cumming 1994: 173).

Questions About Materials

"Shouldn't all books be read in their original language?" (Lena, a Czech mother raising a newborn in Afrikaans, Swiss German, and English)

While many people feel Shakespeare belongs only in English, Cervantes only in Spanish, and Chekhov only in Russian, most critics can find a middle ground. Yes, it is very hard to find Dr. Seuss's *The Cat in the Hat* in many other languages aside from English that carry the rhythm as well (though I have heard a that a very good Latin version exists), and Winnie the Pooh's "rumbly tummy" is hard to translate. Nevertheless, good translations of many children's books do exist. I have found that translated versions of books are often very attractive to children who know the story in the native language, and then find that the same story exists in the second language. My four-year-old son insisted on buying *Robin Hood* in Italian because he had just learned the story in English and wanted more. He was delighted to find that it was the same in Italian as in English. The language was a secondary consideration; what he valued was the confirmation of the story line. This can be used to enhance vocabulary in a target language. Similarly, videos known to the child can be seen in the target language to help children develop fluency.

"Where can I find books in the other languages?"

A number of online bookstores have come into being since the 1990s in order to cater to the growing need for good literature choices in foreign languages. Several online shops with good reputations include those found on my website, www.Multi-Faceta.com, under the reference section. There are also several websites that offer free downloading of support materials for the home in a variety of languages. All the large search engines can put you in direct contact with hundreds of sites of this type as well (search under "bilingual books for children," "multilingual bookstores," "bilingual resources" or "ESL resources"). Maria Johnson's essay in this book, "Bringing Up Bilingual Children in Scarce Language Environments: How the Internet Can Help" is especially helpful. But what if you do not have access to the Internet? While options vary depending on the country you live in, some of the following options may work.

Several families have commented that their relatives in the home countries are only too happy to find age-appropriate reading materials for them. Local bookstore personnel often enjoy the challenge of a good search, and will help find good materials for you as well. This is true of many local libraries that may have books or tapes in your target language(s). Play groups often have their own lending libraries, as do many international church or other religious organizations. Many schools run pen pal exchanges with children from other countries.

While all of these options are not always available to all families, there should be at least one or two from this list that your own family could pursue in order to acquire good age-appropriate, entertaining reading materials.

CONCLUSION

Multiliteracy skills are a lofty but manageable, and often nonnegotiable, goal. In almost all cases of successful multiliteracy development there is a clear family goal, a successful partnership between family and school, supportive materials in the target languages, and, above all, the child's cooperation, if not enthusiasm, for the task. Our job as teachers and parents is to support the child in the task, and to find ways of helping him want to be literate, or multiliterate, on his own.

REFERENCES

Adams, M.J. (1996). *Beginning to Read: Thinking and Learning About Print*. Cambridge, MA: MIT Press.

Baetens-Beardsmore, H. (ed.) (1993). *European Models of Bilingual Education*. Clevedon, UK: Multilingual Matters.

Cumming, A.H. (ed.). (1994). *Bilingual Performance in Reading and Writing*. Ann Arbor, MI: John Benjamin's Publishing Co.

Elkonin, D.B. (1993). *Comparative Reading*. New York: Macmillan.

Ellis, A. (1994). *Reading, Writing and Dyslexia: A Cognitive Analysis*. 2nd ed. Hillsdale, NJ: Lawrence Erlbaum Associates.

Hirsch, E.D. (1988). *Cultural Literacy: What Every American Needs to Know*. New York: Vintage Books.

Liberman, I.Y., D. Shankweiler, B. Blachman, L. Camp, and M. Wefelman (1980). "Steps Towards Literacy: A Linguistic Approach." In P. Levinson and C. Sloan (Eds.), *Auditory Processing and Language: Clinical and Research Perspectives*. New York: Grune and Stratton.

Lundber, I., J. Frost, and O.P. Peterson (1988). "Effects of an Extensive Program Stimulating Phonological Awareness in Preschool Children." *Reading Research Quarterly* 23: 264–284.

Miller, N.E., and J. Dollard (1941). *Social Learning and Imitation*. New Haven, CT: Yale University Press.

Tokuhama-Espinosa, T. (2001). *Raising Multilingual Children: Foreign Language Acquisition and Children*. Westport, CT: Bergin & Garvey.

Ziegler, E. (1986). "Why Our Children Aren't Reading." Foreword to R. Flesch, *Why Johnny Can't Read*. 2nd ed. New York: Harper & Row.

5

Two-Way Immersion Programs in the United States

Jennifer Frengel

Those who intend to make the United States their home need to learn English, but doing so at the expense of their heritage, culture, and native language should not be necessary. Unfortunately, due to the current design of English as a foreign or second language instruction in the United States, when immigrant children are placed in English immersion classrooms, this is exactly what happens. The option of a bilingual education program is no better, for the child generally fails to learn English as well as is necessary to succeed in a monolingual English society. The result of these flawed language designs is that we produce either high school graduates with no sense of cultural identity or those who are unable to read or write fluently in English.

While this is grave in and of itself, it is not the only problem with language learning in U.S. public schools. Language-majority children (those who speak only English) receive an average of two years of foreign language instruction in high school and rarely reach a high level of fluency. In today's world, monolingualism is a detriment to social progress and personal development. Monolingual Americans risk "cultural isolation" in which there is a perceived ignorance about other cultures, as well as the practical difficulty that they are beginning to lose their jobs to more linguistically versatile people who can comprehend cultural subtleties in the business world as a result of their multilingual and multicultural perspective.

THE NEW SOLUTION: TWO-WAY IMMERSION

A solution to this problem is a dual-language or two-way immersion (TWI) program. The objective of his type of program is to turn out a completely bilingual student population from both language-minority and English-only backgrounds. All children will be able to speak, read, and write in two languages upon school completion. The TWI program works by teaching an equal number of language-minority and English-only students in both languages, beginning in kindergarten. For example, a community with a large Spanish-speaking population will have a Spanish/English school. Other language-minority students who attend the Spanish/English school will end up fluent in three languages, provided their native language is still spoken in the home, without risk to their academic achievement (Crawford 1991). Since the community language of the United States is English, the development of the English language will not be slowed (Cenoz and Genesee 1998; Montague 1997). This introduces a second language to English-only students at an early age, and continues mother-tongue fluency in limited English proficiency (LEP) students. Though the concept of two-way immersion schools began in the 1960s, a second look is being taken at this innovative model as American demographics shift, and more and more families have a language other than English in the home.

LANGUAGE ACQUISITION RESEARCH

Probably the largest area for debate in the bilingual education arena is over the most effective way to teach language-minority students with two goals in mind: English fluency and academic achievement. Advocates of bilingual education add that maintenance of the native language should also be a school responsibility, but opponents argue that this should be left to the family. Research shows us that independent of whose job native language maintenance is, fluency in one's first language is a prerequisite for success in second language learning and academic achievement in that second language (Crawford 1991; McLaughlin 1985; Cenoz and Genesee 1998).

For language-minority students, immersion programs in English are generally of a *subtractive* nature (de Cos 1999). What English immersion, or even very rapid transition into English mainstream classrooms, does is *replace* a child's native language with English, thus subtracting from the language skills of that child. If a child is not given the opportunity to develop her native language skills to a level of fluency, even literacy, it will be more difficult to acquire those skills in a second language.

Research also shows that integration with native speakers of both languages increases the child's ability to use the second language properly. In both bilingual education programs and foreign language classes, or immersion programs for language-majority students, the two groups of children are separated and left to learn their second language with little or no exposure to people who actually speak that second language. This division is detrimental in many ways. First of all, it creates a greater division between language-majority and language-minority students. Second, it leaves the students with no access to true usage of the language. They are left to what their grammar workbook says, and they never really see how the language is used in everyday conversation. The more common language and slang that people use in daily interactions is rarely, if ever, taught.

Additionally, "isolation from native speakers has often led historically to *pidginization*—that is, to the development of a simplified form of the target language marked by many instances of transfer from the first language" (McLaughlin 1985: 17). With no exposure to native speakers of the second language, students tend to transfer words and sentences from their first language to the second, even when not grammatically correct. They then reinforce each other's incorrect usage of the second language. According to Fred Genesee, a specialist in immersion research, in "a dual immersion program with native Spanish speakers as 'peer models,' English-speaking children would likely acquire higher levels of proficiency in the second language" (Crawford 1991: 166).

A SUCCESSFUL TWO-WAY IMMERSION PROGRAM

Nichole Montague (1997) outlines seven critical components for a successful TWI program: choice of model, timing of introduction, language combination choices, program reflective of the population, materials, teacher preparedness, and the encouragement of second language use.

The Model

The first one of these components is a clear definition of the model before implementation. There are multiple variations, but the 90/10 model has been shown to be the most successful in the United States. In this model, during 90 percent of the time that children of both language backgrounds spend in kindergarten, they will hear Spanish. (For the purpose of this essay, I will use Spanish/English as the model program. It must be noted, however, that the program works in any two languages and must be implemented based on the need and demographics of the community.) In this model the time gap between the two languages closes by 20 percent each year until the fourth and fifth grades, where the day is evenly divided between Spanish and English. Another model is the 50/50 model, in which children are taught 50 percent of the day in Spanish and 50 percent of the day in English, beginning in kindergarten. Another model uses Spanish 100 percent of the time until the second or third grade, when English is finally introduced. Whichever model the school decides to use, the most important thing to remember is that the minority language should never be taught for less than 50 percent of the day. If it is taught for less than 50 percent of the day, the validity of the minority language diminishes, and it becomes more difficult for the language-majority students to learn their second language.

The way the two languages are divided up can be left up to the teacher(s) (i.e., by subject, days of the week, etc.), but it is very important that the two languages are kept separate. The teacher should not translate between the languages. If children know that the material will not be translated for them, they are more motivated to make out what is being explained in the foreign language

(Crawford 1991). In the lower grades teachers may find it easier to use a visual reminder about which language is to be used, such as a hat or different lighting. Whichever model the school decides to use, and whatever approaches the teacher uses to divide the languages, need to be clearly defined from the beginning. Everyone involved, parents included, needs to know what is expected and when. This is true for any successful curriculum, since a chosen strategy and the consistency with which it is delivered are vital to success (Tokuhama-Espinosa 2001).

Although ideally the proportions of the two languages would be 50/50, most program organizers realize that "schools rarely have the luxury of operating under ideal conditions" (Miner 1999), and find a program can still be successful if one group is represented at least 33 percent of the time, and the other no more than 67 percent of the time (Gold 1988; Crawford 1991). Regardless of the proportions of the students represented, what really matters is the fact that the children are not separated based on language ability. They take classes together, and learn through exposure that one language is just as valid as the other. They also learn that by working together they can overcome the difficulties of learning a new language. If respect and integration are not enough justification for TWI programs, there is sufficient evidence that when one is learning a second language, the presence of and interaction with students who speak that language natively leads to academic success (Gold 1988). When students of both language backgrounds are present, they offer the valuable resource of themselves to each other for practice and support.

Timing

The second component Montague outlines is the necessity of a gradual phase-in of the program. The best way to adhere to this component is to begin the program in either preschool or kindergarten because a child who has already begun his school career in a regular, English-only program may find difficulty in a quick adjustment to a new Spanish curriculum, for example. Another reason to begin early is the window of opportunity, the "critical period" discussed above, that can be taken advantage of at an earlier age (Tokuhama-Espinosa 2001; de Cos 1999).

While the gradual phase-in of the program may seem obvious (most people would not expect fourth graders who have never studied Spanish to automatically be ready to study science in Spanish), what is less obvious is a gradual phase-in of the languages. This is part of the reason the 90/10 model has been so successful. In the study done by Ramirez, Yuen, and Ramey (1991), results showed that students who were abruptly transitioned into English performed worse on math and English (reading and writing) achievement tests. However, since this study was done only on language-minority students who experienced the transition from instruction in their native language to full instruction in

English, it remains unknown whether the same effect would occur in language-majority students. It is true that any disruption in the consistency of a child's education, whether the child comes from a language-minority or a language-majority background, will cause difficulty in the child's academic progress. Research shows that consistency is a key factor to positive development of children (Berger and Thompson 1995; Tokuhama-Espinosa 2001). Children who move more (resulting in constant school changes), and whose parents are inconsistent in their parenting (such as one day permitting them to do something, the next day not), find it harder to adjust to new situations and are often confused by their surroundings, not knowing what to expect. Sometimes the results of this inconsistency can be so severe that the child looks elsewhere, such as to street gangs, to find some sort of consistency. Keeping this in mind, it seems apparent that either the 90/10 model or the 50/50 model would be the most successful in achieving the goals of academic achievement and biliteracy.

Language Combination Choices and Reflecting the Population

Another critical component that Montague lists is that the instruction (i.e., language and course material) needs to reflect the student population of that classroom or school. For example, a Spanish/English program should not be implemented in a school or community that has a very small number of native Spanish speakers but a large number of native Chinese speakers. As stated above, it is also necessary to have a balance (or relatively close balance) between language-majority and language-minority students. An equal balance of students from different backgrounds gives adequate representation of both groups, and equal numbers of role models based on language background. This way one group is never seen as being the dominant or the minority group, and the label of being one or the other never comes into play.

This equal division of students from different backgrounds could pose a problem in communities where there are large numbers of children from a variety of backgrounds such as the San Francisco Bay Area. To solve this problem, many different schools, or different language tracks within one school, could be set up with an emphasis on different languages: Spanish/English, Chinese/English, Farsi/English, and so on. This also gives parents of language-majority students the opportunity to decide which language they want their child to learn. However, the problem remains of what to do within a school when there are small numbers of children from a wide range of language backgrounds. This is an area that could use more research because it is a valid concern in a state such as California, whose minority population, representing at least 100 different languages, is greater than the "majority."

Materials

Montague also stresses the importance of quality materials in each language of instruction. Schools should supply equal numbers of books in Spanish and in English, and both languages should be represented in textbooks of the core curriculum, such as social studies and science. When both languages are represented equally throughout textbooks and literature, students find equal validity in both languages. Textbooks written in Spanish give validity to the language as a professional (scientific, mathematical) mode of communication, and not just a language to tell stories in. Original language textbooks will also expose children to different points of view and different modes of gaining knowledge. For example, a history book written in Spanish (maybe one written and used in Mexico) is going to illustrate the Spanish-American War differently than an American textbook. A Chinese science book may explain gravity differently than an American science book. Not only do textbooks in different languages bring validity to the language, but they also teach children to think about things in different ways. While enhancing cognition by creating a wider background of information accessible for problem solving, language-minority texts also teach children to keep an open mind, reminding them that there are a variety of explanations for each problem, and one is not always better than another.

An argument against TWI programs could be made with regard to cost. It may be difficult or costly to find textbooks written originally in Spanish, Chinese, Farsi, or other languages. Finding literature is not as difficult, and would be essential to the program, though it would not replace the need for texts. Children need to learn that things do not have to be translated into the majority language to become valid. Literature studied in its original text does not lose its meaning through translation. Dr. Seuss stories lose their humor when translated because the rhymes do not translate, and neither do invented words. This is the same for children's stories in all languages. If textbooks are not readily obtainable in other languages, schools could start with foreign literature as a base.

However, through extensive evaluation and research of TWI programs it has been found that these programs are actually very cost effective and are more cost-beneficial than most traditional school curricula. Though initially the right materials may incur a higher cost, once the program gets started its cost is comparable to that of other schools. Most of the 266 schools that have implemented TWI programs across the United States are public schools, so we know by their success that cost is not a problem. Cost-benefit measurements are made not only in terms of savings but also of the improvements in schooling (children are actually *learning* more) and the increased earning potential for bilingual students (Tucker 1995). Dual-language schools actually may save the school system money because of the decrease in remedial classes and special attention needed to help limited English proficiency students, and the lower number of grade retentions seen as a result (Cenoz and Genesee 1998; Tucker 1995).

Teacher Preparedness

The fifth component of a successful TWI program is a well-trained teaching staff. Obviously this component is necessary for any successful educational program, but it is truer for a dual-language immersion program. Bilingual educators are a main constituent of this type of program because monolingual teachers cannot teach in the other language. However, it is possible, and just as successful, to have different monolingual teachers teaching in their native tongues—provided the school could afford two teachers per classroom or had the day organized in such a way that the teachers rotated. It is preferable that the bilingual educators have an ESL certificate because there are important details to be learned only through training. An example is the acknowledgment that simultaneous translation of the material inhibits the child's motivation to learn her second language.

The teaching staff also needs to feel a sense of solidarity within the group. Team teaching is an important aspect of TWI programs, and the staff needs to know how to work well with one another. This is a reason for preferring a bilingual staff. Team teaching becomes difficult if the team doesn't speak a common language. Through teacher training and staff development, this team can be formed, a common goal perhaps being to work toward bilingualism together, with opportunities readily available for monolingual teachers to learn the other language. Teachers who work well and communicate with one another make good role models for students who are supposed to be learning how to work well and communicate with one another.

Montague also stresses the importance of administrative support, not only to the teachers, but to the parents and the community as well. For many language-majority parents, the idea of sending their child to a school in which he will be taught (in kindergarten) ninety percent of the time in a language he does not understand is very frightening. The role of the administration is to ease this anxiety, open communication, and offer support when needed. The administrators act as role models, and parents will find comfort in knowing the administration offers support to them and their children.

Encouraging Second Language Use

The last component that Montague highlights, questions the role of elicited response. This is an area that needs much more research because it is not quite understood what the best method is for teachers to encourage a child to speak in a foreign tongue. However, some things to remember are the importance of getting language-majority students to use the second language, and reducing the fear and stigma that go along with mispronouncing words. Language-majority students will realize that to get through life outside of school, English is all they really need to know. This may lower their motivation and desire to learn the second language. Perhaps a way to counter this reaction would be to teach the importance of knowing both languages to help the children realize that bilingualism really is an asset. The fear of mispronunciation can partially be eased by the fact that all the children are learning a second language, so all the children will mispronounce words at times. The teachers, too, may mispronounce words, since each comes from a different language background. This universality aids in the creation of a comfortable learning environment, one in which ridicule is not permitted.

SUCCESSFUL EXAMPLES

There are 266 documented TWI programs in the United States, four of which are described here. The first experiment with a dual language school in the United States occurred in Dade County, Florida, in the 1960s. In the 1960s, this area of Florida (Miami included) experienced an influx of Cuban refugees, many of them political refugees and most coming from Cuba's upper and middle classes (Stein 1986). By coming to America they sought educational opportunity for their children, and the United States wanted to make it clear that we were concerned with the condition of the Cubans. These two forces working together gained federal funding for the first TWI program in the United States, implemented in Coral Way Elementary School.

The idea for the program came from a mix of successful immersion programs in Canada and American schools in Guatemala and Ecuador that educated children of American diplomats. Coral Way's goal was to create bilingual, well-educated children from both language-minority and language-majority backgrounds. It achieved its goal by creating an environment that was neither compensatory nor remedial for the language-minority students. During this period, school officials recognized not only the needs of Cuban refugees but also the needs of English-only students who could only benefit by knowing Spanish. Fluency in Spanish would give these students the opportunity to "participate in the trade and commerce that had begun to flow through Miami as a gateway to Latin America" (Stein 1986: 21). Evaluations of the program were all positive, showing a high rate of success. Not only were the children bilingual, but they were well-educated as well, scoring high on achievement tests. Word got out, and the program spread throughout the United States (Stein 1986).

A second successful program is Cali Calimecac Charter School (grades K–8) in Windsor, California. Though Cali Calimecac itself is more than 20 years old, it was only recently that it became a charter school. At Cali Calimecac 50 percent of the students are native Spanish speakers, and 50 percent are native

English speakers. Sixty percent of the total population is Latino. Cali Calimecac does not admit students from English-only backgrounds after first grade because the transition into a 90/10 model would be too difficult. However, Cali Calimecac does offer a bilingual education program for late-entry LEP students.

Some of the main goals at Cali Calimecac are academic excellence, equality, and community responsibility. In 1999 more than 60 percent of the seventh grade students scored at or above the state average in math and language. I have had the excellent opportunity of substituting at Cali Calimecac and experienced a wonderful sense of community in the classroom. I found students from both language backgrounds completely proficient in both languages with little or no accent by the fifth grade. On the playground there is no division among the children based on language-background—something one would be sure to see at most other schools.

The San Diego School District implemented some of the first TWI programs in California, and since then there has been a rapid increase in the number of cities that have TWI schools as an option. San Diego's TWI programs begin in preschool and continue through the sixth grade, thus adding two years to most other K–5 TWI programs. Because of the proximity to Mexico and the number of native Spanish speakers in the region, all San Diego programs are Spanish/ English. They run on the 90/10 model, so that fourth through sixth graders study 50 percent of the time in Spanish, 50 percent in English. In kindergarten through third grade a monolingual English-speaking teacher provides English instruction. In these schools the two languages are never used simultaneously in the same classroom or instructional period. San Diego public schools are also fortunate enough to provide each classroom with both a bilingual instructor and a bilingual assistant (*ESEA Title VII* 1985).

A final example is Alianza Elementary School in Watsonville, California. Alianza started in 1980 as a magnet school to target desegregation of Latinos and the more affluent whites in the area. It has received a very positive response from the community, with many parents waiting to get their children into the program. Alianza's goals are to give "all students the chance to be biliterate in both English and Spanish, graduat[e] students who perform at high academic levels, and [develop] a school culture that respects diversity and multiculturalism" (Miner 1999). The philosophy, as in most other TWI programs, is "English-plus." Alianza believes that *all* students should be given the opportunity to be bilingual/biliterate, and that bilingual education should not be viewed as something remedial or compensatory, but rather as a wonderful opportunity for all students. Like all TWI programs, Alianza looks at each student as having a valuable resource (his or her language) to offer, and language-minority students are not viewed as children who need to be "fixed." This builds the sense of pride and self-worth in the students that is necessary for academic and social, as well as personal, success.

THE ADDED BENEFITS OF A TWI PROGRAM

Cooperative Education

Far too often in the school setting, language divides children instead of uniting them. School systems promote the division of children by tracking them according to language abilities, thereby creating division among them. This division comes from both sides of the bilingual debate. All children naturally tend to become friends with the kids who speak the same language, come from the same neighborhood, or run in the same social circles. When there is little or no exposure to the other children in school, integration becomes more difficult.

One of the key components of a TWI program is that children work side by side with one another and see each other as assets who can help with the unfamiliar language. TWI programs integrate children by placing them in classes together and showing them from the beginning that each person has something special to offer: the knowledge of their mother tongue. Beginning in kindergarten, they will see that even though other children are different, they are struggling with the same things while developing a new language. The children will learn to help one another, and this bond follows onto the playground, and then into the community. Children learn that success comes through cooperation rather than competition (Cenoz and Genesee 1998). Benefits of cooperative in contrast to competitive learning expand across a wide range of areas. Test results from children participating in cooperative or collaborative classrooms show that they are more competent and have higher test scores than those in competitive situations.

Love and Love (1995) note that the psychological and social benefits of cooperative learning are valuable. Children in cooperative programs demonstrate "increased feelings of success, enjoyment of the learning process, and self-esteem" (1995: 58). These factors lead to a more positive overall school experience, and less likelihood that the child will choose to drop out before graduation (Leighton, Hightower, and Wrigley 1995). Students in cooperative classrooms are more likely to form interracial friendships, both in and out of the classroom (Kenrick, Neuberg, and Cialdini 1999). Based on these findings, it can be concluded that a cooperative learning experience leads not only to higher achievement but also to less intergroup hostility. According to Kenrick, Neuberg, and Cialdini, "cooperative classrooms can be an important weapon in the fight against negative prejudices, stereotypes, and discrimination" (1999: 428).

Culture and Family

Bilingualism not only helps build an appreciation of culture between children of different backgrounds but also teaches children about their own history, reinforcing their appreciation for their own culture. Children learn to take pride in their language and heritage, which may have otherwise been left behind, in exchange for the mainstream American culture and development of English fluency. Literature that includes people who dress as the students themselves do, or who have names they are familiar with, and beliefs they share will spark much more interest in language-minority students. U.S. language-majority students, most of who came from families that were immigrants less than four generations ago, will find similar pride in discovering their own uniqueness in the melting pot of America.

Respect for one's history and culture follows the language-minority child who is enrolled in a TWI program into the home. This is because she is taught that the language her parents speak at home is a valid and respected language, not something to be forgotten. The United States Committee on Education and the Workforce says, "If children have to choose between English and their home language . . . we will continue to separate families. . . . There are so many families who do not communicate any longer because the families, the parents, speak the home language, and their children are no longer communicating in their home language . . . [but] only in English" (1998).

When immigrant children start attending school in the United States, they realize the importance of learning English, even in a school where they are taught in both English and their home language. Language-minority students often prefer to speak English because they realize that it is the language of success in this country. Slowly they lose their native language abilities, and parents and children no longer communicate in the same language. Many parents, when asked about their relationship with their child as they learned more and more English, complained that by junior high school "they felt as if they were 'living with a stranger'" (from Delgado-Gaitan 1990, published in Borman 1998).

Parents use language to provide primary socialization to their children. Through communication, discussions at the dinner table, and words of wisdom children form their morals, beliefs, and identities. "When parents lose the means for socializing and influencing their children, rifts develop and families lose the intimacy that comes from shared beliefs and understandings" (Wong Fillmore 1991: 343).

McKenna and Willms found that "parental involvement in schooling fosters more positive student attitudes towards school, improves homework habits, reduces absenteeism and dropping out, and improves academic achievement" (1998: 22). If parents and children speak two different languages, this positive parental involvement becomes more difficult. Maintenance of the child's native language in school not only improves relations within the home but also leads to more parental involvement in the child's education and reflects a community value for the home language and parents' heritage. When parents know that they can go to the school and talk to a teacher without having to worry about being understood, when they understand the permission slips and volunteer forms, they are more likely to participate in school activities. According to interviews with Latino parents fighting for bilingual education in Orange County, "The parents felt that a school environment that recognized their language also recognized and encouraged their participation in the life of the school" (Galindo 1997: 182).

CONCLUSION

The debate about bilingual education in California continues to grow more intense. What is the best way to educate the growing number of non-native English-speaking children? Should they be fully immersed in English, or should they be taught in their native tongue? If the first option is chosen, is this portion of the population receiving an education as challenging as its English-only counterpart? If the latter is opted for, the question is what to do about the language diversity of the state. Over 80 percent of the LEP population in California is Spanish-speaking, but what about the other students?

It is becoming increasingly clear that the foreign language education needs by English-only populations are growing as well. Being bilingual allows us to think critically, and it opens doors to job opportunities in other parts of the world, something that is important in today's world. It expands our ability to meet, converse, and exchange ideas with people we would never have known if limited to only one language. In the United States, we require that high school students study a foreign language for two years before graduating. Why, then, do we try so hard to make LEP students drop their native language upon arrival in a classroom?

Both sides of the debate have openly stated that TWI programs work and address their concerns. Bilingual education advocates and opponents alike have acknowledged the academic, social, and linguistic success of the TWI program.

Remaining Questions

There are still many questions left unanswered: What happens to the second language development of the child after elementary school? This may not be an issue for the language-minority students who will be immersed in English for the rest of their lives in the United States, but what about the language-majority students? Will they lose their second language fluency without practice? What happens if a child transfers out of the program, or transfers midway? What does the opposition say? The research has shown only positive results, but before widespread implementation, the concerns of those in opposition would need to be addressed. How is the monolingual child's self-esteem affected (positively or negatively, if at all) by starting kindergarten in a language she does not understand? Does a TWI program separate children with different language backgrounds more by creating a school, or track within the school, for Spanish and English children, and another for Farsi and

English children? Or is there a way that all children can be integrated together? These questions, among others, merit further research.

A review of the literature on dual immersion programs shows that such programs are in fact among the most successful in achieving the goal of teaching language-minority students English while maintaining literacy in their home language. Evidence also shows that test scores for these students, as well as for language-majority students who go through the program, are at or above national averages. The needs of both sides of the bilingual education debate, as well as the needs of the children (both language-majority and -minority) are addressed. Bilingual education advocates concern themselves with making sure LEP children maintain their native tongue and take pride in their heritage. Bilingual education opponents are more interested in seeing that LEP students get adequate preparation in English skills and academic advancement for success in American society. Children need consistency, stability, integration, cooperation, and parental involvement. Language-majority students need a fair opportunity to learn a second language. TWI programs are the only ones that address all of these concerns, and people from all sides of the arena acknowledge that (Gold 1988; Imhoff 1990; Miner 1999).

Hopefully, dual language schools will be the norm some day. Then and only then will we begin to create an integrated, bilingual society more sensitive to the variety of people we see every day, and continue to be a place where people want to come in search of a better life. Language, as a link to, and a reflection of culture can be the bridge used in TWI programs, as opposed to the chasm in the current bilingual education debate.

REFERENCES

Ambert, A.N. (1991). *Bilingual Education and English as a Second Language: A Research Handbook 1988–1990*. New York: Garland.

Berger, K., and R. Thompson (1995). *The Developing Person: Through Childhood and Adolescence*. 4th ed. New York: Worth.

Bilingual Education Handbook (1986). *Learning English in California*. Sacramento, CA: Assembly Office of Research.

Bilingual Education Handbook (1990). *Designing Instruction for Limited English Proficiency Students*. Sacramento: California Department of Education.

Borman, K.M. (1998). *Ethnic Diversity in Communities and Schools*. Greenwich, CT: Ablex.

Cenoz, J., and F. Genesee (eds.) (1998). *Beyond Bilingualism: Multilingualism and Multilingual Education*. Philadelphia: Multilingual Matters.

Crawford, J. (1991). *Bilingual Education: History, Politics, Theory, and Practice*. 2nd ed. Los Angeles: Bilingual Educational Services.

De Cos, P.L. (1999). *Educating California's Immigrant Children: An Overview of Bilingual Education*. Sacramento: California Research Bureau.

ESEA Title VII Directory: Bilingual Education Basic and Demonstration Projects (1985). Sacramento: Bilingual Education Office, California State Department of Public Education.

Galindo, R. (1997). "Language Wars: The Ideological Dimensions of the Debates on Bilingual Education." *Bilingual Research Journal* 21, no. 2–3: 163–201.

Garcia-Vasquez, E., et al. (1997). "Language Proficiency and Academic Success: Relationships Between Proficiency in Two Languages and Achievement Among Mexican-American Students." *Bilingual Research Journal* 21, no. 4 (1997): 395–408.

Genesee, F.H. (1982). "Experimental Neuropsychological Research on Second Language Processing." *TESOL Quarterly* 16, no. 3: 315–322.

Gold, D. (1988). "Two Languages, One Aim: 'Two-Way' Learning." *Education Week on the Web*. www.edweek.org/ew/1988/07410009.h07, 20 January.

Imhoff, G. (ed.) (1990). *Learning in Two Languages: From Conflict to Consensus in the Reorganization of Schools*. New Brunswick, NJ: Transaction.

Kenrick, D.T., S.L. Neuberg, and R.B. Cialdini (eds.) (1999). *Social Psychology: Unraveling the Mystery*. Needham Heights, MA: Allyn & Bacon.

Kessler, C. (1994). *Language Acquisition Processes in Bilingual Children*. Los Angeles: Evaluation, Dissemination, and Assessment Center.

Leighton, M.S., A. Hightower, and P. Wrigley (1995). *Model Strategies in Bilingual Education: Professional Development*. Washington, DC: U.S. Department of Education.

Literacy and Culture: The Problems and Promises of Bilingual Education (1996). Sacramento, CA: The LegiSchool Project.

Love, P.G., and A.G. Love (1995). *Enhancing Student Learning: Intellectual, Social, and Emotional Integration*. ASHE-ERIC Higher Education Report no. 4. Washington, DC: Graduate School of Education and Human Development, George Washington University.

McKenna, M., and J.D. Willms (1998). "Co-operation Between Families and Schools: 'What Works in Canada.' " *Research Papers in Education: Policy and Practice* 13, no. 1: 19–41.

McLaughlin, B. (1985). *Second-Language Acquisition in Childhood*. Vol. 2, *School Age Children*. 2nd ed. Hillsdale, NJ: Lawrence Erlbaum Associates.

Miner, B. (1999). "Bilingual Education: New Visions for a New Era." *Rethinking Schools* 13 no. 4. www.rethinkingschool.org/Archives/13_04/newera.htm.

Montague, N.S. (1997). "Critical Components for Two-Way Immersion Programs." *Bilingual Research Journal* 21, no. 4: 409–417.

Porter, R.P. (1996). *Forked Tongue: The Politics of Bilingual Education*. New Brunswick, NJ: Transaction.

Ramirez, J.D., S. Yuen, and D. Ramey (1991). *Final Report: Longitudinal Study of Structured English Immersion Strategy, Early-Exit and Late-Exit Transitional Bilingual Education Programs for Language-Minority Children*. San Mateo, CA: Aguirre International.

Smith, G.A. (ed.) (1993). *Public Schools That Work: Creating Community*. New York: Routledge.

Stein, C.B. (1986). *Sink or Swim: The Politics of Bilingual Education*. New York: Praeger.

Tokuhama-Espinosa, T. (2001). *Raising Multilingual Children: Foreign Language Acquisition and Children*. Westport, CT: Bergin & Garvey.

Tucker, R.G. (1996). "Some Thoughts Concerning Innovative Language Education Programs." In *Journal of Multilingual and Multicultural Development* 17, no. 24: 315–320.

United States Committee on Education and the Workforce (1998). *Head Start Re-authorization*. Washington, DC: U.S. Government Printing Office.
Wong Fillmore, L. (1991). "When Learning a Second Language Means Losing the First." *Early Childhood Research Quarterly* 6, no. 3: 323–346.

WEB REFERENCES

Campbell Union School District Bilingual Program, Santa Clara County, CA: www.sccoe.k12.ca.us/future10.htm
Educational Demographics Office, State of California: www.cde.ca.gov/demographics
Escuela Montessori de Montopolis, Austin, TX: www.main.org/escuela/dual.htm
National Clearinghouse for Bilingual Education: www.ncbe.gwu.edu/
University of California two-way immersion studies: www.cal.org/cal/db/2way

Part II

Math, Music, and Multilinguals

6

The Relationship Between Musical Ability and Foreign Languages
Communication via Sounds and via Words

Tracey Tokuhama-Espinosa

Is there a correlation between musical ability and the ability to speak foreign languages? This is a question often asked by people who speak many languages, because a "logical" connection between music and language appears to be self-evident. After all, aren't songs just language put to music?

Linguistic studies show that our native language and music are connected in the brain (Lamb 1999), and new technology measuring brain activity confirms that certain aspects of language and music are indeed linked (Hauser 2001), but does musical ability parallel foreign language ability, and vice versa? The short answer to this question is no. However, the long and poetic response reflects on the greater relationship between music and language. A look at the deep, entwined, emotional and physical relationship between music and languages (first, second, or otherwise) will clarify why such a question frequently arises when discussing multilinguals.

THE HISTORICAL MARRIAGE OF MUSIC AND LANGUAGE

About 130,000 years ago, Cro-Magnon, who preceded *Homo sapiens*, finally had throats and mouths that would support speech; and so the human voice was born, and the "first instrument" of man was devised. Darwin believed that rudimentary song was a precursor to language. The earliest example of the marriage of language and music was epic poetry, which was sung. According to Arthur Elson's *The Book of Musical Knowledge* (1927), epic poetry was performed by the trouvères in France and the troubadours in Spain and elsewhere and were probably influenced by the Moors, and in a minor way by the Celts and ancient Romans (1915: 33). These epic poet-musicians were strong until the thirteenth century, then were repressed by the Church, which used music to present the stories of the Scriptures. This may give us a clue as to why children can often sing in foreign languages much earlier than they can speak the language properly: Song lends itself to memorization.

Another way that music and language can appear similar is in the reactions that each elicits. In *Music, Brain and Body*, Storr writes, "Roger Brown, one of the world's experts on the development of language in children, has also studied reactions to music. His research has demonstrated that there is widespread consensus between listeners about the emotional content of different pieces of music even when these pieces are unknown to, or not identified by, the different listeners . . . the general emotional tone will probably be similarly perceived by different listeners" (1992: 29–30). This emotional reaction spills over into the physical as well.

WHERE MUSIC AND FOREIGN LANGUAGE SHARE SPACE IN THE BRAIN

We must ask ourselves, Where do language and music "share" a place in the brain, and where are they distinct? Evidence indicates that language loss almost always concurs with damage to the left hemisphere, and musical loss almost always occurs with damage to the right hemisphere, meaning that musical and linguistic skills are separate neurological capacities. However, there are areas of crossover.

Second, we must look at the many facets that create the whole of music and the whole of language, and see where they share points of overlap in other areas of society, learning structures, and aesthetics. With this in mind, let us begin with the physical structure of sound.

Physical Structures

Physically, sound (music or language) is received in the outer ear, passes to the tympanic membrane (eardrum), then past three small bones called the ossicles. The motions of the ossicles vibrate a small membrane that connects to the fluid in the inner ear in a structure called the cochlea. Once vibrations enter the cochlea, they cause the basilar membrane to move; receptors then generate frequencies and serve to dictate pitch. In the right hemisphere, the auditory cortex specializes in determining hierarchies of harmonic relations and rich overtones. In the left hemisphere, the auditory cortex deciphers relationships between successions of sounds, as in the perception of rhythm (Sancar 1999). Additionally, the frontal lobes "judge" the sound, and the brain stem localizes sound by determining the pitch, intensity, and volume.

The planum temporale is where language development and musical ability share a very interesting role. This area, which originally was associated only with deciphering language, is now recognized as the most likely seat of deciphering perfect pitch as well. "Interestingly, abnormality in this area is presumed to be the cause of developmental dyslexia. From this information, it can be inferred that music and language may be interpreted and deciphered in similar ways as well as by similar brain structures (Sancar 1999).

Two other areas of the brain, the hippocampus for memory and the limbic system for emotional response to music, also overlap with language areas.

On a Theoretical Level

On a nonneurological level, music and language also overlap in theory; researchers now claim that humans may be born with an innate capacity for both of these skills (Pinker 1994; Tramo 1997; MuSICA Research Notes 1997), based on the fact that all cultures around the world have both language and music.

Broadly speaking, there are two kinds of human abilities in every domain: those that are universal, common to everyone (e.g., walking, language) and those that are traditionally called "individual differences" and are acquired by some people but not others (e.g., athletic ability and talent in poetry). My aim has been to delineate those aspects of music that are universally acquired. I have argued that not only "enjoyment" or "preference" or "perception" are universals in music, but that specific processes form the core of understanding common to members of a musical community. In my view, such processes are analogous to acquisitions such as language and concepts of space, time, number, and so on, rather than to special, individual talents found in devotees of sport or poetry. (Serafine 1988: 234)

Musical ability and foreign language ability share territory in that both can be developed, and both find their best success when acquired earlier in life rather than later (Handel 1989: 381). In general terms, however, it is difficult to talk about "music" as a single category, and a similar problem arises when discussing "language." There are many pieces that make up the whole in both cases, and so we must break down their structures slightly in order to understand all of the areas of possible overlap.

The Five Subcategories of Music and Language

When speaking about the relationship between musical abilities and foreign language abilities, there are subcategories that fit logically, and others that seem remote. "The division of function is not so much between words and music as between logic and emotion," writes Anthony Storr (1992: 35). Music touches many other areas of intelligence, and this phenomenon has led to the renowned "Mozart effect" studies proclaiming that early exposure to music can lead to stimulation of the brain. At least five areas that show a positive relationship between music and increased brain activity have been mapped:

1. Music has a relationship to logical-mathematical abilities in terms of composition.

2. Music is related to linguistic abilities in terms of prosody (as in intonation) and the emotion that it elicits.

3. Music is akin to kinesthetic abilities in that it can elicit bodily movements.

4. Music can be said to relate to spatial intelligence because it structures time (as seen in work-gang songs or battle marches).

5. Music can also be said to relate to intrapersonal intelligence and the ability for internal reflection.

Let us take a closer look at each of these five points.

Music has a relationship to logical-mathematical abilities in terms of composition

Musical composition is very mathematical. According to Mari Riess and William Yee, "Musical events differ from non-musical ones in many ways, including their artful construction, which combines explicit use of special frequencies and tonal relationships based on changes along a logarithmic frequency continuum (e.g. as in musical scales) with various temporal constraints associated with tempi, meters, and rhythmic patterns" (1993: 95). When one reads and writes music, it is much like reading a math formula.

"Pythagoras, the Greek mathematician, argued almost 2,000 years ago that music was numerical, the expression of number in sound," writes Joseph (1993: 327). Music's geometrical properties yield pleasing auditory sounds, as when "dividing a vibrating string into various ratios, [Pythagoras and his followers] discovered that several very pleasing musical intervals could be produced," as in the ratio of 1:2, which yields an octave; 2:3, a fifth; 3:4, a fourth; 4:5, a major third; and 5:6, a minor third (1993: 329).

However, the ability to remember the exact melody, intonation, and even gestures related to an operatic performance are the very definition of prosodic linguistic abilities.

Music is related to linguistic abilities in terms of prosody (as in intonation) and the emotions that it elicits

Why is it that children may readily sing in a foreign language, but will not speak in that language? Because when he or she is singing, the child is experiencing language in a very right-hemisphere way. There is no analysis of grammar or deciphering of vocabulary—in fact, many people can sing in a foreign language without knowing what they are saying. I recall reading an interview with Orquestra de la Luz, a Japanese salsa band. They apparently had learned to play, sing, and dance the Latin American rhythm through intense study with masters in the field. They knew all the steps, played all the notes beautifully, and sang with a full Latin heart. But one of the members confessed in the interview that he had no idea what he was saying when he sang. This is something like learning "Frère Jacques" in French, and then years later realizing that "Are You Sleeping, Brother John" is the same thing, in English translation. When one does not have sufficient skills in a foreign language, singing foreign sounds often can be simply a joy of expression, and the language used is not analyzed. When children (or adults) sing in a foreign language, they often simply depend on the vibrancy that successful harmony carries, with no attention to the actual words. Whereas the rules of syntax and grammar are left-hemisphere functions, prosody, or the "texture" of language, is right-hemisphere. Another ironic correlation between foreign language location and music location in the brain has to do with stroke victims. Damage to the left hemisphere in monolinguals usually causes loss of speech abilities. Far greater damage and language loss are reported in right-hemisphere stroke patients who are multilingual, and "musicians who are suffering from right hemisphere damage (e.g. right temporal-parietal stroke) have major difficulties recognizing familiar melodies and suffer from expressive instrumental *amusia*," writes Joseph (1993: 324).

Another example of intonation versus simple syntax is saying the sentence "I am pregnant" in a variety of tones: surprise, exclamation, disbelief, exultation, to name a few. Though the three words are the same, the *ways* they are said reflect very different messages. Similarly, one could play a series of notes in a major key, and it will sound happy or joyful. The same series of notes in a minor key may be perceived as sad or melancholic (Joseph 1993: 321). This area of texture is where music and foreign language skills share territory.

Music can be said to relate to intrapersonal intelligence and the ability for internal reflection

Another area where music and a foreign language converge in our minds is in the realm of emotion. Music moves you emotionally. Certain songs give rise to certain emotions: not only the words they may or may not have, but also the music. Bernstein writes that "when you listen to a warm phrase of Mozart coming at you, something akin to love is reaching you" (1962: 273). This parallels the feeling that speaking a foreign language can have. Some languages have a passion in their melody alone. The romantic feelings that the speaker arouses because of the smoothness of the words used, the delicate curves that the sounds bring to our ears, are close to the sensations brought about by certain types of music. This of course is very personal, as is taste in music. Some languages may seem romantic to certain people and not to others. I know two polyglots who evaluate the effect of the German language sounds in completely different ways. Paula, who speaks Portuguese, Spanish, French, and some English, finds German harsh, cold, unromantic, biting, and rigid. "How can you tell someone you love them by saying *Ich liebe Dich*?" she contends, sputtering out the words as if they tasted bad. Marlene, who speaks German, Swiss-German, English, and French, finds German extremely melodic. "Why

would some of the world's best-known operas be composed using German if it
didn't lend itself to song?" she contends.

Certain musical movements, too, however, may arouse a type of "warmth"
for some people and not for others. Taste in music has its counterpart in taste
in foreign languages, I assume. The emotional quality of the language used,
and of the song heard, is something that one may or may not have the option
to choose. You may, perhaps, be able to decide what to listen to at the moment,
whether it is classical, hard rock, 1950s rock and roll, blues, or salsa, but you
may not be able to choose the foreign language you need to study. If the
language drives you emotionally, like your choice of music, then perhaps it
will bring you the same kind of pleasure.

Music can be said to relate to spatial intelligence because it structures time (as seen in work-gang songs or battle marches)

Music is found in every culture, as is language. What music has been used
for in most cultures, however, is not so obvious. Though Western cultures give
high praise to musical giftedness, and the likes of Beethoven, Bach, and Brahms
are lauded, such talent is unusual. "Historically and cross-culturally," write
Trehub and Trainor, "it has been more common for music to be integrated into
various facets of work and play, with all community members participating
fully" (1993: 281). Gelman and Brenneman postulate that perhaps our universal skills for music grow out of our ability to use language (1994: 375).
Lullabies are sung in every part of the world and are "structurally and functionally distinct from other songs, just as infant-directed speech is structurally
and functionally distinct from other speech" (Trehub and Trainor 1993: 295).
Along these lines, many have postulated that there is something inherent in
humans that drives us toward musical perception (Titon, McAllester, Slobin,
and Lock 1996; Lerdahl and Jackendoff 1996), as well as an inherent mechanism
for language (Chomsky 1988). Still others have discussed the "possibility of
innate perceptual principles for organizing speech and musical output" (Lerdahl
and Jackson 1983).

Music is akin to kinesthetic abilities in that it can elicit bodily movements

Music critics often note the glee with which an audience watches the gestures
of an exuberant conductor, or how they are fascinated at the synchronicity of
the bows in the string section in an orchestra. There is something magical
about the coordinated efforts of music that can be anticipated according to the
song being played. Singing is related to physical movements, not only of
the voice box but also of the whole body. Ellen Dissanayake notes that until
the age of about four or five, children have trouble singing without moving
their hands and feet (1990). It is possible to observe a single hemisphere at
work by sedating one side of the brain (as is done in surgery). If the left

hemisphere is sedated by injecting a barbiturate into the left carotid artery, the subject is unable to speak but can still sing. The opposite is true if the barbiturate is injected into the right carotid artery and the right hemisphere of the brain is sedated; then the person cannot sing, but can speak normally. "Stammerers can sometimes sing sentences which they cannot speak; presumably because the stammering pattern is encoded in the left hemisphere, whilst singing is predominantly a right hemisphere activity," writes Storr (1992: 36). Analyzing the words of a song individually is done in the left hemisphere as normal language processing. However, when words and music are taken together, as in song, they are received in a whole-language fashion in the right hemisphere. A similar phenomenon emphasizing the different locations of different aspects of music and foreign language in the brain is that of melody recognition and naming of a tune versus the ability to recognize the tune alone. The name of the song is stored in a different part of the brain than the melody of the song. One can sing a whole song without remembering its title or recognize the tune without remembering the words (Crowder 1993).

"Music and emotion are directly related to the body and can affect heart rate, and breathing, and can cause us to dance and sway, snap our fingers, or tap our feet. Our bodies are also bathed in music long before birth since we hear the beating of our mother's hearts, the rhythmic pulses of her lungs filling and discharging air" (Joseph 1993: 325).

From Brain to Mind

Aside from these five areas of overlap between music and language in the brain, there are nine additional areas of the mind worth investigating. These include symbols, memory, the human voice, synesthesia, shared learning concepts, individual gifts in music and linguistics, physical limitations to learning, inherited abilities, and music as a tool to learn a foreign language.

Symbols

Both music and foreign languages have symbol systems, though they differ greatly. In the context of Western culture, each word in a language represents something universally concrete and definable (the word's definition), while each letter by itself is meaningless. Each musical note also exists in a vacuum. There is not necessarily a certain sentiment or meaning attached to F minor or A sharp, whereas *luna* is always "moon" from Spanish to English. However, the poetic use of language could be said to resemble the musical use of notes. Words can be organized within poetry in a freer way, and the meanings are "liberated" by the author's use. The sun can "bathe" the flowers, poetically speaking, though literally this is absurd. Similarly, Howard Gardner (1975) writes of cases where patients have lost the ability to read words but can still read musical notation.

Broken down at the individual sound (not word) level, things look a bit different, however. In language, the physical characteristics of phonemes (sounds) vary as a function of the context. "For example," write Gelman and Brenneman, "the actual 'b' sound depends on which phonemes come before and after. In music, tones are defined by their frequency so that context does not affect how middle C (or any other note) is formed and produced. These differences are reflected in the fact that it is easy to specify the note that sounds like middle C on the piano but not at all easy to specify the phoneme that sounds like *ba* across the different words that share this same speech sound" (1994: 376). To complicate things further, this is only within a Western structure. If looked at on a cross-cultural scale, the comparisons become even more complex, because musical notation differs from country to country (North Indian music notation is vastly different from North American notation, for example), as does the alphabet or symbol system of written languages (Korean uses a different symbol system than French, for example). Such cultural variations, it is hypothesized, emerge from the role of music and the role of language in each society. Each culture has the symbols it needs to represent the language it has, and the language reflects the needs of the society, just as each culture uses musical notation (for example, to indicate pitch) depending on the music, and that reflects the musical needs of that society. And taken to a further extreme, most music has never been notated or recorded; it has relied strictly on aural transmissions (Brenneis 1990: 173).

Memory

According to studies of memory, music and languages differ in terms of recall. Musical recall is more problematic than verbal recall. Musical recall demands additional points of reference, such as pitch, tone, and meter, as well as differences in symbolic notation used to note recall (Sloboda 1985, as cited in Crowder 1993: 129–130). It is easier for people to recognize a written note in a melody than to recognize the wrong pitch. Similarly, it is easier to recognize the wrong word used in a sentence than to recognize wrong intonation.

Gelman and Brenneman write of the universal qualities of music, one being that it "serves to efficiently organize information that cannot be written down." For example, Gardner (1983) describes a possible role for music in organizing religious rites and work groups in the Stone Age, and Sloboda hypothesizes that music provides "a mnemonic framework within which the structure of cultural knowledge and societal relations is stored and communicated" (1985: 369).

The human voice

Another area of auditory memory shared by language and music is related to the parallel between timbre in music (the differing sounds of a tenor saxophone and a bassoon, as Crowder mentions 1993: 138) and the variations in human voices. In both cases "the fundamental frequency itself is not at stake, but rather resonant frequency characteristics" (Crowder 1993: 138). Even further differences were found to emerge when gender differences (male versus female voices) were taken into account. These differences, Crowder notes, are much subtler than the differences found, for example, between accents (a Texas and Australian speaking the same English sentence).

Synesthesia

Perhaps another area in which musicians, or those who are musically inclined, converge with polyglots is synesthesia. Many a musician writes of experiencing different "colors" or smells when contemplating various musical pieces. Leonard Bernstein writes in *The Infinite Variety of Music*:

Every work, every real work of art, has a world of its own that it inhabits, where there's a certain smell and a certain touch. Even various works by the same artist differ if they're really important works. The Second Symphony of Brahms—I see different colors when I just say those names. "The Second Symphony": I smell something; I feel a texture; I see colors; I have certain synesthesia responses. It's altogether different when I say "Symphony No. 3 by Brahms." So that this textural atmosphere, or climate, is a vitally important thing. (1962: 266).

Foreign language learners often use synesthetic devices for memory enhancement to remember words.

Shared learning concepts for music and language

The use of previous knowledge for creation and utilization

Another area that speakers of many languages may share with the musician is the definition of musical composition. As Bernstein writes, "All musicians write their music in terms of all the music that preceded them. All art recognizes the art that preceded it, or recognizes the presence of the art preceding it" (1962: 272). This is very much what Kenji Hakuta wrote *Mirror of Language* (1986: 123): "Who, when faced with an unfamiliar language, would not make the most of an already familiar language? By using knowledge of the native language, second-language learners would be following a principle of human development." So learning new musical concepts would be built on known musical concepts, and learning a new language would be built on the native language.

Music and foreign language perhaps share a mechanism in memory construct as well. McLaughlin and Nations (1986) showed that polyglots use their previous knowledge of language X to learn language Y (they build on the general rules of language construction that they have learned from previous language study), and many musicians claim inspiration from other musicians in their compositions. On the other hand, Sloboda (1985) showed that when testing auditory memory skills, there was a "powerful proactive inhibition (earlier melodies intruding into recall of later melodies)" (Crowder 1993: 130). This means that whereas knowing one foreign language tends to help you learn a new foreign language, and knowing many tunes can help you learn other tunes, recalling phrases from one language or remembering specific tunes can meet with interference from other languages or other tunes. On the other hand, recalling certain aspects of languages or pieces of tunes can experience interference from previously learned languages or tunes. It has been established in neurology and linguistics that there is a theory of separate representation (Ojemann and Whitaker 1978), and/or a dual language hypothesis (Albert and Obler 1979), and/or a language overlap hypothesis (Paradis 1983) in which language A is located in its own space in the brain and language B has its own place, but there is a place of overlap in which they share space. Perhaps such a phenomenon exists for musical tunes. "Frère Jacques" has a space in your brain, as does "Twinkle, Twinkle, Little Star," but they may also have a point of overlap. This would explain why the wiring sometimes gets crossed and we confuse tunes, or parts of languages, that we know.

The variety of musical and linguistic gifts

The technology exists to measure the parallel aspects of music and foreign languages in the brain. Since musical gifts are varied, they may not always be found together in the same person. For example, having a good ear and a talent for distinguishing sounds does not necessarily mean that you like music or want to be a musician. The opposite is true as well. You may love music and enjoy it immensely, but have no talent for producing it. And there are people who have no ability to remember a song's title or the composer's name, nor how the tune begins, but once offered a friendly start, can remember the tune completely. Or those who can "hear" a full piece or music in their heads but, when they open their mouths to sing the tune, find that their "internal" voice is far superior to their "external" voice. (I once met a woman who asked if her *in*ability to sing was correlated to her high aptitude for foreign languages. She spoke five languages "fluently" but had been told by many a friend and foe alike that, though she thought she could sing, she was actually awful at it!) "People who score highly on a test of musical aptitude tend to show left hemisphere advantage, regardless of training," according to Sloboda in *The Musical Mind* (1985: 264).

This shows that musical analysis, executive skills, and criticism related to music are in the "logical-mathematical" area, or left hemisphere, whereas the emotional response remains in the right hemisphere. As mentioned earlier, musical composition is in the left hemisphere, as are native language abilities (for the average, left-hemisphere-dominant person—95 percent of right-handed people and 70 percent of left-handed people fall into this category). But the emotional intonation, pitch, and volume with which one sings a song are in the right hemisphere. This goes for speech as well. The ability to inflect

surprise, anger, or other emotions into speech is housed in the r
sphere. Anthony Storr writes, "There are many similarities between p
communication and music. Infants respond to the rhythm, pitch, intensity, a
timbre of the mother's voice; all of which are a part of music" (1992: 9). In
this sense music and language are the same for monolinguals and for multilinguals.

The physical limitations to learning music and language

Physically, do we all have what it takes?

Our brain's interpretation of the physical world is impacted by the actual
structure of the ear and our ability to hear clearly. Those with blocked or
impaired hearing in the left ear, for example, may have a hard time appreciating
the emotional quality of music or the intonation in spoken sentences. Those
with a physical defect in the right ear may have trouble with sensing the
mechanics or structure of a written piece. But given "normal" hearing and a
"normal" brain, do we all have the ability to speak foreign languages and to
be musical? Elizabeth West Marvin of the University of Rochester in New York
believes that you do not have to be born with perfect pitch; all of us have the
potential to improve what we have and our understanding of musical tones
(Brown 1999). Yet other recent research suggests that all babies are born with
perfect pitch, confirming Janet Werker's hypothesis that all babies are born
"universal listeners" and can differentiate sounds from any language when
first born (1997). Most linguists and all language instructors would vouch for
everyone's ability to learn a foreign language (barring the physical problems
mentioned earlier). Can everyone learn to be musical and/or learn a foreign
language, then? No. But probably more for reasons of motivation and inspiration than of physiology.

Is ability inherited?

This leads to another realm that musical ability and foreign language ability
share: genetic inheritance. Is musical ability inherited? Is foreign language ability inherited? Both questions invite a good deal of speculation, and many studies argue in favor of a positive answer. Do they share the same gene, proving
their codependent state? No, as far as we know, though it would be a convenient
find. While absolute pitch has been shown to run in families—Nelson Freimer's
study quoted in Brown (1999) gives a good example of current research showing this—the inherited gift of foreign language ability has not yet been so fully
documented, though many informal accounts by hundreds of polyglots seem
to lean in this direction. Research shows that ability in music, like ability in
foreign languages, is not an "all or nothing" scenario; some people have a great
deal of talent while others, perhaps due to lack of opportunity, show only a
hint of such a talent. In both cases, there is no doubt that early musical training

n languages aid in exploiting whatever level of
ith.

New School for Social Research in New York be-
s of music are in the verbal exchanges between
t year of life. She writes, "No matter how important
ng eventually becomes, the human brain is first or-
to respond to emotional/intonational aspects of the
published paper). In this sense, language *is* the "sing-
language and music are part and parcel of what is de-
livereu   rough such exchanges. These types of exchange "are
concerned with en.. onal expressiveness rather than with conveying factual
information" (Storr 1992: 8). Such "goo goo" and "gah gah"-ing or cooing is
the basis for the small child to communicate feelings of love and warmth, not
necessarily words and grammatically correct exchanges. This may give us a
clue as to why the TeleTubby Babies became such a hit. Pediatricians and linguists agonized over the incorrect sentence structure and the monotonous repetition found in the TeleTubbies' "speech," but what they really were conveying
to children were emotions, and those were clear to the infant listener because
of, not in spite of, the playful gurgle sounds that replaced words.

Music as a learning tool

Finally, the use of music to learn foreign languages has grown significantly
since the 1990s. Music can be used to enhance foreign language learning in at
least two ways, and though the research to back up these ideas is still being
documented, it is well worth noting here.

In the first case, music can be used through song to enhance at least some
aspects of foreign language learning, such as vocabulary. It has been shown
that the frequency of exposure to a language, in both the spoken word and the
lyrical form (within music) aids in firm mental representation, and therefore
in recall. "If this were the case, then listeners exposed to different musical
systems would acquire different musical schemas just as listeners exposed to
different languages acquire different speech and language schemas" (Trehub
and Trainor 1993: 296). This has been difficult to prove universally, for studies
in non-Western music are scarce. However, neurological research lends weight
to this possibility: "Even when the entire left hemisphere has been removed
completely, the ability to sing familiar songs or even learn new ones may be
preserved—although in the absence of music a patient would be unable to say
the very words that he or she has just sung. The preservation of the ability to
sing has, in fact, been utilized to promote linguistic recovery in aphasic patients
and acquisition of speech by the damaged hemisphere, that is, melodic-
intonation therapy" (Joseph 1993: 324).

The second way that music can be used is through secondary stimulation.
By playing music while studying a foreign language (or any other subject),

you open the brain to stimulus not usually received while learning that language. Background music triggers neural connections that would not normally be "in action" when learning a foreign language. Unless the language learner is very young (under eight) and learning the language "naturally," the study of a foreign language is very grammar-dependent and at least part of foreign language learning means an analysis and deciphering of syntax. This is very left-hemisphere work. If the language learner plays music while studying, the right hemisphere is stimulated. This means that areas of the brain which are not normally part of the language learning process are "open" while learning the new language, and therefore information is being stored in areas of the brain that would not normally be associated with foreign language learning. Such a learning process means that neural connections have been forged in areas of the brain not normally associated with foreign language learning, creating a facilitation of recall when retrieval is required. In computer terms, this is "inputting" information onto several files instead of the single "language learning" file, which makes retrieval easier because you can enter through numerous files instead of one.

Springer and Deutsch write in *Left Brain/Right Brain* that "certain combinations of tasks are relatively easy to do together, while other tasks seem to interfere with each other. For example, many people can listen to music and read simultaneously, although the same people are unable to follow a conversation and read simultaneously. . . . Intuitively, it seems as if tasks that call on different areas of the brain show less interference when performed together than tasks that rely on the same general areas" (1997: 99). Other studies conducted since the 1970s show how vast improvements on standard tests of puzzle making, reading, and math are directly related to musical stimulation (Hurwitz et al. 1975; Lamb and Gregory 1993). Others write of the "cognitive spin-offs" (MuSICA 1994) from musical exposure while performing other tasks (Draper and Gayle 1987). Thus background music may allow concepts (foreign language) to enter, or cause connections between neurons in the brain that would not normally be there, and therefore led to a greater efficacy in learning. Certain types of music have been purported to have greater benefits than others, such as classical rhythms that are synchronized to sixty beats a minute, as in Vivaldi's *Four Seasons* "Spring" movement. The theory is that such a rhythm is in sync with a human's natural heartbeat, and is therefore naturally conducive to assimilating learning.

CONCLUSIONS

In effect, there is no correlation between musical abilities and the ability to speak foreign languages, though in terms of emotion, the underlying beauty of one is often reflected in the other. Though music and language overlap in areas of emotion, intonation, communication, location in the brain, and hereditary patterns, there is no evidence to suggest that having a gift for languages means you should also have a gift for music or vice versa, though instinct tells us otherwise.

John Corry wrote of the musician Cole Porter that "His words and music weren't just joined, they were inseparably married" (*New York Times*, 29 July 1987). Perhaps this is true of all humans. While there seems to be no end to the areas where music and language overlap, ranging from the neurological to the poetic, there is no conclusive evidence to suggest that one causes the other, and so, sadly, we must conclude that while married in verse, they remain bachelors in their own domains in the mind.

REFERENCES

Albert, M.L., and L. Obler (1979). *The Bilingual Brain: Neuropsychological and Neurolinguistic Aspects of Bilingualism*. New York: Academic Press.

Bernstein, L. (1962). *The Infinite Variety of Music*. London: Weidenfeld and Nicolson.

Brenneis, D. (1990). "Ecology and Culture." In M.A. Runco and R.S. Albert (eds.), *Theories of Creativity*. London: Sage.

Brown, K.S. (1999). "Striking the Right Note." *New Scientist Magazine* (London) 164, no. 2215: 38–41.

Chomsky, N. (1988). *Creating Curriculum Music*. New York: Prentice Hall.

Cromie, W.J. (1997). "How Your Brain Listens to Music." *Harvard Gazette*, 13 November. Available: www.news.harvard.edu/gazette/1997/11.13/HowYourBrain Lis.html.

Crowder, R.C. (1993). "Auditory Memory." In S. McAdams and E. Bigand (eds.), *Thinking in Sound: The Cognition Psychology of Human Audition*. Oxford: Clarendon Press.

Dissanayake, E. (1990, August). *Music as a Human Behavior: A Hypothesis of Evolutionary Origin and Function*. Paper presented at the Human Behavior and Evolution Society meeting, Los Angeles, CA.

Draper, T.W., and C. Gayle (1987). "An Analysis of Historical Reasons for Teaching Music to Young Children: Is It the Same Old Song?" In J.C. Peery, I.W. Peery, and T.W. Draper (eds.), *Music and Child Development*. New York: Springer-Verlag.

Elson, A. (1927). *The Book of Musical Knowledge: The History, Technique, and Appreciation of Music, Together with Lives of the Great Composers*. Boston: Houghton Mifflin.

Gardner, H. (1975). *The Shattered Mind*. New York: Knopf/Vintage.

Gardner, H. (1983). *Frames of Mind: The Theory of Multiple Intelligences*. New York: Basic Books.

Gelman, R., and K. Brenneman (1994). "First Principles Can Support Both Universal and Culture-specific Learning About Number and Music." In L.A. Hirschfield and S.A. Gelman (eds.), *Mapping the Mind: Domain Specificity in Cognition and Culture*. Cambridge: Cambridge University Press.

Hakuta, K. (1986). *Mirror of Language: The Debate on Bilingualism*. New York: Basic Books.

Handel, S. (1989). *Listening*. Cambridge, MA: MIT Press.

Hauser, M. (2001). Department of Psychology, Program in Neurosciences, Mind, Brain, and Behavior, Speech and Hearing Sciences Faculty, MIT–Harvard–MGH. www.wjh.harvard/edu//~mnkylab/LabPersonnel.html.

Hirschfield, L.A., and S.A. Gelman (eds.) (1994). *Mapping the Mind: Domain Specificity in Cognition and Culture*. Cambridge: Cambridge University Press.

Hurwitz, I., P.H. Wolff, B.D. Bortnick, and K. Kokas (1975). "Nonmusical Effects of the Kodaly Music Curriculum in Primary Grade Children." *Journal of Learning Disabilities* (Lincolnshire, UK) no. 8: 45–51.

Joseph, R. (1993). *The Naked Neuron: Evolution and the Languages of the Body and Brain*. New York: Plenum Press.

Jourdain, R. (1997). *Music, the Brain and Ecstasy: How Music Captures Our Imagination*. New York: William Morrow.

Lamb, S.J., and A.H. Gregory (1993). "The Relationship Between Music and Reading in Beginning Readers." *Educational Psychology*, 13, 19–27.

Lamb, S.M. (1999). *Pathways to the Brain: The Neurocognitive Basis of Language*. Amsterdam: John Benjamins Publisher.

Lerdahl, F. and R. Jackendoff (1996). *A Generative Theory of Tonal Music*. Cambridge, MA: MIT Press.

McAdams, S., and E. Bigand (eds.) (1993). *Thinking in Sound: The Cognition Psychology of Human Audition*. Oxford: Clarendon Press.

McLaughlin, B., and R. Nation (1986). "Experts and Novices: An Information-processing Approach to the 'Good Language Learner' Problem." *Applied Psycholinguistics* 7, no. 7: 41–56.

MuSICA Research Notes (1997). "The Musical Infant and the Roots of Consonance." Music and Science Data Base 4, no. 1. www.musica.cnlm.uci.edu/index.html.

Ojemann, G.A. and H.A. Whitaker (1978) "The Bilingual Brain." *Archives of Neurology*, no. 35: 409–412.

Paradis, M. (ed.) (1983). *Readings on Aphasia in Bilinguals and Polyglots*. Montreal, Canada: Didier.

Pinker, S. (1994). *The Language Instinct: How the Mind Creates Language*. New York: William Morrow.

Riess, M., and W. Yee (1993). "Attending to Auditory Events: The Role of Temporal Organization." In S. McAdams and E. Bigand (eds.), *Thinking in Sound: The Cognitive Psychology of Human Audition*. Oxford: Clarendon Press, 1993.

Runco, M.A., and R.S. Albert (1990). *Theories of Creativity*. Newbury Park, CA: Sage.

Sancar, F. (1999). "Music and the Brain: Processing and Responding." Response to Biology 202 at Bryn Mawr University. Web published at http://serendip.brynmawr.edu/bb/neuro99/web1/Sancar.html.

Serafine, M.L. (1988). *Music as Cognition: The Development of Thought in Sound*. New York: Columbia University Press.

Sloboda, J.A. (1985). *The Musical Mind*. London: Oxford University Press.

Springer, S., and G. Deutsch (1997). *Left Brain/Right Brain: Perspective from Cognitive Neuroscience*. New York: Worth.

Storr, A. (1992). *Music, Brain and Body*. New York: Free Press.

Titon, J.T., D.P. McAllester, M. Slobin, and D. Lock (eds.) (1996). *Worlds of Music: An Introduction to the Music of the World's Peoples*. New York: Shirmer Books.

Tokuhama-Espinosa, T. (2001). *Raising Multilingual Children: Foreign Language Acquisition and Children*. Westport, CT: Bergin & Garvey.

Tramo, M. (1997). Quoted in W.J. Cromie, "How Your Brain Listens to Music." *Harvard Gazette*, 13 November. www.hno.harvard.edu/science/archives/biology/brain_ music_13.Nov.97.html.

Trehub, S.E., and L.J. Trainor (1993). "Listening Strategies in Infancy." In S. McAdams and E. Bigand (eds.), *Thinking in Sound: The Cognitive Psychology of Human Audition*. Oxford: Clarendon Press.

Werker, J.F. (1997). "Exploring Developmental Changes in Cross-language Speech Perception." In D. Osherson (ed.), *An Invitation to Cognitive Science*. Vol. 1, *Language*. 2nd ed. Vol. eds. L.R. Gleitman and M. Liberman. Cambridge, MA: MIT Press.

Worringer, W. (1963). *Abstraction and Empathy*. Trans. Michael Bullock. Munich. FUNDUS.

7

Language, Math, and Thought
Vygotsky's Concept of Inner Speech

Tracey Tokuhama-Espinosa

If you speak more than one language, what language do you do math in? And why does it matter?

The language one uses to do math is intriguing on three levels. First, from a counseling perspective, when a child seems to be having academic difficulties, knowing whether or not a child's multiple languages are to blame, or whether or not math skills are really lacking, helps counselors to guide students properly. Second, from a policy perspective, knowing whether or not languages need to be taught in their own time, or whether or not they can be combined with other subject areas, can determine curriculum. That is, English language instruction can be achieved by teaching math *in English*, for example. Third, addressing this question offers a new angle on an old philosophical question: Do we think using words? While whole books could be written on all three aspects, this brief essay is limited to the last question. Are math problems solved using words?

Such intrigue raises questions more akin to philosophy than to linguistics that initially appear to be as infinite as the mind itself, though there are only four possible answers. Multilinguals do math either (1) in the native language, (2) in the language one was schooled in (if not native), (3) by choice (i.e., they choose which of their languages is most suitable), or (4) using no language at all. Since the purpose of this essay is to stimulate debate, ideally all forms of mathematical skills would be considered. However, the immediate discussion will be limited to addition exercises in order to simplify the options.

PHILOSOPHICALLY SPEAKING: DO WE THINK USING WORDS?

An Old Question

From Plato and on through St. Augustine and Descartes, man has wondered about the associations made in the mind, and has questioned the connection of thought to words. Scholars, linguists, and philosophers have long debated "why there has to be a private language" (Fodor 1975: 55–64) that utilizes "the vocabulary of internal representations" (1975: 124–156). In terms of developmental psychology, a similar question has been posed with regard to children. If thought requires words, and infants cannot speak, does that mean infants cannot think?

We now know that the ability to categorize differing numbers of objects is a preverbal skill found in infants with no apparent verbal language skills (Gallistel and Gelman 1992; Brannon 2002); meaning that the ability to count and classify pre-empts the ability to speak. Infants can respond to numerical differences without language. When, then, do children develop "thought," and how does this reflect on words, languages as a whole, and ultimately the language of mathematics?

Endophasy

Endophasy has been defined as many things over the years. Initially it was recognized as "verbal memory," later as "speech minus sound," then as the all-encompassing "motives of speech" and the indefinable "nonsensory and nonmotor specific speech experience" (Vygotsky 1962: 131). Vygotsky chose a simpler definition himself. Endophasy (literally, inner speech) is speech for oneself. External speech is for others (Vygotsky 1962: 131). He felt that the absence of vocalization is only a consequence of the specific nature of inner speech. *External* speech is the turning of thought into words; *inner* speech is speech into thought. Children experience a stage of egocentric speech, identified by Piaget, that proceeds inner speech, usually between the ages of three and seven. As speech for oneself becomes more sophisticated, "its vocalization becomes unnecessary and meaningless and, because of its growing structural peculiarities, also impossible. Speech for oneself cannot find expression in external speech" (Vygotsky 1962: 135). This does not mean that Piaget's egocentric speech has stopped occurring; rather, it has become sophisticated with the growing understanding of the child about his world, and with his growing vocabulary that leads to a "progressive development, the birth of a new speech form" (Vygotsky 1962: 135)—in effect, endophasy.

Vygotsky developed his theory concerning the internalization of dialogue into inner speech and thought to contrast the then popular point of view of Piaget on speech development as the suppression of egocentrism. Vygotsky believed that "speech and thinking are not interrelated. A prelinguistic period in thought and a preintellectual period in speech undoubtedly exist also in the development of the child. Thought and word are not connected by a primary bond. A connection originates, changes, and grows in the course of the evolution of thinking and speech" (Vygotsky 1962: 119). This relates to thoughts about all subjects, including mathematics.

A New Question

An E-mail exchange on the *Ask a Linguist* page (www.linguist.org/~ask-ling/archive-most-recent/msg00489.html) asked: "Can mathematics be described as a language? Or is it the other way round? Similarly, can mathematics exist without language—and can language exist without mathematics?"

One response read:

Mathematics can certainly be defined as a language in the formal sense; it is composed of a set of terms and a set of rules for the combination of those terms. However, it can't be defined as a "natural" language. And language cannot be defined as mathematics, no; it's a one-way relationship. In my opinion, language could exist without mathematics . . . but mathematics could not exist without a language in which to express the terms and rules. (Suzette Haden Elgin, 9 February 2000)

Another linguist responded to the same question by saying:

If you define "language" as a means of communication of complex ideas through the use of arbitrary symbols to encode these ideas, then you could say that mathematics is a language. If you decide mathematics only deals with numbers, then yes, you could have a language without math. And I believe you could have math without "language," but I don't know how you would talk about it. Cheers, DKR. (Deborah D. Kela Ruuskanen, 17 February 2000)

IS THERE SUCH A THING AS "MATHEMACY" OR A LANGUAGE OF MATH?

Symbols

Whereas the concept of 2 may be universal, how 2 is written is not the same around the world. Does this difference in symbolic representation influence the "ease" with which different school systems teach math? Do different symbols lend themselves to different mathematical interpretations? On a very simple level, the Chinese and Japanese symbols for one, two, and three as a single line for one, two lines for two, and three lines for three seem much more obvious than the Arabic 1, 2, and 3, which have to be associated without reference to a set. The differences in these symbols however, should not detract from the overriding concept that "math" is a singular domain of the human mind, whether done in Japanese, English, Turkish, Hindi, or some other language.

Interestingly enough, math skills are generally located in the left hemisphere, as are numbers; however, the symbol recognition of letters is in the right hemisphere (Joseph 1993: 169). So while the concept of 2 is in the left hemisphere, acknowledging the similarities and differences between 2 and 22 is in the right hemisphere.

Cummins's view about mental representations is expressed thus:

The essence of mental representation is an isomorphism between representations and their contents. My fundamental take on the problem is still the same: what makes sophisticated cognition possible is in the fact that the mind can operate on something that has the same structure as the domain it is said to recognize. The mind, in short, must be able to model the world, not just denote things in it. (Cummins 1994: 297–298)

That is, the mind thinks by referring to a domain of knowledge, and learns new things based on what already exists in the domain. If I understand the numbers 1 through 4, then I can grasp that 2 + 2 could equal 4. But this still begs the question of whether I hear the number 2 in English when I see this problem, or simply see the symbols and use no language at all.

THE QUESTION: IN WHAT LANGUAGE DO BILINGUALS DO MATH?

There are four possibilities:

1. People do math better in their native language.
2. People do math better in the language they were schooled in, regardless of what their native language is.
3. People choose the language they feel is more appropriate for the task.
4. People do math at least partially by depending on visual symbols (the numbers), using metalanguage skills and not words.

How can each of these views find backing? Isn't there a "right" answer? And is there only one right answer? What are the reasons for each of these four possibilities, and which is most likely to be true?

Option 1: People Do Math Better in Their Native Language

Since children begin to speak about 12–18 months of age, albeit in a fragmented form, and "by the time a child has reached the age of 3 she or he is capable of making simple calculations" (Joseph 1993: 177), one would think they were doing math in the native language. "Counting is important in knowledge acquisition because it aids in the ability to determine what is, versus what isn't, and thus to form categories consisting of abstract notions" (Joseph 1993: 177). *Thinking* and *talking to ourselves* are ontogenetically linked. Before children are able to think in words, they must be able to *hear* them, in order to know what the words sound like. Because of this, in part, people first learn to think out loud as children. "It is only over the course of the first seven years of life that verbalized thought becomes progressively internalized as the private dialogue that we all experience as our train of thought" (Joseph 1993: 279). This is due to the maturation of the corpus callosum, which facilitates the communication between the two halves of the brain. This explains why young

Hold Receipt

Malik Tiwana

Namra

05/10/2019 23:59:59

Date	28/09/2019 12:34:32
Last Name	Malik Tiwana
First Name	Namra
Call Number	404.2 MUL
Title	The multilingual mind : issues discussed by for and about people living with many languages /
Item Barcode	0060343000
Expires	05/10/2019 23:59:59
Pick up	Harcourt Hill Library

Thank you for using your Library.

children "think out loud" and narrate their actions. This argues in favor of the idea that people use their first language to do math.

When the question of math and language arose in an international E-mail exchange on bilingualism, one person responded:

I can tell you my personal experience. I am 33 years old, and I am originally from Taiwan. I moved with my family to the U.S. when I was 11 years old. So, I learned my numbers: addition, subtraction, multiplication, and division all in Chinese first. I memorized the multiplication table in Chinese in the 3rd grade. When I first moved to the U.S., the only English that I knew were the "ABC"s, "hello," and "good-bye." It took me one year to become fluent in English and one more year to acquire native-like fluency. Now, when people hear me speaking English here in the U.S., no one ever guesses that I wasn't born in the U.S. and English wasn't my first language. I actually think in English now. However, to this day, when dealing with numbers, I still think in Chinese. It's difficult for me to recite the multiplication table in English. If I had to do it, I would have to think about it and translate it! Needless to say, that would be a slow process! (March 2001)

One might conclude from such testimonials that math is then done in one's first language, however evidence to the contrary is also readily available.

Option 2: People Do Math Better in the Language They Were Schooled in, Regardless of Their Native Language

There is much evidence to back this: "The argument is that learning is facilitated by the presentation of multiple exemplars of inputs that share the same structural description" (Gelman and Brenneman 1994: 382). This means that the language of the environment where there is more time for practice, which is usually school for math skills, is the language in which a person does math. So if a child is a native Spanish speaker but attends school in English and therefore has more time to practice math in English, that child will use English as his "math" language. If we presume that the child has more math practice in school than he does at home, it would make sense that the language used to do math would be the school language.

A copy of an E-mail exchange provided one mother's testimony about her children's language skills:

. . . my older daughter, she prefers doing it in French, but I feel that's because she spends all day in French, and it can be very hard to change language modes. French is becoming her domain language for school. Actually, I said "prefer," but I suppose I shouldn't use that term since she's never said that. I should say she does math most often in French. And by the way, now she's learning lots of things that she doesn't know how to say in English: algebraic equations, geometric shapes, etc. I don't know all of them or remember them myself, as math was never my favorite subject. That makes it quite hard for her, if not impossible, to switch back to English. (March 2001)

This person's experience supports the idea that bilinguals do math in their school language, but avoids the question of whether or not family support, or the lack thereof, can influence the language in which the child chooses to do math.

Option 3: People "Choose" the Language They Feel Is More Appropriate for the Task

When adding without the use of paper ("in your head"), some bilinguals may lean toward the language system that lends itself best to the task. For example, if you learned to use "units" when doing math, such as ones, tens, and hundreds, then language systems such as the Japanese and the German are arguably linguistically more appealing because they effectively divide numbers into units (twenty-one in German is *ein und zwanzig* (1 + 20), and *ni ju ichi* in Japanese (literally 2 × 10 + 1). However, this may not have any particular advantage when it comes to other types of math problems.

Another woman wrote in an E-mail exchange:

This is interesting to me. I always had a feeling that math (simple arithmetic in particular) seems easier in Japanese linguistically in comparison with English or German. Since I'm no specialist and do not know how children learn arithmetic in English or German, this is based on my limited observation of how English-/German-speaking people process simple calculations. Japanese words for numbers are short (1502 for instance is *sen go-hyaku ni*, in comparison with one thousand five hundred and two), and for the basic multiplication table we have a song-like memorization aid, which goes like *ni-nin ga shi* (2 × 2 = 4), *ni-san ga roku* (2 × 3 = 6), . . . *ku-ku hachiju-ichi* (9 × 9 = 81). My (largely unrooted) theory is that such simpleness of the number system in the Japanese language, with short and easy-to learn expressions for basic multiplications, makes it easier (or quicker) to do simple arithmetic. (March 2001)

So one might conclude that some languages lend themselves to math more than others, and that bilinguals actually choose which to use. Is this choice a conscious one? Would the same child who would prefer to do addition in her native language of Japanese switch and use the school language to do algebra?

Option 4: People Do Math at Least Partially by Depending on Visual Symbols (the Numbers), Using Metalanguage Skills and Not Words

"What is this?" A girl aged seven years and four months is shown "7 + 6" on a piece of paper. After a moment she says, "Thirteen."

"How did you know that? How did you figure that out? Did you hear it in your head, for example?"

"I don't hear it out, I just know what 6 + 6 is, so then seven is one more, but not in words" (May 2000).

This reminded me of a quote from Piaget's work in which he discovered that "grammar precedes logic." In this case, this girl's understanding of the math result preceded her ability to decipher the content of the answer.

Another E-mail exchange about languages in math struck at the heart of this question.

As a trained mathematician, who taught math in Polish, French, and English, I found the question very interesting. So I tested quickly what I do. And it turned out that I do math in "math." I always had. If I can't get rid of the noise of any language, I can't solve the problem. I can start in any language I know, translate it into total abstraction with no language attached, solve it, then I can tell the result in any language I know again.

What does it mean for trivial things like multiplication? Say I tell myself "fifteen times fifteen" (in English), I don't see any 15's but 225 in digits flashes in front of my eyes, and immediately I say "two twenty five." I tested it in Russian, which I know but never use. Same thing; I "see" the result and then automatically I translate it in Russian, so the first answer is some sort of picture in my head, the second answer comes in the language the question came in, even if I never use this language. Then I tried something harder, something I don't have memorized: 32*32. I still did it in pictures of the numbers, but I ended up storing the partial results in my head in the language I asked myself the question in.

Then I thought of some hard stuff, open problems, and again it was pictures, lines, who knows, but not much of any language. Then I thought of more verbose open problems (like P = NP? if anybody knows what I'm talking about) and I was getting lost in the words and couldn't think about it.

So I came to the conclusion that I do math in "math" and maybe that's why I always liked it since I'm horrible in languages. (March 2001)

This excellent illustration gives weight to the idea that the language of math may be dominant over other languages in the mind of bilinguals and multi-linguals.

SO WHICH OF THE FOUR POSSIBILITIES ARE CORRECT?

As we can see from the examples here, they all are. While this question is one that no doubt will be raised again and again (I do not profess to answer something that Plato could not), I will conclude by laying my bets with Vygotsky, who wrote that "The relation of thought to word is not a thing but a process, a continual movement back and forth from thought to word and from word to thought" (1962: 125)—meaning that yes, we *do* use words, but the words live in a constant exchange with the thought they are reflecting. In this sense, the words are not static; they are alive and changing. "In that process the relation of thought to word undergoes changes which themselves may be regarded as development in the functional sense" (Vygotsky 1962: 125), and I would argue that this occurs in all of the languages available to a person, for knowledge about concepts is increased independently of the language they are learned in. As a nonmathematical example of this same concept, I believe my understanding about "fish" increased when I visited the Tokyo Fish Market when I was a teenager; I saw fish I had never seen before, ate fish I never knew existed, smelled odors I never knew—and all in Japanese. In a sense, my understanding of "fish" is also the Japanese *sakana* due to my experience.

Vygotsky continues: "Thought is not merely expressed in words; it comes into existence through them. Every thought tends to connect something with something else, to establish a relationship between things. Every thought moves, grows and develops, fulfils a function, solves a problem" (1962: 125). I therefore believe that the language we do math in is the language of "mathematical thought." Just as my understanding of "fish" is a multilingual experience, so math would be—and a dynamic experience it is. As my daughter begins to do more and more sophisticated math in German, and I continue to try and keep up with her, my own concept of 2 is influenced by my new learning of math in German. The 2 I used to do math in Japanese while on university exchange, and the 2 in Spanish I used while living in Ecuador for six years, and the 2 I use at the supermarket in France is combined with this new German 2 to enhance my understanding of 2 as a concept. I admit that I hear 2 in English as I write this essay, but I hear it in German as I help my daughter with her homework.

We have a personal way of interpreting language in that we can preserve the power of the word in a personal dialect. We know what whole concepts are without having to define them word for word. I understand "freedom" without having to break it down into a lengthy definition. "The language of thought is known (e.g., is the medium for the computations underlying cognitive processes) but not learned. That is, it is innate. Language of the mind is understood, not learned" (Fodor, 1975: 65).

Bilinguals do math in all four forms: in the native language, in the school language, in the language chosen by the bilingual, and without language at all (as many individual testimonies state here). A unifying concept of these four choices comes with Vygotsky's definition of our inner language: "speech for oneself." The beauty in this answer is in its ambiguity: There is no simple answer because there are no simple human beings. What language bilinguals do math in needs a complex, multichoice answer, because individuals fluctuate in their language dominance and in developmental stages of language, thought, and math abilities. Math, like thought and language, evolves in complexity throughout the life span and builds cumulatively.

REFERENCES

Brannon, E.M. (2002). "The Development of Ordinal Numerical Knowledge in Infancy." *Cognition* 83: 223–240.

Cummins, R. (1994). "Interpretational Semantics: Representations, Target and Attitude." In S.P. Stich and T.A. Warfield (eds.), *Mental Representations*. Oxford: Blackwell.

Fodor, J.A. (1975). *The Language of Thought*. New York: Crowell.

Gallistel, C.R., and R. Gelman (1992). "Preverbal and Verbal Counting and Computation." *Cognition* 44: 43–74.

Gelman, R., and K. Brenneman (1994). "First Principles Can Support Both Universal and Culture-specific Learning About Number and Music." In L.A. Hirschfield and S.A. Gelman (eds.), *Mapping the Mind: Domain Specificity in Cognition and Culture*. Cambridge: Cambridge University Press.

Horgan, T. (1994). "Computation and Mental Representation." In S.P. Stich and T.A. Warfield (eds.), *Mental Representations: A Reader*. Cambridge, MA: Blackwell.

Joseph, R. (1993). *The Naked Neuron: Evolution and the Languages of the Body and Brain*. New York: Plenum Press.

McAdams, S., and E. Bigand (eds.) (1993). *Thinking in Sound: Cognition Psychology of Human Audition*. Oxford: Clarendon Press.

Stich, S.P., and T.A. Warfield (eds.) (1994). *Mental Representation: A Reader*. Cambridge, MA: Blackwell.

Vygotsky, L.S. (1962). *Thought and Language*. Ed. and trans. E. Hanfmann and G. Vakar. Cambridge, MA, and New York: MIT Press and John Wiley & Sons.

8

Multilingual Mathematics

Marie Petraitis

Mathematics is the only language shared by all human beings regardless of culture, religion, or gender. All of us share this language called numeracy, and it is this shared language of numbers that connects us with people across continents. The language of math is numbers, not English or French or German.

(Annenberg CPB Project 1998)

If a child speaks, reads, and writes fluently in two languages, is it necessary for that child to do math in both of these languages, or is it just adding an extra burden? Do bilinguals think in a "numeracy," as Annenberg suggests, visualizing the numbers instead of hearing the name for the number in either French or English in their heads? Do my children, for example, use their school language (French), or do they use their "mother tongue" (English)?

One evening, when my children asked me to quiz them on the multiplication tables, I chose to do so in my native English and they had no problem producing the responses (also in English). Upon reflection, I wondered if it would be better to work in their school language, so I began drilling them in French. This did not faze them at all; they could reply in either language. How was this occurring in their minds, and were both children channeling the information in the same way?

I began observing other children's language choice for math. Would they use their mother tongue, or would they feel stronger in their school language? I quizzed fourteen children in my class according to their age-level math abilities. All were French-English bilinguals between the ages of six and fourteen. French is the school language of all the children; their ability to write in English varies.

Using a series of simple math questions that varied according to their abilities I administered a test and then asked the children which language they had used to solve the problems. I expected to find that children whose school language was French would use French to do the math, but realized that the school language was not necessarily the language that math skills were first taught in, and so turned to the question of binding to mother tongue or school language. Additionally, I observed the hand use of the children to see whether there was a correlation for language preference based on cerebral dominance.

INTRIGUING RESULTS

By and large, these fourteen children's experiences supported the conclusion that math skills were bound to language at the time of acquisition, and were not affected by the home versus school language question. The children who had greater exposure to English while infants have stronger numerical skills in English. This is probably owing to the fact that often the parents introduced the math skill in English before it was taught in school in French. It also may be due to the parents wanting the child to be capable of doing math in English, so they repeat the skill in English.

For example, Jacqueline was born in the United States and had both English and French until she was three and a half, at which time her family moved back to Switzerland and the language around her became mainly French. Jacqueline's mother encouraged her exposure to English through educational videos and reading classes until she was six years old; then the family had an English speaker around Jacqueline full-time. As a result of this strategic English exposure and the fact that math skills are taught in the schools beginning at age six in her village, Jacqueline was first exposed to her numerical and reading skills in English. She said that she did her math in English.

Other examples are teenagers Ashley and Steve. While both are developing their math skills at school in French, they originally learned their basic skills in English, and continue to use it when doing math.

This means that the language in which the child learned the skill is the language the child uses to do math, in my group. For example, Sandra was born in Switzerland to a French-speaking family. The family was living in Australia when Sandra first learned her addition skills in school. Since then the family has moved back to Switzerland. Sandra still does basic addition in English, but the more complex skills were learned after her return to Switzerland and therefore she uses her school language, French, for them. Haley, her older sister, has similar skills even though Haley had begun more complex math skills before leaving Australia; the skills have been reinforced in French.

Roseanna's family moved to Switzerland two and a half years ago, and Roseanna adapted to speaking French at school rather easily. It is possible that to help herself in the French language used at school, Roseanna has found the "number" language and uses her English as a backup. Unfortunately, Roseanna's family will be moving back to Australia. If they were to stay in Switzerland, it would be very interesting to see if she would develop her numerical abilities in French or would continue to stay with her "number" language. And in the long run, in which language would she be faster at doing the calculations?

Charles and Steve are brothers whose language usage is very different. Steve, the older, learned his primary number skills while the family was living in the

United States, and his only language was English. Charles, on the other hand, started his schooling in Switzerland in French and developed a strong basis in French.

PRELIMINARY THEORIES OF MATHEMATICS AND LANGUAGE CORRELATION

Math skill and language are "bound" at the age of acquisition. According to Lawrence, "Studies of the brain have gradually revealed what educators and parents have known instinctively for years: that the experiences children have in the early years of their life have a direct effect on the quantity and quality of connections made in the brain" (Lawrence 1998: 15)

It is possible that the age of acquisition of the math skill is related to the language used when the math skill is first acquired. For example, if a child is taught a skill in English and it is well integrated into the child's brain, the child will continue to use English because it is associated with the skill, even though the child may learn to speak more languages. A child is most sensitive to learning pathways in language during the first six years of life (Lawrence 1998: 16), the time when a child learns ordering skills and basic addition and subtraction.

Table 8.1
Bilingual Children in Math Survey

Name	Years Old	Hand Use	Birthplace	Choice of Language for Math
Thomas	6½	Right	Switzerland	French
Annabelle	6½	Right	Switzerland	English
Jacqueline	7	Right	USA	English
Roseanna	7½	Right	Australia	English and "numbers" language
Helene	8½	Right	Switzerland	English
Sabrina	9	Left	Switzerland	Combination of English and French
Sandra	9½	Right	Switzerland	English for addition and subtraction but French for multiplication
Emma	11	Left	Switzerland	Combination of French, English and "numbers" language
Roger	11½	Right	Switzerland	English
Heather	12	Right	in Switzerland	English for addition and French for subtraction, multiplication and division
Charles	13 y	Left	Switzerland	French
Haley	13½	Right	Switzerland	English for addition; subtraction multiplication and division in French
Ashley	14	Right	Switzerland	English
Steve	14	Right	Switzerland	English

Children naturally reinforce their skills in their primary language by continuously repeating the pathways in order to refine and develop them. "Pathways that are not reinforced wither away around the age of ten, leaving only what is strong and functional to develop" (Lawrence 1998: 15). This would lead us to conclude that a child who repeatedly uses two languages for skills such as communication and numerical thinking will develop mathematical skills (via the logical thinking pathway) in both languages at an equal ability.

Why then, do some of the children who were brought up with schooling in both languages tend to choose to do their math in only one of the languages? Or why do they do one mathematical skill (addition) in one language and another mathematical skill (multiplication) in their other language? To answer this, we need to look at the age of acquisition of the skill. Regardless of whether the child can fluently speak two languages, the language choice for mathematics depends more on the language that the math skill was taught in.

The counterargument is made that multilinguals who have learned more than one language after the age of six often say that they are able to add and subtract in their second languages. On a closer look at these claims, we may find that few of these adults can stay in their second language when they are doing continuous and complicated equations. They may "naturally" slip into using their first language, which was learned at a younger age. This is an intriguing question that requires further research among multilingual adults before firm conclusions can be drawn.

Maternal Influence

A factor that was not controlled for the study but may be applicable is the influence from the children's main caregiver; in my group's case this was always the mother. Some of my initial findings are reported below. When I asked the children how much their mothers helped them with learning their multiplication tables, Roger said his mother drilled him with flash cards. Flash cards are neutral in their language use. They allow children to develop their visual or auditory skills in their thinking and evaluating process. The interesting fact for Roger was that his mother asked him to repeat what was written on the cards and that he always answered in English, thus strengthening his mathematical skills in English. She also translated his math into English so that he would learn to use his maternal language to do sums. Interestingly, Roger's English skills did not block out his teacher's French; instead, they learned to coexist. Roger actually learned the math skills in both languages.

Ashley's mother also helped her greatly in learning her math skills at an early age by introducing the skills directly in English. This experience must have come at a time when Ashley was clearly ready for it and was therefore very positive for her, since she has since kept her maternal language as her stronger math language.

Jacqueline's mother chose not to teach Jacqueline any math skills in French; instead, she allowed a native English speaker to help her develop these skills. This instruction was supplemented by English television, *Sesame Street* videos, and English computer software.

As for my own girls I visually taught them math concepts that were reinforced in English before they learned them in school. It is likely that they "relearned" the material in school in French, and subsequently have two languages that perform fairly equally.

Hand Use As a Factor in Language Binding

According to the theories of localization of brain functions, mathematical abilities are in the left hemisphere (Tokuhama-Espinosa 2001: 92). I expected to find that right-handed children would be more strongly bound to their choice of language for mathematics, whereas in left-handed children, I expected to find a less strong binding. Language was directly related to skill acquisition, though interestingly, in my survey the right-handed children were found to do math skills in the language of the school. This was true regardless of the child's speaking another language and moving to a country where the other language was dominant.

If the right-handed children are left-hemisphere dominant and it is this hemisphere that holds the facilities for logical thinking, mathematics, and language abilities, then how do left-handed children find the pathways to integrate language and mathematical problem solving? Since 70 percent of left-handed individuals also have their main math areas in the left hemisphere, only a small percentage of left-handed people should have math skills in another area of the brain.

These preliminary observations sought to investigate the manner in which hand use was related to the binding of language use and mathematical problem solving. Though no definite conclusions can be drawn from such a small sampling, it is interesting food for thought. The right-handed children tended to be more definite in their language selection. They would do the skill in the language in which they acquired the skill, but not go back and forth between the two. For example, Haley used English for addition but stayed in French to do subtraction, multiplication, and division.

The girls who were left-handed used a combination of their two languages to do the math. They would go in and out of French and English or number symbols without any seemingly conscious preference. Is it possible that as left-handed children they have learned to develop the pathways between the languages so that there is no difference between them? Charles, the one left-handed boy who was tested, said that he did the quiz in French because he wanted to block out the language in the room so he could concentrate more, and at school he often used English for the same reason. This would suggest that the left-handed girls were more flexible than the boy in using language.

Switching Languages

One of the reasons we have such a rich vocabulary of thinking is that words teach concepts and thereby create paths for thinking to follow. The more ways of describing thinking that are available to language learners, the more paths learners will have along which to direct their thinking. (Tishman, Perkins, and Jay 1995: 8)

Is it possible that a child who is able to do math in two languages is able to be more precise in his thinking, and therefore calculating, or would he be hindered by extra vocabulary? Is the child who chooses the language that he wants to work in able to work faster than those who have taken the school language as their stronger math language? The internal logic of the children as they expressed it seemed to be that it just "felt better" one way or the other. When did the children switch, why did they switch, and what strategies did they use in choosing the language with which to do mathematical problems?

Charles used the opposite language as a way of blocking out the noise around him; since I had been speaking to him in English, he used French in order to block me out and concentrate more. He added that he felt more comfortable checking his work by using French. Roger relates the language to the environment. For example, at school he will do his work in French without thinking that he uses this language to follow the teacher or his classmates. At home he will naturally use English for his homework even though the text may be written in French and he does not necessarily have anyone speaking to him in English.

Math Abilities and Syntax Structure

As a preliminary hypothesis I wondered if syntactical ability in a language (maternal or school) was related to the choice of language in which the children did mathematical problems. Would greater syntactical ability increase the use of the language in which they do their math? That is, would syntactical abilities align with logical thinking, which would determine the language used in math?

I investigated the relationship between the children's written syntax in English and their use of language when doing their math, but I did not find that children who were very capable of writing good sentences would only use English. Nor did I find that it made a difference if the math was written horizontally or vertically—except for Roger, who did his vertical math in French even though he was doing them in his English environment.

Why did children's syntactical abilities have no apparent influence on their language choice? Is it possible that some of these children could alter their choice of language in which to do math when the mathematical problems became more difficult, and simultaneously their logical abilities and syntax became focused in one language? These and other questions are ripe for further research.

For Further Exploration

These observations were limited in the way that the children were tested on their language choice and the speed with which they calculated the responses to the mathematical problems. It would be beneficial to test the children in English and French environments (i.e., speak to them in English first and then have them do the test, then repeat the test after having spoken French to the children). It is possible that the results of this survey were partial to English because I had spoken English to the children and they knew that the environment was English before doing the test. The idea of two languages being a burden on the child's ability to perform logical thinking is perhaps better tested in an environment where the speed of their brain patterns could be judged and compared, as is being done in current research in Switzerland (www.uni-bas.ch/themultilingualbrain/2001). Two elements that clearly could be tested further are the accuracy of the math solutions and the amount of time spent on each problem. Other areas in which the research could be expanded would be to test other language combinations, and to have a standard questionnaire for the parents, to capture family information.

Conclusions

The fact that some of the children chose one of their languages in which to do their math shows that they are most comfortable in that language. The children I tested did not communicate that they felt an extra burden in speaking two languages, but they made choices for their logical thinking patterns in mathematics. Perhaps the definitive answer lies in new studies now being conducted that monitor participants' brain patterns when performing reading, speaking, verbal recall, logical thinking, and math in both of their languages. The variables seem great, and each individual's life experiences, including the age at which and the language in which they first learned math skills, seem to impact the answer to the question. What language do bilinguals do math in? Further studies in this field, as well as acknowledgment that the true answer may vary in each individual's case, may lead to a clearer understanding of the relationship between math and multilinguals.

REFERENCES

The Annenberg CPB Project (1998). "The Universal Language: Math in Daily Life. How Do Numbers Affect Everyday Decisions?" Available: www.learner.org/exhibits/dailymath/language.html.

Lawrence, L. (1998). *Montessori Read and Write*. London: Ebury.

The Multilingual Brain: www.unibas.ch/themultilingualbrain/.

Tishman, S., D.N. Perkins, and E. Jay (1995). *The Thinking Classroom*. Boston: Allyn and Bacon.

Tokuhama-Espinosa, T. (2001). *Raising Multilingual Children: Foreign Language Acquisition and Children*. Westport, CT: Bergin & Garvey.

Part III

Degrees of Multilingualism

9

In the Beginning Was the Word
Language and the Womb

Andrea Bader-Rusch

Words can touch feelings, and can even touch our senses by richness of texture.
(Segal 1995: 8)

Having had the pleasure of witnessing my two daughters develop language and begin to speak, I am now immersed in this experience with my grand-daughter. All are multilingual, bilingual since before birth. Although their personalities and circumstances differ, their process of language acquisition has been similar.

What has always remained the same for me in this process is the profundity of connection and relationship that language brings with it. Whether it be the language of a rhythmic kick from a fetus still in the womb, a newborn's recognition of her mother's voice, a new sound repeated over and over again, a little echo trailing behind me, or two words suddenly strung together, the joy of mastery expands from the center of a child's being, sweeps across her face, and radiates a kind of knowing; a child's kind of knowing that allows entry into a hidden world. She knows that there is something in language that connects her to others. Words play an integral part in her exploration of how to relate. Her brain bursts with an eagerness to learn. Her little hands offer me a chewed and worn favorite book, her way of asking for my voice and the rhythm of sound. The strength of our relationship strikes deep within my heart.

How did this all begin? When do learning and language acquisition really start? Although we have no definite answers to these questions, we do have fascinating research related to the brain and learning that sheds light on how we as humans develop language and what supports that process. It all begins in the womb.

A NATURAL ENVIRONMENT FOR LEARNING

The importance of prenatal communication and music came into my awareness after the birth of my youngest daughter over eighteen years ago. As an infant she loved classical music and seemed to be soothed by the pieces I had repeatedly played when she was in my womb. At four years of age she announced that she wanted to play the "big violin." I was later to learn what this was as she stretched her ten fingers in front of me and proclaimed that she had "cello fingers."

It was not until I started working with parents-to-be, however, that I increasingly began to observe more incidents of what I termed "prenatal memory." I intuitively knew that prenatal memory was real, and I was eager to know more. I thus began to explore current theories and related brain research with the intent of joining intuition with scientific knowledge. Extensive documentation exists that not only supports reports of memories of pre- and perinatal events, but also confirms the existence of prenatal memory. Most interesting is that these studies particularly lend credence to the importance of the role of prenatal communication in the development of the brain and language acquisition. P.G. Hepper (1996), researcher at the Foetal Behaviour Research Centre in Belfast, concludes that the fetus does possess a memory, with possible functions including practice, recognition of and attachment to the mother, promotion of breast-feeding, and language acquisition.

Life in the womb is extremely active. The fetus is submerged in a stimulating environment of sounds, vibrations, and movement. Recordings of uterine sounds by researchers reveal that it is not a particularly quiet place to take up residence. The mother's body is constantly digesting food, pumping blood, and conveying the sound of her voice as rhythm, melody, pitch, and intonation reverberate through her bones. Outside sounds are conducted through the amniotic fluid to the fetus. "It's kind of like listening to a stereo next door," says William Fifer, associate professor of developmental psychobiology at Columbia University in New York. Fifer has found that when the mother is speaking, the fetal heart rate slows down, indicating that in addition to hearing and recognizing the sound, the fetus is calmed by it. Amazingly, the fetus also likes to hear her speaking in her native tongue rather than in a foreign language (Hendricks 1998).

A six-month old fetus moves its body rhythmically to the pattern of the mother's speech, an early lesson included in the complex development of language, preparing the child for language acquisition after birth. But how does a baby build upon this rhythmic foundation?

Peter Jusczyk, former professor of psychology at Johns Hopkins University and author of a book on how children acquire language, discovered (with psychologist Peter Eimas) in the 1960s that babies at one month of age were distinguishing between the sounds "pa" and "ba." Subsequent studies by other researchers report that this is happening at birth, even with babies born to speakers of a language without the pa/ba sounds. "Babies come equipped with basic speech perception, as if it were hardwired," concludes Jusczyk (Hendricks 1998).

Perhaps the calming effect of the mother's rhythmic voice and words spoken directly to the fetus are the very beginning. The unborn child listens attentively to communications from outside the womb as well as to those from within. A baby in a breech position during the last weeks of pregnancy, for example, often can be safely encouraged to turn to headfirst by gentle coaxing from a familiar voice. I've known fathers who have placed themselves near the lower abdomen and "talked" the baby down. Who knows, she may go down there so she can hear better!

THE GIFT OF ATTENTION

Infants as young as seven months can abstract simple rules from language-like sounds, according to cognitive scientist Gary Marcus. Ninety percent of the infants included in his research study were able to recognize sentence structure that they had heard before. At this same young age, they also focused longer when they heard a voice saying words they had heard before, consistently paying attention to rhythm, sound, and structure. How many of us have found ourselves grinning at an infant, repeating words or strings of words in a high-pitched voice in an attempt to get the slightest response? Jusczyk identifies the high-pitched, singsong voice that adults often use with babies as emphasizing "certain aspects of the structure of language that a baby should pay attention to" (Hendricks 1998). Goethe said that the gift of attention is the only thing that differentiates the genius from the average human being. How much attention are we paying to life in the womb?

SOUNDS OF LANGUAGE

Language involves an intriguing complexity of components. The levels of learning confronting the fetus are both diverse and sophisticated. Not only does each culture express a distinct worldview, but each language has its own set of rules and patterns for understanding things. In addition, of the estimated 6,000 languages spoken worldwide, each has a distinctive rhythm and sound of its own. As in music, they all use the same base tones, which range between 125 and 250 hertz (a measurement of pitch). The overtones, however, differ according to each language, as shown in table 9.1.

While British English uses a lot of high-pitched tones, French is distinguished by primarily lower tones. Base tones are produced by the vocal cords and travel through the mouth cavity, where the overtones are formed. Within the mouth cavity the tongue plays the important role of splitting it into two sections, generating overtones. Although the fetus hears its mother's voice, it sounds different from her real one, stresses French researcher Dr. Alfred Tomatis. The amniotic fluid around the fetus acts as a sound filter and lets only the high-pitched sounds through, providing the fetus with the composition of its "mother tongue."

Table 9.1
Language Tones Measured in Hertz

Language	Hertz
French	1,000 - 2,000 Hertz
British English	2,000 - 12,000
North American English	800 - 3,000
German	100 - 3,000
Slavic	100 - 8,000
Spanish	100 to 500, - 1,500 to 2,500

Sound, defined as vibration in a medium (usually air), has intensity (loudness), rate of vibration (pitch), rhythm, and duration. Loudness is measured in decibels (dB). The human ear, fully functioning when the fetus is only four and a half months old, has a hearing threshold (intensity at which sound is perceived) of approximately 40 dB at twenty-seven to twenty-nine weeks of gestation. This decreases to a nearly adult level of 13.5 dB by forty-two weeks of gestation. The range of sound within the womb is estimated anywhere from 30 to 96 dB (a normal conversation is about 60 dB). Just imagine what effect sound has on the fetus as it is surrounded by the energy fields created by all the resident activity. Hearing impairment has been documented in children whose mothers were exposed to consistent and excessively loud noises during their pregnancy. At the very least, startling noises can make the fetus jump. Reactive listening begins as early as sixteen weeks of gestation, eight weeks before the ear is structurally integral.

Although it is difficult to study language perception in the womb, it is known that fetal sound stimulation causes the brain to operate at a higher level of organization. The study of infant speech perception and the newborn's reactions to sounds imitating those of the womb is being pursued. Studies confirm that newborns are able to distinguish one language from another; they suckle more vigorously when they hear their native language as opposed to one they haven't heard before. Again, babies indicate preference for the sound of their mother's voice to that of another.

It has been proven that we have an aptitude for hearing the sound of a language. We do have an "ear" for a language. The mother's voice provides a strong foundation upon which the listening process and the development of language unfold. The sophistication of the language spoken is matched by an already keen intellect on the part of the unborn child, and the baby begins to learn her "mother tongue." It appears that sound shapes us, both inside and out. The first language lessons are in the womb.

MUSIC AND THE MIND

In specific cultures the community traditionally gathers around the soon-to-be mother while singing and playing music to the unborn baby, careful not to say "bad" things that the fetus will hear. Michel Odent, director of research for the Primal Health Research Center in London, believes that women have a deep need to sing to their babies. The inflections of the mother's voice convey her mother tongue through song and complete the direct communication of emotions through melody and rhythm with words. Whatever our beliefs, we all know that music affects our mood. Prenates exposed to lullabies seem to be calmed by them, and four-month-old infants prefer harmonious to disharmonious music. Babies who have moved in rhythm to music while in the womb remember these tunes and are comforted by them after birth. Mozart's music seems to be the most ideal choice. But why Mozart?

Recently it has been postulated that music has a stabilizing effect on the neural connections of the brain. Born with 100 billion unconnected or loosely connected neurons (nerve cells), babies immediately begin to undergo a strengthening of or coupling between these cells with each new experience. In addition to a parent's loving touch or mother's soothing voice, Mozart's complex and richly patterned music has been shown to have a soothing effect upon the brain, causing changes in the brain's wiring. The link between music and learning has only begun to be studied, although it has been used for years in connection with foreign language learning such as the Tomatis method and Suggestopedia or Super-Learning. Now we are recognizing it as a boost to mental skills used for mathematics as well, and we consider it a prelinguistic language.

The term "Mozart Effect" was coined from the neuroscientific and musical studies of Dr. Francis Raucher, a researcher and former concert cellist, and Dr. Gordon Shaw, at the University of California, Irvine. A causal link has been discovered between music and spatiotemporal reasoning, which is used when we turn images around in our minds or calculate fractions. The results of these studies and others have encouraged educators to rethink their school music programs. Don Campbell, author of The Mozart Effect for Children, offers exercises for using music to stimulate creativity from prebirth to ten years, basing his work largely on the pioneering work of Tomatis. It is now an accepted fact that music, recorded as patterns in the brain, affects creativity, learning, and health. Simply stated, sound and vibration interacting with matter create either beauty or chaos. Mozart's music seems to increase in the alpha rhythm frequency and to offer the most balance, energetically. This is optimal for therapeutic use, healing, and learning.

PROFOUND IMPRESSIONS

My granddaughter seems to be the vehicle to my past, allowing me once again to listen to other forms that language can take. I am reminded of Richard

Lewis's words when he said, "As children we relied much more on the transparency of feelings. We watched and listened, not so much with the intent of speaking about things, but with immersing ourselves in the feelings we had from things" (1995: 27).

It is my feeling that very often the babies born to my clients—parents-to-be with whom I have intently focused on the baby and impending birth—recognize my voice. It is not an egotistical desire, but a knowing. When I first dared to mention this to a new mother as I held her baby for the first time, her authentic response was, "Of course she does." I've not been so shy about my feelings since then.

Psychiatrist Stanislav Graf, among others, reports that he has had clients who have spoken in a foreign language that they heard only before birth, an example of fetal memory amazingly translated into language. The famous American-born violinist Yehudi Menuhin attributed his musical talent in part to his parents, who were always singing and playing music before he was born. "I've been hearing fiddle music since I was in the womb, I'm sure," says Nathalie MacMaster, a leading Canadian female fiddler representing Celtic culture. "My mother had this tape recorder going then. I started playing fiddle when I was young" ("Fiddler MacMaster," 1999).

Young mother and health professional Susan Mantegani has always been curious about the issue of prenatal voice recognition and memory. Just one hour after she gave birth to her daughter, they lay together in the dimly lit room nose to nose. "I was there with her, right at her level, her eyes looking into mine, blinking. I lay talking away to her as she looked at me intently. I'll never forget the impact of that moment and the feelings it aroused." Susan had begun playing a favorite piece music to her unborn daughter about halfway through her pregnancy. The first time she played it after her birth, the baby turned her head toward it with eyes wide open. "It was the only thing that calmed her down. When I played other music, she just didn't react as strongly" (personal conversation, 2000).

Rosel Wälchli remembers receiving Rod Stewart's *Rebel Heart* in the last weeks of her pregnancy and playing it regularly. She was then pregnant with her son, Benjamin, who was an extremely high-need baby after birth. "I couldn't place Benjamin down without him screaming. I even had to push the pram and carry him in my arms. It was a very difficult time. The only thing that seemed to put him to sleep was playing *Rebel Heart*. It worked quite soon, actually. By the second song he would be asleep. It's still my favorite music of Rod Stewart's, and Benjamin enjoys it as well" (personal conversation, 2000).

Dhruti Dholakia, child-development specialist and mother of two young daughters, recalls the time that she and her husband spent talking and reading to their unborn baby during each pregnancy. Fluent in five languages, Dhruti knows the power of the word. "I would sometimes read the newspaper to them; it didn't have to be a children's book . . . although the books I did read are still their favorites today. I wanted them to hear my voice and know me. My husband would speak and also play with the various sounds of a drum. In India it is traditional to communicate with the unborn child" (personal conversation, 2001).

My own little cello-fingered cherub is today a healthy, extremely bright young woman of eighteen. She still has a passion for Mozart, and I am convinced she formed a close relationship with his music while in my womb. I remember being particularly fond of listening to string instruments and Mozart's compositions all through my pregnancy. I am not at all surprised at her passion for languages. I intuitively know that this has had a positive effect on Elana's intellectual development and her gift for learning languages. Perhaps this has been the real inspiration for my pursuit of research in language development; the search for scientific evidence in support of my theory.

The womb is indeed a classroom. It is also a place where we have the opportunity to form a strong relationship and bond with our baby. Stimulation of the senses in utero assists our children in arriving in this world prepared for their next steps in language acquisition and development. All they strive to do, all day long, is to communicate with us. Yes, in the beginning was the word; and the way we approach the word is as important as the word itself.

REFERENCES

American Academy of Pediatrics (1997). "Noise: A Hazard for the Fetus and Newborn." *Pediatrics* 100, no. 4: RE9728.

Benziger, K. (2000). *Thriving in Mind: The Art and Science of Using Your Whole Brain.* Dillon, CO: KBA.

Campbell, D. (1997). *The Mozart Effect for Children.* New York: William Morrow & Co.

"Fiddler MacMaster Uses Voice for 'In My Hands.' " (1999, November 8). CNN.

Fuller, R. (1995). "Parabola: Myth, Tradition and the Search for Meaning." *Language and Meaning* 20, no. 3: 33–38 (August).

Gerritsen, J. (1996). *How the Tomatis Method Accelerates Learning Foreign Languages.* Paris France: Tomatis Listening and Learning Center. Available: www.tomatis.com/English/Articles/languages.htm.

Hendricks, M. (1998). "Origins of Babble." *John Hopkins Magazine*, February. Available: http://www.jhu.edu/~jhumag/0298web/baby.html.

Hepper, P.G. (1996). "Fetal Memory: Does It Exist? What Does It Do?" *Acta Paediatrica* supp. 416: 16–20.

Hopson, J. (1998). "Fetal Psychology." *Psychology Today* 31, no. 5: 44.

Jusczyk, P. (1997). *The Discovery of Spoken Language.* Cambridge, MA: MIT Press.

Lawrence, R. (1995). *How the Tomatis Method Affected My Violin Playing.* Available: www.tomatis.com/English/Stories/violin_playing.htm.

Lewis, R. (1995). "Parabola: The Magazine of Myth and Tradition." *Language and Meaning* 20, no. 3: 27.

National Research Council, Committee on Hearing, Bioacoustics, and Biomechanics, Assembly of Behavioral and Social Sciences (1982). *Prenatal Effects of Exposure to High-Level Noise*. Report of Working Group 85. Washington, DC: National Academy Press.

Odent, M. (1992). *The Nature of Birth and Breastfeeding*. Westport, CT: Bergin & Garvey.

Segal, W. (1995). "Parabola: Myth, Tradition and the Search for Meaning." In *Language and Meaning* (August), 8.

10

First Choice Option
From Birth

Tracey Tokuhama-Espinosa

When parents think about raising their children in a multilingual environment and about sharing two different languages with their son or daughter from birth, they pass through at least one gripping moment of doubt. Should we take the plunge? Should we really challenge our little baby with two different languages from the start? Won't we be wearing out her little brain too quickly? Isn't more than one language a mental burden she shouldn't have to bear until later in life, say in high school, when she can get her language requirement out of the way as well? Ultimately, wouldn't it be better for our child to speak one language skillfully than two languages with flaws?

Everyone knows the benefits of bringing up children with more than one language, but what are the drawbacks? Children who can switch gracefully from tongue to tongue, depending on their company, impress us all, but haven't we seen enough kids who barely speak at all, or who mix their languages incessantly? How do we get the goodies without buying into the host of problems that "other" people's bilingual children have? How do we get to *multilingualism* without failing and falling into *semilingualism*, where little Susie can't speak either of her languages well? Maybe two multilingual family examples can shed some light.

I once received a concerned couple in my home who were worried about their daughter's study skills. They began explaining their worries about Maria to me in a mixture of Spanish and English, both parents chiming in at different points in the conversation, usually with half a sentence in Spanish and the rest in English. Maria's parents blamed her current dyslexia and shyness on the fact that she had always heard Spanish, Hebrew, and English as a mix since she was little. And now, they feared, she was "handicapped for *vida.*"

On the other hand there is Sanjeeta, who was in my senior class group in an international school in Tokyo where instruction was conducted primarily in English. Her mother is Indian and her father is Japanese. She speaks Hindi,

Japanese, and English with no accent and has never had confusion with her languages.

Both of these seventeen-year-old girls had three working languages in their lives, but they had very different levels of success. Why? What did Sanjeeta's parents do that worked, and for goodness' sake, what did Maria's parents do so we can avoid it? Many factors come into play.

In speaking to parents who are contemplating bilingualism for their children, there are a great number of concerns: "Learning another language will be too much for him"; "Too many languages will confuse her"; "I don't want him to get behind in his first language because he's learning a second one." Often their worries boil down to the idea that acquiring too many languages at one time will somehow "overload" the brain. Is it possible that all these well-meaning mothers and fathers could be right? Yes, it is. But, interestingly enough, it could be that the opposing camp is *also* correct.

The other camp is the group of people who push the idea that a second language opens up the brain to greater stimulus, that one's chances of thinking with a wider scope are heightened, that making friends from other lands and enjoying movies and books and customs from other countries are increased with the ability to speak another tongue. Not to mention the later marketability of polyglots in comparison with others in today's workforce.

In researching multilingual children I have come to believe that there are problems with the reasoning of people in the first camp. First of all, getting back to Maria, bilingualism does not cause dyslexia or shyness. These are language developmental, personality, and neurological problems that would have been present had she spoken just one of her three languages. Researchers have now proven there is no correlation between societies with high levels of bilingualism and high levels of dyslexia. While it is true that a second language can aggravate dyslexia and even shyness, it is not true that multiple languages cause them. Those who believe there are reasons not to raise children bilingually base their decision on "facts" that are decades old.

Much of the first research on bilingual individuals was based on intelligence tests given to immigrant populations in the 1950s. The tests "proved" that people who split their language capacity between two languages were on the whole less intelligent than monolinguals. The tests were given to people of all ages, primarily from Europe, who learned English subsequent to their arrival to America. Unfortunately, some linguists and a few pediatricians too many have bought into these "proofs." Why do I say "unfortunately"? Because the new arrivals scored low for a variety of reasons, including that many came from less educated backgrounds, many did not understand the purpose of the test, and the IQ tests were given in English, which was unfamiliar or unknown to many of those who were tested. Additionally, we cannot fail to recognize that those immigrants and our children are very different groups of people, due not only to social, economic, and educational opportunities but also to the times in which we live and the age at which the foreign language is undertaken.

Can we compare a middle-aged Italian or Polish economic immigrant in the 1950s with your child in today's world? A few differences come to mind. Giovanni and Jan came to the United States right after a major world war with the goal of bettering their economic status. Their primary aim was not to learn English as a second language. English "happened" to them as an aside to improving their economic status and fulfilling their dreams of offering their children a more prosperous life.

Your infant son at the opening if the new millennium has an entirely different goal when it comes to learning a language. He wants to communicate with the most loved person in his life, you, and you want to help him know both his parent's culture(s) as well as understand the culture where he lives. If you and your spouse happen to speak different languages, he will have to learn to communicate with each of you. He is not looking for a *change* of life; he is looking to *share* your life. In your family situation, the focus is not about cultural absorption, where English eclipses an old language; it is on fostering the cognitive abilities of your son to find the means of transmitting his messages to you, whether in one, two, or ten different languages.

Another argument against early second language learning involves the question of "brain overload." Parents ask, "Wouldn't we be better off just using what 'brain space' we have devoted to language to completely develop our mother tongue?" "Aren't there a number of bilinguals who are less than 'fluent' in either of their languages?" In extreme cases these people are labeled *semilinguals* and never fully develop any of their languages. Because they do not have a native tongue, they do not have the tools in which to think profound thoughts, nor the ability to express what they do think with clarity. Parents' worries are plainly spoken: "What is the point of speaking many languages poorly, when we can focus on speaking just one brilliantly?"

While the concerns are very legitimate, I think they have been strongly refuted by current neurological research. Scientists now know that humans use approximately 20 percent (you may be more, you neighbor maybe less) of the brain's potential. That is, synapses occur between just 20 percent of the neurons we are born with. It used to be thought that there was just a single language area in the brain, and that by learning more than one language, we were dividing out total capacity for language. What is now evident from new research, such as studies being conducted at the University of Basel in Switzerland, is that while most people's language centers are in their left frontal, temporal, and parietal lobes, bilinguals and multilinguals generally have their languages spread over a greater area of the brain, employing many areas in the right hemisphere as well (www.unibas.ch/themultilingualbrain). Given how much potential is left for development, should "overloading" children still be a concern?

No, *nein, non,* say many polyglots. But what about these kids who "know" several languages but cannot speak in any of them clearly? The counterargument of linguists is that bilingual people who express themselves poorly would have been monoglinguals who expressed themselves poorly; some people just have poor verbal expression. Neurologists boost the idea that there is no known limit on the number of languages the human brain can learn. And demographers point out that most of the world is bilingual, so it is not such a lofty goal as we may believe. To top this off, fascinating new research shows that multilinguals use more of their right hemisphere than monolinguals, who generally have their language centered in the left hemisphere. This means that rather than "overloading" the brain, multilinguals use parts of the brain that would otherwise go unemployed.

So, should you, mother-to-be or parent of a small baby, take the plunge into raising your child in an environment with more than one language? I believe that to avoid problems such as Marie's, and to foster success such as Sanjeeta's, timing is of the essence. There are times in your child's life when the brain is better prepared to learn a new language, and birth is the first window of opportunity.

If multiple languages are learned from birth and the parents are consistent in a conscious strategy (for example, one-parent, one-language, which is a well-documented method), you have begun a recipe for successful bilingualism. It's a simple formula but one many parents are afraid to adhere to.

Many parents, for example, appear to doubt their importance in their child's life. They cannot believe their exchanges with their child are enough for him to learn their language. Doesn't he need a class, or a "real" instructor, to learn a language? What you believe is less important than what your baby thinks in this case, and she thinks you are enough.

Some parents lapse into using more than one language because they doubt the child really understands the conversation. What is more likely is that the child doesn't want to hear what is being said. I remember watching an amusing exchange as a mother at school tried to get her polyglot five-year-old son to put on his coat. "Put on your coat. How many times do I have to ask you the same thing?" No response. Then in French. No response. Then in German. No response. The mother then pleaded with him in a mixture of the three, as if language was the problem. Putting on his coat was not a language problem; this was an example of lack of discipline, not vocabulary!

What should be encouraged and what should be avoided, then, when raising multilingual children? First, begin at birth. The easiest way to ensure successful bilingualism is to employ it from the moment your child arrives in this world; it only gets more complicated to do as the child gets older. Third or fourth languages can be undertaken later in life in other windows of opportunity, but there is nothing like starting at the very beginning to become a successful bilingual.

Be consistent. Mom, speak only your native language; Dad, do the same. I have met a number of families who, for various reasons, chose to speak in a language that was not their own. This may seem peculiar at first, but their justification was usually well-intentioned: "English isn't my native language, but I thought it would be more useful than Portuguese"; "English isn't my native language, nor my husband's, but we decided to use it because we were living in the United States at the time my daughter was born, and it just stuck"; "English isn't my native language, but we live in America now, and I want my kids to be American, speak 'American.'" Problems that arise from this strategy include nonnative speakers having grammatical flaws in their speech that they then pass on to their children. In many cases, they also mix their native language with the language they are trying to share with the child, which leads the child to mix languages as well. And finally, the kids usually figure out the charade, and they find it quite disturbing to know that Mom has never let them in on her "secret" language. In the early years, children's language will reflect the quality of the input, which is usually received from parents or other primary caregivers. If parents mix languages, so do children, because they assume this is a legitimate language structure. Since the mixed language appears to be understood by all in the family, the child presumes it is a single language. However, when confronted by people who do not know all the languages involved (such as the pediatrician or grandmother), the child appears to be "confused," whereas he is just using the language he has been exposed to.

I have never had a more satisfying professional moment than when I heard from one of the parents quoted above after she decided she was going to speak to her son in her native Portuguese after nearly six years of speaking to him in English. Her son knew his grandparents, uncles, and cousins back home spoke Portuguese, but had never spoken with his mother in that language. The mother had not spoken Portuguese to her son from birth because "We didn't want to confuse him, and English seemed more useful." When the family finally decided to have Mom use her native language, the mother asked her son what he thought about learning to speak Portuguese, "to be able to speak with your cousins, grandma, grandpa, and Uncle So-and-so, and because it's Mommy's language." They began in a dedicated and consistent manner, and she said he caught on like wildfire. In just a few weeks he was speaking to her in limited Portuguese, and was highly motivated to do more. She said she cried when he said his first sentence to her in her own language: "It was like hearing my baby say *mama* for the very first time." This is a kind of satisfaction that shouldn't be denied any parent.

Finally, use your child's inborn motivation at birth to communicate with you. He desires to be with you, wants you to understand his needs, and wishes to know you. Go on, take the plunge and give him the gift of a tongue.

11

Bilingualism from Birth

Manuela González-Bueno

I am from Spain but have lived more than a dozen years in the United States as a professor of Spanish and foreign language methodology. Because I live in a foreign culture, I struggle with communicating in a borrowed language. Through my profession, I am acquainted with most teaching methods, strategies, and techniques that are available to help formal learners express themselves minimally in a foreign language. But three years ago I faced the challenge of facilitating the process of language learning in a different type of learner: a newborn, my daughter.

Our family goal is that she becomes a perfectly balanced bilingual. The challenge is to be able to adapt current techniques, and to learn new ones that enhance the bilingual acquisition process of this spongelike, but ever so fragile, communicating being.

THE LANGUAGE LEARNING PHENOMENON

According to Krashen (1982), learning and acquiring a language are two completely different processes. Adults *learn* languages; children *acquire* them. What is so special about acquiring a language in infancy as opposed to learning it as an adult? Sociological, psychological, even physiological aspects have something to do with the ease or difficulty with which the language learning process takes place. In fact, these aspects are said to be responsible for the striking difference observed between children and adults only when it comes to pronunciation.

THE "MOTHER TONGUE"

In a bilingual from birth situation there is no such thing as a first versus a second language, but what De Houwer (1998) refers to as bilingual first language acquisition. Research has shown that full-term fetuses can react to external stimulus (van Heteeren et al. 2000). And after birth, even when two languages surround the infant, the mother's language is more important to the child and therefore bears a special meaning.

Alma Flor Ada (1997) tells the story of a three-year-old orphan girl with whom she used to volunteer to interact and play when she was a college student. She would tell the children stories in English, since it was assumed they had all lost their Spanish, despite being Mexicans. "One Saturday afternoon, as I was telling stories with the little girl on my lap, she whispered in my ear: 'Speak the other way, please, speak the other way.' I realized that she was asking me to speak in Spanish, and I was surprised by her request. 'Why do you want me to speak Spanish if you don't understand it?' I asked. And then, with a feeling in her voice that moves me to this day, she said: 'I don't understand it, but that's the way my mother used to sound'" (1997: 3). It is questionable if this little girl ever regained an active use of Spanish. Changes in linguistic context do not have to be so drastic that they cause language loss, however. We have seen the cases of semilinguals, and even of individuals who, having at their disposition the necessary tools to become balanced bilinguals, do not do so. In some bilingual situations, there are factors that work against children's keeping a perfectly balanced bilingualism. The literature warns us about "input-poor environments," in the form of limited situational vocabulary, that leave some bilingual children without the tools they need to communicate. If the caregiver addresses the child only to make her eat, sleep, or pick up the toys, in the context of a kitchen, a bedroom, or a bathroom, the vocabulary of the child will be limited, and the majority language will overshadow the minority language.

Is there anything we can do to prevent this loss, and to enhance the opportunities of our children to become bilinguals?

THE "MASTER" EAR

My career work has concentrated in the field of pronunciation. In the current situation of foreign language learning and teaching, proficient communication is the paramount goal for many language learners. Even in the field of pronunciation, authors introduce their respective methods and techniques by stating that, within the communicative frame, the pronunciation goal should be intelligibility versus nativelike accuracy (Celce-Murcia et al. 1996; Dalton and Seidlhofer 1994). The difference in pronunciation achievement between children and adult learners is of great interest to researchers. After all, pronunciation is the aspect of a language that is most impacted by the existence of a critical period due to physical limitations in the auditory cortex.

Many researchers (Eimas 1985; Flege 1981; Pennington 1992) have pointed out that we cannot produce sounds that we cannot perceive. We are born with the ability to perceive all humans sounds (Werker 1997). However, as soon as we are exposed to a particular linguistic environment, our ear starts to concentrate on sounds that are significant in that language, and we lose the ability to perceive sounds that are not part of our linguistic repertoire. When we try to produce foreign sounds, we do it through the filter of our own language. For an adult, it takes awareness and a lot of training to be able to perceive, and later correctly produce, these subtle phonemic distinctions, all of which involves training the ear. Eimas writes that the gradual loss of the ability to detect distinctions which do not occur in the native language does not completely deactivate unused perceptual mechanisms, meaning that with proper training it is possible to approximate the foreign accent desired.

Children brought up bilingually from birth, however, approach the task differently. It seems that being consistent in exposing the child to enough aural input would do the trick; however, the type of auditory input is crucial. Does that mean that just by listening to the radio, for example, children will learn the language? Not at all! This is where the importance of keeping the cognitive aspects of learning a language apart from the purely physiological ones comes in. As we know, in order to learn a language, learners have to interact, communicate, be understood, use the language actively—not only mechanically producing it but also listening to it with a purpose. Some studies suggest that infants start attuning their perception capabilities to those sounds present in their linguistic environment very early in life (Eilers, Gavin, and Wilson 1979; Eilers, Oller, and Benito-Garcia 1984; Oller et al. 1997; Werker and Tees 1984; Werker 1997). We have to assume that infants are only capable of decoding those impulses into physical descriptions, since they do not posses cognitive linguistic knowledge to assign. However, the ear training is still taking place at the perception level. Adults, on the other hand, might have to assign meaning to those new sounds in order to become able to discriminate them and "reactivate unused perceptual mechanisms" (Eimas 1985).

Nerve endings that are not stimulated through repetition of certain sounds die. What causes the unused nerve endings to become atrophied? There are two answers to this question. The first one suggests that synaptic connections are discarded because of lack of use. This "pruning" of neurons is part of the normal developmental process in which the growth in synaptic density observed during the first few years of life is slowed to a more adultlike rate. In fact, synaptic loss might be fundamental to normal brain development (Bruer 1999). Furthermore, Bruer goes as far as to say that "creating more synapses or preserving as many of them as we can into adulthood may be neither possible nor desirable," incredible as that may sound. He explains that the number of neurons is not equivalent to capacity to learn and reason. In fact, as stated before, the elimination of synapses allows for the establishment of new and more complex forms of thinking. It is not clear whether the neurons that are capable of decoding foreign frequencies are part of this massive neuron discharge.

Another theory has to do with language aptitude. High aptitude language learners, who are found about as frequently as people with high aptitudes for such other skills as ballet, physics, music, math, and drawing (approximately 10 percent of the population), are able to reproduce foreign languages without an accent. Those who are born with a high aptitude for foreign languages are able to take exposure to a foreign language when young, and apply those neuron connections later in life to the ability to speak without an accent (Tokuhama-Espinosa 2001).

The other type of perceptual mechanism referred to in the literature is located not in the inner ear and the nerve ends, but in the middle ear, particularly in the muscles attached to the hammer and stirrup bones. According to Gerritsen (1996), whose theory is based on Tomatis's (1996) work, these muscles prevent us from being able to focus on sounds rarely used in our mother tongue, further emphasizing the benefits of acquiring a language from birth, rather than learning it later. Adults are "deaf, so to speak, to the foreign frequencies of languages not heard regularly." As Tomatis points out:

To perceive these [foreign] frequency zones correctly, without the risk of introducing distortions through our auditory receiver, which operates as a filter, we have to adjust or, better still, condition ourselves to perceive in such a way that our optimal selectivity reaches that of the frequencies desired in our emission. (1996: 103)

For adults to be able to perceive foreign frequencies, we need to train our ears in the same way we train for a sport competition. Tomatis's method involves a series of "sit-ups" with these little muscles of the medium ear. The method consists of making learners listen to a tone or frequency not found in their mother language. The source of this tone might be a native speaker's recorded speech, music, and even the learners' own speech, presented in such a way that the unwanted frequencies are filtered out, lest the still imperfect production introduce unwanted distortion. This tone is continuously switched on and off, in a "sit-up" manner, forcing the muscles to alternately stretch and relax. This exercise strengthens the muscles until they are capable of making the hammer and stirrup bones vibrate to the foreign tones. Synapses for languages are created throughout the life span, and in differing areas of the brain, depending on when the languages were learned (Paradis 1983). In the case of the bilingual child, the inner ear learns to vibrate to the frequencies of two different sets of sounds from birth; therefore, synaptic connections responding to both kinds of stimuli will be established and, most important, never discharged. If it is true that only connections which are used repeatedly will be kept, then we can be confident that a constant exposure to the target sounds will assure a continued ability to perceive, and therefore produce them. It follows that in addition to consistency and continuity in the approach to maintaining bilingualism (or multilingualism) in the family, a well planned, articulated sequence of language education experiences may guarantee the long-term preservation of the synaptic connections responsible for decoding sounds from more than one language.

How early does the ear conditioning start? Van Heteeren et al. (2000) conducted an experiment that involved fetal habituation to repeated vibro-acoustic stimulation to assess fetal memory. Fetuses were able to learn, and showed a short-term memory of at least ten minutes and a long-term memory of at least twenty-four hours. Although fetuses were able to memorize the stimuli, they may need more than one stimulus to establish recognition, a further indication of the need for consistency and continuity in the language experience we provide our bilingual children.

Very Early Production

With regard to speech production by young bilingual children, research has tried to establish when we can expect children to show some indication of their double ability. Oller et al. (1997) reported that infants reared in bilingual and monolingual environments start babbling (produced well-formed syllables), an event related to speech development, at a very similar age. That is, babbling of bilingual infants is not fundamentally different from that of monolingual ones.

It might not be until the age of two that children can significantly show differences in production of either language. Eilers, Oller, and Benito-Garcia (1984) followed the production of voice contrast of two groups of monolingual infants (English and Spanish respectively) and children aged one and two years old. At the age of one, neither group showed any difference in production, but by the age of two, some subjects from both groups started to show characteristics of their native languages in the production of the voice contrast. On the other hand, and as Watson (1991) speculates, perfectly balanced bilinguals might start with an averaged system that has contrastive patterns and perceptual category boundaries intermediate between the two target systems, and slowly and more or less simultaneously move away from this in either direction toward the differential phonologies. Watson grants the possibility that bilinguals may use both strategies, the only difference being one of emphasis (cross-language interferences and differential separation) (1991: 36).

My Own Recipe

When the birth of my daughter was imminent, the fact that I was going to "teach" her Spanish was a given. But I saw a problem. On the one hand, I knew that simply by addressing her in Spanish, I was guaranteeing that my daughter would learn Spanish, but I was concerned about the level of fluency she would achieve. In continuing my research, I realized the culprit was a question of opportunity: In most cases, a minority language—in my case, Spanish—was going to have a hard time competing with the majority language, English (Kravin 1992). Thus, I started an unequal fight by trying to compete with Alicia's exposure to English. I wanted to enhance the chance that my daughter would become a complete bilingual, and borrowing Tokuhama-

Espinosa's (2001) metaphor. I tried to combine the different ingredients in one or more of the recipes available. After reflection, our family decided to follow the "one parent, one language" strategy, which we found was quite easy to use consistently. Since my husband does not speak Spanish, he had no alternative but to speak English to her. In my case, falling back into my mother tongue was a relief, since I felt so much more at ease in that language. My efforts meant speaking exclusively in Spanish when addressing her (the only exception being the hard-to-get-rid-of expression "OK"). I have to confess that it was hard at times, particularly when I could not find a Spanish equivalent (e.g., "driveway," "deck") or could not remember; it took me a while to come up with the Spanish translation for "rattle" (*sonajero*), which I had not thought of in years.

When I first knew I was pregnant, I began a conscious effort to use Spanish with her. I listened to Spanish music and often sang in Spanish. I talked to her, confident in the good hearing skills of my baby and in the good conductivity of my amniotic fluid. Tomatis goes as far as to use recordings of patients' mothers' voices in his therapy, in order to re-create the patients' "linguistic rebirth" (Gerritsen 1996). He believed that only high-frequency sounds traveled through the amniotic fluid, and that the low-frequency ones were filtered out. Conveniently, women have high pitched voices, and some, like myself, have higher pitches than others. It might be the case that the quality of mothers' voices has an impact in the effectiveness of this acoustic bonding.

Once Alicia was born, I followed the advice found in every article and book I read: Talk to your baby. My husband complained: "Must you verbalize everything?" "Yes," I responded. I was putting the first coat of what I wanted to be a permanent color on my daughter's walls: Spanish language, without an English accent. When you paint a wall or a door, you can hardly see the first coat. It feels like it is worthless, so why bother? But we know that the next time the color will become thicker and more defined, thanks to that first coat. That is the way it is with language. In order to see the second coat, we have to have a first coat. I knew that my daughter could not understand the intricacies of my monologues. But several things (coats) were happening: She was listening to my voice, my intonation; she could see my face and my mouth moving at the same time I was emitting sounds, human sounds (versus sounds produced by kitchen utensils or car engines). I also knew from my research that her hearing nerve ends and middle ear were being exposed to the frequency of the Spanish tones, in addition to those of English coming from Dad, Grandma, and everybody else around her. But the most miraculous thing: She was learning vocabulary—indeed, sentences. Months later, I would notice that she could recognize or even utter a word that I had not used since her early days being diapered on the changing table. Now she sings to her sleeping dolls the same lullabies that I used to sing to her when she was still too young to ask for a book before going to bed.

Active Comprehension Training

The authors of "Signing Babies" put forth the idea of teaching babies how to communicate with gestures. In their experiments, they concluded that children who had been communicating from an early age with the help of signs, made the jump to oral language quicker than those who had not. The reason was that the former very early discovered the arbitrary relationship between sign and meaning (Acredolo and Goodwyn 1996). I tried with the "eating" sign (moving the fingertips pressed together toward the mouth). I made that gesture every time I offered her food: "Do you want to eat [gesture]?" We also sang José Luis Orozco's song "Y ahora vamos a cantar" (Now Let's Sing), from *Diez deditos* (Ten Little Fingers). The second stanza goes: "Y ahora vamos a comer, a comer, a comer. Y ahora vamos a comer, a comer a comer" (Let's eat now, eat, eat. Let's eat now, eat, eat). The repetition provided by the song allowed for an easy and effective establishment of relation between the word *comer* (eat) and the gesture.

By the time she was eighteen months, I learned that they were using sign language at her daycare center. Not surprisingly, the "eating" sign was the same one we were using at home. I had read that because bilingual children discover earlier the arbitrary relationship between meaning and symbols (the action of taking nourishment can be expressed both by the English word "eat" and the Spanish one *comer*), they are also early readers (Bialystok 1997). I felt that the fact that she was experiencing the same gesture when simultaneously hearing the words "eat" and *comer*, depending on the speaker, should have the same effect. So I asked the teacher to teach me all the other signs they were using for other concepts. And so I started rubbing my chest circularly every time I said *por favor* (please), and putting my hands together at the fingertips to say *más* (more). It took a few trials to get Alicia to utter the Spanish words whenever she used the signs, by saying "What does Mummy say?" After two or three attempts, she was accompanying the gestures with English words when she talked to Daddy, and with Spanish words when she talked to me.

I also put to use everything I knew about the Total Physical Response technique. This method, developed by Asher (1983), is based on the fact that children go through a period of silence before starting to produce any language, though they respond and react to the language by acting upon it. I consciously started giving easy-to-follow commands to Alicia, such as "Bring me the red ball" or "turn the light off." After all, I was not doing anything that a regular mother would not do to teach her child her first language. But mothers usually have the support of the environment, which I do not enjoy. Instead, I felt that I had to win a race against it. I had noticed that my mother-in-law was doing a good job of teaching Alicia some of her first English words, and she understood more and more English. Alicia loves Grandma with passion; people who are highly relevant in a child's life have the greatest impact on that child's language development (Tokuhama-Espinosa 2001). Alicia was even using English baby talk, imitating Grandma: "Yummy-yummy in my tummy," she would say whenever she was enjoying some food. I was jealous. I did not have an equivalent expression in Spanish to teach her. What could I do? In addition to missing expressions, I also had far less time with her than her English caregivers. That was when I made the decision to take a one-semester leave of absence. I am sure that this period of time spent exclusively with me, listening to me speaking in Spanish, and away from the daily English influence of daycare, helped establish a solid base of Spanish language that would catapult her bilingualism forward in the months to come.

Production

The first word that Alicia uttered was, for my pride, *mamá*, and soon thereafter *agua* (water). For a while, and as it is reflected in the literature (Watson 1991), she had one word only, in either language, for each concept. I had to conclude that her criterion to select either language was ease of pronouncing the word in question: *Agua* is easier than "water," but "cookie" is easier than *galleta*, and so is "book" versus *libro*. I could not help feeling great whenever Alicia chose to use a Spanish word versus an English one. The feeling was different, though, was she asked me for a "cookie" instead of a *galleta*. In those cases, the one-person, one-language approach came into action: "*¿Qué dice mamá?*" My husband supported this process wholeheartedly and would often ask Alicia, "What does Mommy say?" even when it was not necessary (she would be talking to him, after all). This strategy resulted in Alicia consistently talking to Daddy in English, and to me in Spanish. Moreover, she often translates into English sentences she says to me, so Daddy can understand, and vice versa, even though I understand the English sentences aimed at my husband. One time, after I reacted in Spanish to something she had said to my husband in English, she reprimanded me: *No, estoy hablando con papá* (No, I'm talking to Daddy), as if I was not supposed to interfere in her English conversation. Out of the house, she was soon aware of who spoke English and who spoke Spanish. There is a growing population of Spanish speakers in our community, and it is not uncommon to hear Spanish here and there in the store or the post office. Alicia announces: "*¡Habla español!*" whenever she hears somebody speaking in Spanish. And when nonnative Spanish speakers playfully say "*Hola*" or "*Adiós, amigos*," she reacts with surprise. This awareness, which, according to the literature, does not manifest itself until around the age of two, came about not without some intervention. I would reinforce her sense of Spanish community by helping her remember the names of everybody (friends and family members, albeit abroad) we know who speak Spanish.

In the beginning, when talking to other English speakers, it was necessary to remind her to "say it in English; he doesn't understand Spanish." Nowadays, if an English speaker gives her something, and I say to her in Spanish "*Dile gracias*," she will say "Thank you" in English without hesitation. Döpke (1992)

writes that "The accomplishment of the adult standard of language separation
. . . might only be possible for the older preschooler" (1992: 483). Alicia is almost
three now, not much different in age from Döpke's subject. This might be only
another indication of the variability likely to be found among individuals.

Continuity

While these successes were encouraging, I still knew that Spanish was going
to be at a disadvantage in Alicia's life. It was apparent that my efforts to talk
to her only in Spanish were not going to be enough. I designed a plan that
included the acquisition of as many props and tools I could get, locating as
many Spanish-speaking friends in Alicia's age range as I could, and bringing
my monolingual Spanish family into the picture.

Friends and Family

Because I work at a big university, there are many international families
(faculty, graduate students) with little children growing up bilingually. The
Hispanic population is the largest. We started to get together with a Puerto
Rican family with a small girl whenever our hectic schedules allowed. I would
interact with the mother, and her daughter would play with Alicia. We both
were trying to show our daughters that Mommy was not the only person that
spoke "that funny language."

I also began doing a bilingual storytelling session at the local bookstore, and
another Spanish-speaking mother approached me, expressing her interest in
meeting more bilingual families. Bingo! From then on, I met several Hispanic
families with children ranging from less than a year to six years old, a perfect
age range for Alicia's Spanish ability to develop and grow (she was one year
old by then). Finally, my family came into the picture. My relatively small
family lives in Spain. It is not very convenient for me to visit them often, nor
is for them to visit us in the United States. However, I feel strongly that it is
our duty, both linguistically and culturally, to make those visits happen as
frequently as possible. The first time Alicia went to Spain, she was seventeen
months old. She did not talk much at the time. I do remember, though, that
during this visit she starting saying her own name. It was a short stay, and
although Spanish-speaking people surrounded her, she heard a lot of English
between my husband and me. Still, I think this experience must have had a
great impact on her incipient bilingualism.

The family event that has had the greatest impact on Alicia's Spanish development has been my sixteen-year-old niece's one-month visit. Alicia was
two at the time. Her language had recently started to grow, and then this fallen-
from-the-sky monolingual angel came. Alicia was ecstatic, as was I. Blanca, my
niece, would play with Alicia, take her for walks, put her to sleep, and take
naps with her. During this time, Alicia's Spanish flourished.

Games, Books, and Videotapes

Children's music has always been an ally. Alicia is capable of remembering the Spanish lyrics of songs from her infancy even though we do not play them often anymore. She also sings English songs that she learns in daycare. When she sings a popular English song, I try to come up with a similar one in Spanish—to remind her that it is as much fun to sing in Spanish as it is in English. Every time she wants to sing and play "Ring Around the Rosie" I counter-attack with "El patio de mi casa," for example.

The children's music market is full of possibilities, some better than others. Bilingual artists, aware of the need to enhance bilingualism and biculturalism, have produced numerous recordings of old and new folk songs; songs that, in spite of having been composed almost a century ago, teach vocabulary, spelling, or math with the best of the pedagogical approaches. But, most important, Alicia likes to sing and make up her own lyrics, which she does by looking around and incorporating any vocabulary that comes to her mind. There is no rhyme, there is no rhythm, but it is definitely music. And she does it in Spanish.

Then came the books. We have several books in Spanish, or Spanish-English bilingual versions, that we have acquired since the very beginning of Alicia's life. At that time, I believed that the language did not really matter. I could easily translate the English picture books. However, translating longer sentences and descriptions became more and more difficult, and I realized that it was time to get books consistently in Spanish. This is also because Alicia is now learning the function of print, and the relation of the words to the page, so translating is not recommended. Alicia loves to be read to, and she can spend a great deal of time in front of a book, turning page after page—adding the cute gesture of wetting her finger. And when she pretends to read aloud, she does it in Spanish when she is at home—and one time that I surprised her at daycare, she was doing it in English. Alicia is a reader.

I also felt I needed "talking" toys, for example, an electronic toy that claimed to teach languages to children as young as two. Languages can be selected by changing a cartridge. The toy is interactive, the language is accurate, and the whole thing is attractive, user friendly, (and a little expensive). Another product made by the same company claims to expose infants to foreign language sounds in the form of babbling. Based on theories which suggest that early exposure to foreign sounds will prevent loss of the ability to perceive them, this toy kind of makes sense. These "linguistic" toys were only the beginning. Soon after, I found Izzy, a soft doll that can be made to talk in Spanish and English by pressing on her hands and knee (French, Italian, and Chinese versions of this doll are also available). And even the little interactive gremlin that "learns" how to talk like you, in your own language (Spanish, French, or German)! A whole cohort of bilingual toys live in our house, constantly reminding Alicia that there are two accepted and validated ways of talking in our family, and she manages both.

Eventually, I had to give in to other media sources. I consciously decided that Alicia would watch television only in Spanish, with videos of my own choice as the first option. Alicia is familiar with some Disney movies, which we found mainly in Spanish versions. I have to confess that hearing Snow White and Jiminy Cricket talking in Spanish after so many years (since my own childhood) was a little bit of a flashback, and I was happy to share these moments with Alicia.

Commercial video programs to teach foreign languages to children are available. Those produced by the BBC are of great quality, and my daughter likes them. Moreover, I can tell that some of the vocabulary and expressions she has incorporated into her own language comes from those videos, not from me. That is when I resorted to the Spanish version of *Sesame Street* on the Hispanic Channel. These programs are an excellent source of entertaining education, and I confess we have around twenty hours worth of *Plaza Sésamo* on video.

All of this has meant that Alicia is exposed to Spanish, not only through a few friends and me but also by the media. But then I started to think of her bilingualism as a two-way process. Did Alicia comprehend that not only were there people who spoke English and people who spoke Spanish, but also bilinguals like herself? I found a solution in children's programs in English with bilingual characters. The amount of Spanish in those programs is very small, but the concept of bilingualism is well represented, I think. And Alicia loves those cute little characters who can speak in English and in Spanish—like her!

Finally, the computer came into play in the form of interactive CD-ROMs. As with everything else, there are good ones and not so good ones. Alicia has learned many expressions and vocabulary items from them that I do not use.

Talk To Your Cat!

One of the maladies of a linguistic input-poor environment is that complete paradigms are not represented naturally in the scarce available input. For example, Alicia's interactions with me involved mainly the use of the second person singular, referring to her, and the first person singular, referring to myself. I started including Mini, our cat, in our Spanish conversations—Mini did not seem to mind. Sentences like "Mini, ven con nosotros" (Mini, come with us) helped introduce the plural into Alicia's Spanish input.

From the very beginning, I considered it extremely important to teach Alicia words that would help her control and manipulate her surroundings. In the bathtub, we often play with her plastic toys. We take turns hiding the rubber whale, and then pretend to call "Ballena, ¿dónde estás? ¡Ven!" (Whaaaale! Where are you? Come here!). Soon, she was using *ven* to call me or to call others, even when the others would not understand Spanish (at the time, she was not yet aware of the difference).

Only recently she has been able to figure out that when she wants to go with me, she has to say *contigo* (with you) and not *conmigo* (with me). She was initially exposed to *conmigo* because I would be the one who said, "¿Quieres venir conmigo?" So she would generalize the use of *conmigo* to the situations in which *contigo* would have been appropriate: "Mamá, quiero ir conmigo" (Mummy, I want to go with me). She was being potty-trained at that time, so sometimes I would offer to stay in the bathroom with her by saying, "¿Quieres que me quede contigo?" She caught on soon, and now uses *conmigo* and *contigo* correctly.

With Friends Like Mom, Who Needs Enemies?

One day when Alicia was about twenty-four months, she uttered her first affirmation of possession: "Mine!" she said, referring to a toy that I had just taken away from her. (Well, what she really said was "mi's," as a hybrid between "mine" and the Saxon genitive " 's".) I was about to give the toy back to her, but her use of the English word stopped me. How could I promote the use of Spanish in this situation? If I gave her the toy, her hypothesis would be proven that the word "mine" would do the job. But when and where was she going to hear somebody fighting for a toy and saying the Spanish word "mío" instead of "mine"? It looked like a job for *mamá*. So I refused to give it back to her and said "No, ¡mío!" Once she learned that I was not being serious, she caught on to the joke, and now she likes to perform it frequently. She loves role-playing, which has the same teaching effect: She can switch roles and therefore hear, and use herself, language that she would not use normally. For example, when it is my turn to be her, and she is I, she gets to say "¡Alicia, no toques nada!" (Alicia, do not touch anything!). The same applies to role-playing with dolls. Every time I have caught her in individual playing, she is talking in Spanish. However, when I asked my husband whether he has caught her in similar situations when only he is around, he said that she would be talking in English. Finally, I have taken advantage of every opportunity to role-play with puppets, particularly felt or paper finger puppets representing favorite characters.

Now, in her third year, we have added a Spanish teacher who goes to Alicia's daycare on Fridays. She is aware of the interest of others in learning Spanish, and proud of being able to recite the numbers, and name the colors and the letters in Spanish.

What I have learned from the process of facilitating my daughter's balanced bilingualism is that learning a language is a very broad concept, and we compartmentalize it in different subfields in order to make it more manageable to study and research, and ultimately to apply to our teaching. But these subfields overlap, because learning a language is a human function that happens on many levels: in the classroom (in a foreign language, bilingual, or immersion situation), in the family, as a minority language, and as a majority language. Ultimately it is the same process of learning to communicate in more than one way, and even of living and thinking in more than one way. It is very clear to me that with my daughter I have not had to use any strategy that I would not use with classroom students, and vice versa. The following quote from Corder (1981, cited in Lee and Van Patten 1995) might apply equally to language teachers and parents of multilingual children: "We have been reminded recently of von Humboldt's statement that we cannot really teach language, we can only create conditions in which it will develop spontaneously in the mind in its own way" (1995: 22). I hope I have provided Alicia with the best conditions possible.

REFERENCES

Acredolo, L. and S. Goodwyn (1996). *Baby Signs: How to Talk to Your Baby Before Your Baby Can Talk*. Chicago, IL: Contemporary Books.

Ada, A. F. (1997). "Mother-tongue Literacy as a Bridge Between Home and School Cultures." In J. Villamil Tinajero and Alma Flor Ada, *The Power of Two Languages: Literacy and Biliteracy for Spanish Speaking Students*. New York: Macmillan/McGraw-Hill.

Asher, J. (1983). *Learning Another Language Through Actions: The Complete Teacher's Guidebook*. Los Gatos, CA: Sky Oaks Productions.

Bialystok, E. (1997). "Effects of Bilingualism and Biliteracy on Children's Emerging Concepts of Print." *Developmental Psychology Journal* 33, no. 3: 429–440.

Bruer, J. (1999). "Neural Connections, Some You Use, Some You Lose." *Phi Delta Kappan*, December: 264–277.

Celce-Murcia, M., D.M. Brinton, and J.M. Goodwin (1996). *Teaching Pronunciation: A Reference for Teachers of English to Speakers of Other Languages*. Cambridge: Cambridge University Press.

Dalton, C., and B. Seidlhofer (1994). *Pronunciation*. Oxford: Oxford University Press.

De Houver, A. (1998). "By Way of Introduction: Methods in Studies of Bilingual First Language Acquisition." *International Journal of Bilingualism* 2, no. 3: 249–263.

Döpke, S. (1992). "A bilingual child's struggle to comply with the 'one parent-one language' rule." *Journal of Multilingual and Multicultural Development* 13, no. 6: 467–485.

Eilers, R.E., W. Gavin, and W.R. Wilson (1979). "Linguistic experience and phonemic perception in infancy: a cross-linguistic study." *Child Development* 50: 14–18.

Eilers, R., D.K. Oller, and C. Benito-Garcia (1984). "The Acquisition of Voicing Contrast in Spanish and English Learning Infants and Children: A Longitudinal Study." *Journal of Child Language* 2: 313–336.

Eimas, P. (1985). "The Perception of Speech in Early Infancy." *Scientific American* 252, no. 1: 46–61.

Ellis, R. (1985). *Understanding Second Language Acquisition*. Oxford: Oxford University Press.

Flege, J.E. (1981). "The Phonological Basis of Foreign Accent: A Hypothesis." *TESOL Quarterly* 15: 443–453.

Gerritsen, J. (1996). *Learning Foreign Languages*. The Tomatis Listening and Learning Center (http://www.tomatis.com).

Krashen, S. (1982). *Principles and Practices in Second Language Acquisition*. Oxford: Pergamon Press.

Kravin, H. (1992). "Erosion of Language in Bilingual Development." *Journal of Multilingual and Multicultural Development* 13, no. 4: 307–325.

Lee, J.F. and B. Van Patten (1995). *Making Communicative Language Teaching Happen.* New York: McGraw-Hill.

Lenneberg, E.H. (1967). *Biological Foundations of Language.* New York: John Wiley & Sons.

Oller, D.K., R. Eilers, R. Urbano, and A.B. Cobo-Lewis (1997). "Development of Precursors to Speech in Infants Exposed to Two Languages." *Journal of Child Language* 24: 407–425.

Paradis, M. (ed.) (1983). *Readings on Aphasia in Bilinguals and Polyglots.* Montreal, Canada: Didier.

Pennington, M.C. (1992). "Recent Research in Second Language Phonology: Implications for Practice." In J. Morley (ed.), *Perspectives on Pronunciation, Learning and Teaching.* Alexandria, VA: TESOL.

Schneider, A. (2001). "A University Plans to Promote Languages by Killing Its Language Department." The Chronicle of Higher Education, 9 March: A14.

Snow, C.E., and M. Hoefnagel-Höhle (1978). "The Critical Period for Language Acquisition: Evidence from Second Language Learning." *Child Development* 49: 114–128.

Tokuhama-Espinosa, T. (2001). *Raising Multilingual Children: Foreign Language Acquisition and Children.* Westport, CT: Bergin & Garvey.

Tomatis, A. (1996). *The Ear and Language.* Trans. B. M. Thompson. Norval, Ontario: Moulin.

van Heteeren, C.F., P.F. Boekkooi, H.W. Jongsma, and J.G. Nijhuis (2000). "Fetal Learning and Memory." *The Lancet* 356, no. 9236: 1169–1170.

Watson, I. (1991). "Phonological Processes in Two Languages." In E. Bialystok (ed.), *Language Processing in Bilingual Children.* Cambridge: Cambridge University Press.

Werker, J.F. (1997). "Exploring Developmental Changes in Cross-Language Speech Perception." In D.N. Osherson (gen. ed.), *An Invitation to Cognitive Science, Vol. 1, Language, 2nd ed.* Cambridge, MA: MIT Press.

Werker, J.F., and R.C. Tees (1984). "Cross-Language Speech Perception: Evidence for Perceptual Reorganization During the First Year of Life." *Infant Behavior and Development* 7: 49–63.

12

Trilingualism
A Study of Children Growing Up with Three Languages

Suzanne Barron-Hauwaert

Much research has been done on bilinguals, but relatively little on trilinguals. This is primarily because comparative testing and longitudinal studies are difficult to administer with three languages. Additionally, it is hard to find a sample of trilinguals using the same three languages, at roughly the same competence levels, with similar backgrounds. Individual case studies of trilinguals exist, but they are limited in number and scope. However, the increase in mixed marriages and in families relocating to another country for economic or political reasons has recently drawn attention to such multilingual families (Nullis 2001).

I began work on trilingualism out of a personal interest: I am English, my husband is French, and we have lived as expatriates in Hungary, Egypt, and Switzerland. My husband and I spoke our own languages to our children alongside third language input from local child care, friends, and daily interaction in the neighborhood. Therefore our young children began to speak in trilingual environments. I wanted to find out how the family as a unit copes with three languages and cultures, so I looked at how languages are acquired and used by each family member. I asked about parental attitudes to social and cultural questions that arise from daily contact with two or more languages and cultures, and the educational choices of the parents.

SCOPE OF THE RESEARCH

While questions of trilingualism come from all areas of cognitive science, the focus of this essay is mainly on linguistics, psychology, and sociology. I questioned ten families using three languages on a daily basis. A typical family has two parents, each speaking a different language, and lives in a third language country. I describe the languages of the family in the order of *mother/ father/country*. For example, a trilingual child with an English mother and

French father and who lives in Germany is listed as *English/French/German*. All ten families lived in Europe—France, Switzerland, Germany, Belgium, and England (see table 12.1 for details). While this limits the scope of the conclusions, parallel research being conducted in other parts of the world reflects similar findings (Southeast Asia: May 1994; Africa: Chick 1999; United States and the Americas: McCarthy and Watahomigie 1999).

In the first part of this essay I briefly review some of the research on trilingualism. In the second part I present the findings of my study.

A REVIEW OF RESEARCH ON TRILINGUALISM

Trilingualism is generally discussed as another "type" of bilingualism. Academic research into multilingualism is a relatively new field, and encompasses disciplines such as psycholinguistics, neurolinguistics, and sociolinguistics. The links between language and culture, social status, and mental processes are still being investigated. Inevitably the studies are linked to the languages they describe, and there is some argument over generalizations made in the context of one country or language that cannot be replicated. Differences in alphabets or scripts, and perceived linguistic and historical differences between the two or three languages, can affect usage and competence as well.

One of the first researchers to write about bilingualism was Bloomfield (1933), who defined bilingualism as "native-like control of two languages," although he adds that the "distinction is relative." The concept that bilinguals are ultimately aiming for double native speaker proficiency has continued, though, and society still expects bilinguals to behave as "double monolinguals."

The practice of "alternative use of two or more languages by the same individual" proposed by Weinrich (1953) and Mackay (1968) is a more realistic viewpoint. This takes into account the fact that a bilingual uses language in the appropriate domain or situation. One language may be used exclusively at school and another at home, for example. Both authors positively acknowledge the existence of multilingualism, and Weinrich also notes that "all remarks about bilingualism apply equally to multilingualism." Baetens-Beardsmore (1982: 4) states, "There is no evidence to suggest that the fundamental principles affecting language usage are any different whether two, three, or more languages are being used by one and the same speaker, and the major question is whether they differ significantly from cases where only one language is being used."

The question of how different a bilingual or multilingual is from a monolingual has been the emphasis of many studies. Mackay (1968) suggested that factors such as age, sex, memory, intelligence, attitude, and motivation affect the level of bilingualism. These are the main themes of recent linguistic research, which since the 1970s have provided clues to how bilinguals function. There are two main branches of research: the longitudinal case studies conducted on one or two children (usually the author's own children), and the wider-ranging age, sex, and educationally matched comparisons of bilinguals to monolinguals.

In research written specifically about trilinguals, there are some case studies on trilingual children written by a parent/linguist, such as Hoffmann (1985), Widdicombe (1997), Oksaar (1977), and Elwert (1959). Laboratory studies exploring cognitive and acquisition processes have been done by Klein (1995), Abunuwara (1992), Magiste (1986), and McLaughlin and Nation (1986). A long-term study is currently being carried out, with trilingual families in Australia, by Clyne (1997). Baetens-Beardsmore (1993) and Byram and Leman (1990) explain models of trilingual education in Europe. The neurological dimension of trilingualism was examined by Michel Paradis (1995), and the societal angle and "challenging world needs" are interpreted by Byram (1997), Visser (1997), and Woods (1999).

However, there is a lack of data specifically comparing monolinguals or bilinguals with trilinguals, and little research on the social or cultural effects of using three languages, or on how the family as a unit uses three languages. Many bilingual theories simply cannot be transferred to trilinguals. Trilingualism is unusual because the three languages (or cultures) cannot be "balanced" or equal, as in a bilingual. One (or two) languages are always at risk of becoming underused or "passive."

The Learning of Two or More Languages

There are at least four types of trilinguals:

1. Children or adults living in a trilingual or multilingual community
2. Children with parents speaking two different languages and living in a third language country
3. Children with parents speaking two different languages who use a third language as a "language of communication" within the family
4. Fluent bilinguals who have learned a third language at school or for other reasons.

Most of these individuals do not have much choice of whether they wish to be trilingual; it is a fact of their particular circumstances.

However, simply being exposed to two or three languages does not guarantee multilingualism. Some countries that are noted for multilingualism are Switzerland (German, French, Italian, and Romansch), Finland (Finnish, Swedish, and English), Israel (due to immigrants learning Hebrew and/or Arabic and English), India (Hindi, Urdu, and English are commonly required within an individual's schooling), Indonesia (dozens of languages), and North Africa, most notably Morocco (where Arabic, French, and the local Berber languages are spoken). The inhabitants may have a good level of comprehension, but not all are fluent in all languages, unless it is necessary for social communication, work, or tourism.

To acquire a language, a learner needs to have specific input, that is, a good range of verbal examples from different people, alongside media such as books, songs, and television, to reinforce the language. This is important in the trilingual family, because each parent is responsible for his or her language. Peer group learning is very strong from age two on, particularly at school, where the language used can become the dominant language of the child.

Language Domains

A trilingual usually has very specific domains or people who link to each language. For example, language A is used only with the mother and her family, language B at school, and language C with the father and his family. Whole chunks of vocabulary can be missing in one or more languages due to lack of input and opportunity for use in meaningful situations. For example, if we imagine that a mother likes cooking, she will pass on a wide range of cooking vocabulary to her child, which he or she may never learn in the father's language or at school.

The language acquisition process in a child is a tremendous achievement: to go from a mute newborn baby to a fluently conversing five-year-old. For trilingual children this process is remarkably similar, and they go through the same stages or developmental milestones as monolinguals (Slobin 1992). There may be some initial delay or confusion of the languages, which can be attributed to outside effects such as choice of kindergarten or to parental linguistic input, but generally young multilinguals are fluent by around age five if all of their languages were introduced from birth in a consistent strategy.

Charlotte Hoffmann (1985) described in detail the acquisition of three languages (German/Spanish/English) by her two young children. Her daughter, Christina, acquired English later, after her German/Spanish bilingualism was established, while her son, Pascual, learned all three simultaneously from birth. Christina was aware of the differences when she was two and a half years old, calling them "so wie Mama" (like Mummy) and "como dice papá" (as Papa says). She then learned English "holistically," that is, in whole sentences/phrases, and never went through the stages of holographic (one word) or telegraphic speech (two or three words), which usually precede actual speech. Pascual babbled for a long time and began to be aware of the linguistic differences at age two and a half. Eventually English became their overall dominant language of community life, school, and peer groups. Hoffmann also cites personality factors and their positions in the family (the second child having linguistic exposure from his sister) as having an effect on the rates of acquisition and output in her children.

Code-Switching and Mixing Languages

Many bilinguals change language mid-sentence or to suit the person they are talking to. This fast "processing" often disturbs monolinguals, who cannot imagine changing language in this way. This is described variously as *code-switching, interference, mixing, borrowing*, or *language overlap*, and generally it is seen as a sign of language weakness or inability to separate the languages by monolingual observers, though there are initial periods in a child's language development when these are part of normal, developing language skills.

Recent research using sophisticated sound recordings and videos of bilinguals have shown *code-switching* to be completely normal for a bilingual and part of daily language usage with other bilinguals. All code-switching retains the grammar of the corresponding language and is rule-governed, even in small segments. It has now been recognized as an intrinsic part of a bilingual child's development.

Young children under age five are usually described as *borrowing* or *mixing* languages. This can be because the child doesn't know or has forgotten the equivalent word. Some words are deeply linked to one culture and are used in every language. It can be annoying for parents who may think the child is making mistakes. In fact it is a cognitive skill because the child is actually practicing code-switching techniques and testing the use of both languages concurrently. Milroy and Muysken (1995) consider that bilinguals aged around three years mix languages on purpose, as a way to hone translation skills. The bilingual child may well be swapping words across languages in the way a monolingual would use a synonym or rephrase a sentence. It is a sign that the child has grasped the potential of playing with two or three languages.

Susan Widdicombe (1997) described the code-switching of her five-year-old trilingual English/Italian/French child. At home the parents use English and Italian, while French is the language of school and the community. He sometimes uses all three languages in one sentence, although usually he uses a combination of two languages, with French "as the most favoured language" for switching. Some examples are the following

(trilingual): "Mum, DEVO FARE BOUCLES D'OREILLES" (. . . have to make [Italian] some earrings [French])

(trilingual): "I can't see you behind this and then ANCHE COMME ÇA I can't see you, you see?" (. . . like [Italian] like this [French]. . . .)

The child appears to have a competence in all three languages, and chooses selectively to code-switch for effect or communication. He often repeats a word in two or three languages, perhaps to clarify parental comprehension or to translate. He also changes some verb endings (e.g, *criato* from *crie*) or pronunciation to make them "fit" the language, which is not correct but is a cognitively creative step. Widdicombe notes that more switches were made using French, although his parents do not switch or use French at home. In a trilingual family the likelihood of mixing or interference seems inevitable and part of the development process.

Parental Involvement in Early Multilingualism

Several books have been written for families: De Jong (1986), Harding and Riley (1986), Arnberg (1987), Baker (1996, 2000), Andersson (1999), and Tokuhama-Espinosa (2001). In general, books recommend the "One Person, One Language" or the "One Language, One Environment" approach. They advise that each parent consistently use his or her native language. They imply confusion and speech retardation otherwise, although this has not been proven, and mixing is prevalent in bilingual communities such as Alsace in France (Gardner-Chloros 1991).

The factor of parental involvement is somewhat underrated in academic work on bilingualism because it is assumed that children will automatically acquire the parental languages. However, parents with different languages do not necessarily pass them on to their children. In a "mixed language" family usually one language is chosen for communication between the parents (see Andersson 1999). In my situation as half of an English/French couple, we speak English together simply because we are more fluent in it. The other language exists in a "passive" sense, restricted to use with relatives or friends, or when visiting France.

Often a couple will use the language they used before the children were born. As a new parent, the parent with the passive language may decide to increase usage at home or *not* to use it at all. This depends on whether he or she is linguistically marooned within a second language community, or has social contacts in the first language. Some new parents who are used to communicating with their partner in a second language find going back to their first language rather strange. A family "language strategy" is recommended by Tokuhama-Espinosa (2001) to regulate and clarify choice of language to suit the situation or each parent. However, circumstances can change, and each strategy must be flexible to allow for differing stages of child language development and parental agreement.

"Prestige" Languages

There is also the issue of a family with a majority or "prestige" language coupled with a minority language. De Jong (1986) gives examples such as Danish, Dutch, or Swedish in Europe as "minority," although it is a matter of personal judgment. The minority language person may decide to stop using it, especially if there are few chances to practice, or it is noticeably "foreign" in public, or he or she thinks that the child will struggle to learn the language. This happens particularly to minority-speaking mothers. Harding and Riley (1986) point out that the mother is normally given the responsibility for the child's bilingual ability. In the average family the father statistically spends less time with the child, so the language input is unbalanced from the start. To compensate, the mother can use the father's language and/or the country language.

School and Social Factors Influencing Language Choice

Parents bringing up children bilingually usually begin to have problems when the child starts to talk. The child then has to learn that there are two ways of saying every word, and that can be overwhelming or frustrating. Families writing to *The Bilingual Family Newsletter* frequently ask for advice on toddlers or preschool children growing up with two languages. In child development terms, preschool children are renowned for their truculence or rebelliousness, and can use language as a way to annoy or upset parents. Refusal to speak a language to a parent is one of the commonest problems, and the family may need to temporarily redefine its language strategy. Andersson (1999) gives explicit advice on this issue.

Although it is now clear that multilingualism does not cause stuttering, dyslexia, or a gamut of other speech impairments (Wei, Miller, and Dodd 1997), the concern expressed by parents is often validated by their children's slower language development. Around the age of two to three years children begin to have a *metalinguistic awareness* of the two language systems. However, families and friends often expect a "double monolingual" level of vocabulary from a child and are disappointed at a bilingual child's output.

Often when a child begins full-time preschool or kindergarten, the language of play and social world becomes dominant over the mother's language. A parent may find that the child answers in the language of the preschool or refuses to respond to the parental language. When the child starts school, the mother or father may not be able to keep up with the language demands of the primary or secondary school, and feels limited in conversations or when helping with homework.

Early child bilingualism can be affected by the attitudes of the parents. I have noticed in letters written to *The Bilingual Family Newsletter* that the most successful families are the ones where each parent speaks a good part of the other's language or the language of the country where they live. They are positive role models for their children and show appropriate language use to suit the situation.

Some Case Studies of Trilingual Families

Tracey Tokuhama-Espinosa (2001) gives twenty-two case studies of multilingual families, many living in Switzerland, where she is based. She has direct experience because her family is quadlingual: She speaks English; her husband, Spanish; and they live in the French-speaking part of Switzerland. Their three children, aged eight, five, and three, attend a German-language school. She gives a detailed diary account of the three children's acquisition and use of each language that shows some of the difficulties and positive aspects of bringing up children multilingually.

Arnberg (1987) has one Finnish/Kurdish/Swedish case study that shows the effect which school has on languages. For the two children, aged six and four, Swedish is the dominant language. The parents make an effort to speak their languages, but in public they are considered "minority" in Sweden. They accept that they can only "keep up" the Finnish and Kurdish, not use them actively. Lack of contact with relatives and few visits to the home countries makes them seem distant to the children, too.

A case study of an expatriate Austrian/French family living in Brazil and Chile shows trilingualism in a domain-related way. The family has two children, aged four and two, and their language of communication is French. The family had a Portuguese-speaking maid in Brazil. This made the order of the older child's languages Portuguese/French/German, reflecting usage and exposure. The older boy answered his mother's German with French. When the family returned to France, the Portuguese disappeared in a few months and French became dominant. The study shows that continuing with the parents' languages in a third language environment does help the child on returning to the home country, and his ability to separate—and, if necessary, drop a language—shows a high cognitive level of understanding in the child (Harding and Riley 1986).

Philip Riley (in Harding and Riley 1986) also raises the issue of sibling language use. In his family, Swedish/English/French are used. At home the three children use Swedish alongside the country language of French. The two older children often speak English to each other. This seems to help the mother and father keep their languages "alive" within the home.

Cultural Attachment to Two or Three Languages

Society requires a high level of cultural awareness alongside a linguistic knowledge of a language. The ability to be both bilingual and bicultural is often the true test of fluency. A major concern for parents is whether their bilingual child will develop a double identity alongside intellectual capacities in two languages. Pressure to conform culturally is subtle, and can come from a country or from a parent. Children with parents who use two languages are under the same pressure to be bicultural from each parent as children growing up in a second language country.

Living with two or three cultures can cause a conflict of emotions or anomie (the breakdown or absence of social norms and values that an individual associates with a certain situation). One of the first studies on biculturalism was by Child (1943), with teenage Italian-Americans. Both cultural groups have strong identities and pull adolescents toward a certain lifestyle, expecting commitment and following of certain traditions or cultural norms. As second-generation children of Italian immigrants, they were all able to speak both languages fluently. Child recorded "symptoms of bewilderment and frustration" and "conflict of loyalties and aspirations." The young adults consequently withdrew from the Italian community or American society. Some refused to attach themselves strongly to either identity, seeing themselves as hybrids or *Italo-Americans*.

This stage of anomie can be temporary, but it often causes a reappraisal of the languages. The bilingual may consciously, or unconsciously, drop one language if he or she feels it will be impossible to live up to the standards expected. Families using a minority first language appear to have less anomie if they keep the minority culture active. Wei (1998) spoke about the language patterns of Chinese/English bilingual teenagers, which showed that bilingual language skills were considerably higher for children whose parents spoke Chinese and English at home, and had equal cultural links. The parents were good role models by being comfortable with both languages/cultures. Families using only Chinese at home frequently had children who rebelled linguistically, and used English as their first language.

Therefore the level of *cultural understanding* between the parents and empathy for the other culture are important. Sometimes the gap between parental cultures is not recognized until children are born and a parent begins to assert his or her culture as the language is acquired (Gordon 1966). Although a child needs a wide range of cultural input from society in general, "It is far more difficult to arrange for children to acquire knowledge of a culture in the same un-contrived way. While parents alone can give children a second language, they will not be able to give them a second culture without the help of others and the support of society" (Andersson 1999: 85).

In some situations a child may become closely attached to one culture, thereby isolating the other parent. Ideally both parents want to see their children not only speaking their language, but also appreciating cultural jokes, family histories, fairy tales, and songs or participating in celebrations of special occasions such as birthdays, Christmas, Easter, Carnival, or Ramadan. The bilingual or multilingual family must accommodate all these cultural issues, and compromise to suit all family members, in order to build their own individual family culture.

Lambert (1977) studied French-Americans from mixed marriages for signs of conflict and indifference to one culture. Expecting results similar to those of Child, he found a fourth group who coped well with both cultures. This group had healthy attitudes and showed no signs of personality disturbance, social alienation, or anxiety. He compared these bilinguals with homogeneous monocultural children and found no differences. The bilinguals had developed a "dual allegiance that permits them to identify with both their parents." Whether all children are able to develop such attitudes is not known, because this research has mostly been done with additive prestigious language bilinguals. This reference to "additive" bilingualism applies to children who benefit socially from bilingualism and do not lose their mother tongue due to bilingualism. They are also referred to as elite bilinguals.

The book *The Third Culture Kid Experience* (Pollock and Van Reken 1999) describes the new phenomenon of children who grow up, or spend a significant part of their childhood, abroad. The children have cultural acquisition from their parents, from the countries where they lived and from a "third" culture that is an amalgam of the cultures experienced. It is a pattern particularly seen in expatriate families, such as those of diplomats, who change countries often and educate their children in private international schools. It can be positive in that such children or *global nomads* are flexible thinkers and linguistically plural, but they can suffer from continuous change and, as adults, feel rather rootless.

In my family, our two children, aged four and two, were born, respectively, in Budapest and Zurich, and have lived in Hungary, Egypt, Switzerland, and France. They have had baby-sitters and child minders who spoke French, Arabic, Pilipino, and Swiss-German, and have already experienced a range of different and often contradictory cultures. Marc (age four) finds a great difference between cultural norms such as greetings. He is often unsure how to react: kissing on the cheek, as he does with French people; only saying "hello," as with English-speaking friends; or using a Swiss-German child's greeting of *hoy* (hi!). His indecision is sometimes seen as rudeness or indifference. Switching cultural codes is often more difficult than switching languages.

The Silver Lining

A trilingual child with parents who speak different languages and who lives in a third language country seems almost sure to experience some anomie or language anxiety. The trilingual child may even be caught among three competing languages, all exerting powerful cultural ties.

On the other hand, parents who willingly decide to bring up their children trilingually may take extra care that cultures are passed on carefully and with respect for the other parent and/or country. Trilingual families living as expatriates in a foreign country are in the unique position of being able to educate their children triculturally. Unlike trilingual families in Africa and Southeast Asia, they can travel often, provide extra books and media, and pay for extra private education if necessary. Living away from their home country cultures can help parents make more of an effort to preserve their own cultures, although how the third culture is represented depends on length of residence, appreciation of the third culture, and general adaptability in the family.

Education of a Trilingual Child

Finding an ideal school is often a difficult issue for families, regardless of their language status. With trilinguals, the problem is complicated further. The choice of educating a child in the mother's, the father's, or the country's language is a difficult one. It is restricted by a lack of multilingual schools or, more important, multilingual teachers and educators. However, some schools that emphasize trilingual education do exist.

One such school is the European School, which is funded by the European Economic Community for its staff and related employees. Ten European Schools are specifically designed to promote multiculturalism. The largest school, in Brussels, has eight languages. The school aims to guarantee the development of the child's first language and to "promote European identity" in at least two languages, with compulsory learning of a third language and options regarding a fourth (Baetens-Beardsmore 1993).

In this school model, the child's first language is maintained throughout schooling, although usage may decrease with age in many cases. The compulsory second language (English, German, or French) is introduced as a subject in the primary grades. Classes such as sports, music, and art are taught in the second language. This use of language in a "cognitively undemanding and highly contextualised context" aims to create a natural setting, and to aid peer group learning. The third language begins in secondary school, and is also a taught subject before it is a medium. Examinations can be taken in any of the three languages.

However, many parents do not have the option of the European Schools. Private, fee-charging bilingual or international schools do exist across Europe, but for many families the only choice is a monolingual state education in the language of the country where they live.

Another model of trilingual education is the Foyer Project in Brussels, a scheme to help young minority children become bicultural and trilingual. The children's first languages are Moroccan Arabic, Italian, Spanish, or Turkish. They learn Dutch (Flemish) as a second language and French as a third language. The languages have distinct domains: their first language is the home/family, Dutch is for education, and French is the "street" language (for state information, socializing, and work). Some areas of Brussels are 80 to 90 percent foreigners. About a third of all immigrant children start school with little or no knowledge of Dutch or French (Byram and Leman 1990).

In kindergarten, children have about 50 percent first language input (in a separate ethnic group) and 50 percent Dutch (for "non-demanding activities"). After three years the children begin primary school and are "partially immersed" in Dutch. In the second year Dutch is used for oral activity work and some mathematics. By the third year Dutch is used for nearly all curriculum work. "French as a foreign language" is then introduced for a few hours per week.

Byram and Leman found that one major problem is to validate French for the children. This is because in many second-generation immigrant families, French is the first language. The language of origin exists, but in an "affective" way, and the children are more focused on French for their everyday lives. In the school French is relegated to third place, as a foreign language. In reality children hear and speak considerably more French than the other languages, but it remains a lingua franca for them. The immigrant parents participate in preserving the home language, in case they decide to return to their country of origin, but in interviews they admitted that their children will probably never return to the country of origin.

One important factor is the teacher, who is a strong role model, especially if he or she has the same or similar languages to those of the children, or knowledge of bicultural issues (Tokuhama-Espinosa 2001). Bilingual teachers are employed in many schools across Europe; less widespread is the trilingual or multilingual teacher. However, an understanding native speaker teacher can be a strong role model to a child, and help reinforce a parental (possibly minority) language. Ideally, children learn to speak fluently and to read and write in two or more languages. Skills of comprehension, reading, and writing are required to pass final examinations in bilingual or multilingual schools. To reach this high level, help from the parents at home and/or extra private language teaching is often necessary. In the future there will be a need for schools to promote multiculturalism as society encompasses more nationalities and languages (Visser 1997).

FINDINGS OF THE STUDY ON TRILINGUAL FAMILIES

I contacted trilingual families across Europe through advertisements in the *Bilingual Family Newsletter*, the *Zurich International Women's Association Newsletter*, and international schools in Switzerland, Belgium, and England. Respondents were judged for suitability with the following criteria:

1. The family must use three separate languages (not regional dialects)
2. Residency in a country with a language not connected to either parent for more than a year
3. Children aged over two years old, who could be judged for language acquisition.

Questionnaires were then sent out to ten selected families, with an overall range of fourteen languages and children aged from two to ten years (see table 12.1).

Which Language Comes First? The Language Order

All multilinguals have a *language order*, with the most fluent one being considered the "first" language. Bilinguals may have equal usage of each language, but for a trilingual the choice of first, second, or third is due to circumstances, which can change language frequency. For example, the language of the kindergarten or school may become the first language because the child spends a large part of the day there. A summer vacation spent in the country of one parent could upgrade a language from second or third to first. Socializing with friends who speak one of the languages will have an effect, too. The trilingual child therefore uses each language to suit the current situation.

In my study, 50 percent of the children spoke the language of the country as their first language. These children were aged between six and twelve, and also used this language at school. I labeled these families *Country-Language Dominated*. They were long-term residents of the country and usually both parents spoke three languages, too. The other children were *Family-Language Dominated*, with a parent's language being the first one. This was clearly linked to age, because most of these families had children under the age of four who spoke the mother's language because they were mainly at home with her. However, some children aged between four and six years had the father's language as their first. This could be because the child had already established the mother's language and was now practicing the father's language. The children can follow various patterns, as shown in table 12.2.

In the trilingual family the parents have to establish a language of communication among themselves. The importance of conversations between the parents, although not directed at the child, should not be underestimated in the child's overall language development. The choice of the father's or mother's language as the one most used in the home could affect the child's language

Table 12.1
Summary of the Families Involved in the Study

Family	Mother's language	Father's language	Language-Country	Age of Child/ren
1	German	English	French - *Belgium*	3 yrs
2	Spanish	English	French - *Belgium*	3 yrs
3	Swiss- German	English	French - *Belgium*	4 yrs
4	Catalan/Spanish	English	French - *France*	3.5 yrs
5	Bulgarian	Hungarian	French - *Switzerland*	10 yrs
6	English	Dutch	German - *Switzerland*	3.5 yrs
7	English	Swiss French	German - *Switzerland*	10 yrs
8	Polish	English	German - *Germany*	8 & 6 yrs
9	Czech	Italian	English - *England*	9.5 & 3 yrs
10	French	Dutch	English - *Nepal*	2.5 yrs

Table 12.2
Country-Language Dominant Versus Family-Language Dominant Trilinguals

Country-Language Dominant		Family-Language Dominant
1st **Country** language	or	1st **Mother's** language
2nd **Parental** language	or	2nd **Father's** language
3rd **Parental** language	or	3rd **Country** language

order. When the parents talked to each other, 70 percent of them chose to use the father's language. Many fathers spoke an "international" language such as English (a high percentage), French, or Italian. This tended to overwhelm "minority" languages such as Polish, Dutch, Catalan, Swiss-German, and Czech, and the mother's language would take second or third place. In the case of parents with two equally "prestigious" languages (English with German, Spanish, or French) no pattern is seen; probably a choice has been made due to parental proficiency and personal preference for a particular language of communication. The dominance of the father's language is clearly shown in Figure 12.1.

Trilingual children generally used the appropriate language to each parent unless on parent did not understand the other's language. Families can have rather bizarre conversations with at least two languages being used in the same conversation if several members are present, and so parental knowledge of each language seems to be important in a trilingual family. Between siblings a mix of parental and country languages were used depending on the situation; role-playing of the mother would be mimicked in her language, vice versa for the father. Role-play involving a local person, such as a doctor, would be done in the language of the country.

Juggling Three Languages at Home

Bearing in mind that the trilingual potentially has three labels for every object, verb, and expression, some delay in verbal competence is natural because trilingual children decide which language to use with which person. Children can also seem rather reticent to talk—they wait to see which language they should use with each person. All the parents use the one person, one language approach at home. They were asked, "How do you react when your child uses the 'wrong' language?" Table 12.3 shows their replies.

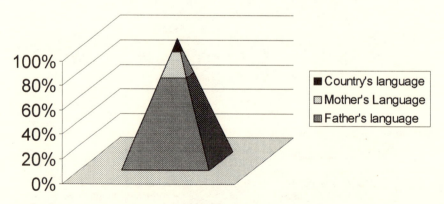

Figure 12.1 Dominant Language Between Parents in Trilingual Families

Faced with this situation, the majority of parents in my study would ignore the child's inconsistent use of the languages, and then repeat the right word in context to the child. This showed that many parents are sympathetic to the child's linguistic trials and can understand what he or she is saying, so the child is not frustrated by not being able to communicate. More important, it shows a high level of linguistic knowledge in parents, especially with older children who have a wide vocabulary.

Translation can make children feel as if they are making mistakes and demoralize them. If a translation is necessary, parents generally personalize it. To Marc I could say, for example, "Mummy says milk, et Papa dit lait," to highlight the difference. With younger preschool children most parents used themselves as language role models, saying "Mama spricht Deutsch." Later, parents introduce the concept of the language's name: "In English we say . . . " or "A l'école on parle français." One respondent wrote that she explained geographical language use for her trilingual child as "We speak English in Dublin, Dutch in Brussels, and German in Zurich," which shows how complicated life can be for trilinguals, especially in Europe!

Social Influences on a Trilingual's Language Choice

Which language does the trilingual family use with a visitor? This can be a tricky situation with simultaneous translation not at all conducive to natural conversation. Most families chose a lingua franca or common language. A third chose to use the language of the visitor to make them feel at home. Table 12.4 highlights the choices made.

The one person, one language approach was criticized by parents in daily life because each parent speaking his or her own language is considered strange and unnatural by visitors, especially if they do not understand one of the

Table 12.3
Parents' Responses to Use of "Wrong" Language

	Mother	Father	Total
Correct the child	0	0	0
Translate the word for the child	1	1	2
Ignore it, but repeat back in the right language	6	8	14
Ignore it, and continue the conversation	3	1	4

Table 12.4
Use of Language with Visitors

	Mother	Father	Total
Each person speaks his/her own language	2	2	4
One or some people translate	1	0	1
The language of the visitor is used	3	3	6
A language that everyone knows is used	4	5	9

languages. It is an issue rarely mentioned in advice books for parents, and the data suggest that parents prefer a lingua franca to excluding or translating for the visitor. As children get older, the one person, one language approach may be frustrating for the trilingual child who would rather use a lingua franca than be addressed differently by each person. Parents serve as strong role models for children, and showing they can change languages to suit the situation is a good example for future trilingual children.

Social Support for Trilingual Families

Support is important for trilingual families, and most families in my study knew at least one other trilingual family in their area. These families gave each other most support, supplemented with books on bi/trilingualism, and family and friends from the home country. Many parents subscribed to the international quarterly publication *The Bilingual Family Newsletter* for general advice and features on bringing up children multilingually. Web sites for bilingual and multilingual families also were mentioned for contact with other families. Parents are all very committed to helping their children practice language at home, with a most encouraging 90 percent of the fathers being involved! The sources supporting language development were, in order: videos, films, books, music, and songs. Some parents also listed day-to-day habits of watching TV in a certain language and playing games together.

Living with Three Competing Cultures in a Trilingual Family

Language is closely linked to culture, and it is necessary to have some cultural knowledge to sound authentic. It allows children to enjoy jokes, puns, and cultural expressions when they are visiting family and friends, or with other people from a particular country. In this study all the parents expressed a wish to "pass on" their culture to their children, describing it as "the reason for my existence and upbringing, and an essential part of myself" or saying "It is important for my children's identity." They provided this input with books, films/videos, songs, and some special things like nursery rhymes, cooking together, or looking at photo albums of the family and home country.

As figure 12.2 shows, most families are juggling two cultures (parental) and the country culture.

Cultural identity is seen as a way to pass on personal identity, but it was stressed that passing on a culture should not be an effort, but something that happens naturally. Families made efforts to keep cultures "alive" alongside the other parent's culture and the country culture. Because the trilingual family is potentially at risk of losing one or more parental cultures to the country culture, efforts are made to sustain the cultures. The parents seem to be asserting their language (and culture) in more or less equal doses.

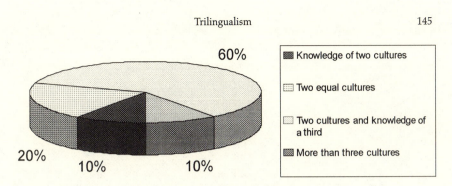

60%

	Knowledge of two cultures
	Two equal cultures
	Two cultures and knowledge of a third
	More than three cultures

20%
10%   10%

Figure 12.2   Cultural Definitions of Trilingual Families

The Influence of Peer Groups on Older Children

Being bicultural or even tricultural can be difficult for older children or adolescents who want to fit into their peer group. Therefore the effect of the peer group may bring the culture of the country into the family, whether they like it or not. As with language order dominance, one culture may eclipse another at certain times. The child cannot be culturally plural in all three cultures at the same time, because he or she cannot speak three languages at the same time. But he or she will always be pulled between attachments to at least two cultures. Luckily, as the world becomes more of a global marketplace, cultural icons like the Winnie the Pooh or the Teletubbies can be seen in English, French, and German. Children's films and books are often translated almost simultaneously. Trips to visit friends and family also can give children deep cultural knowledge. Sixty percent of parents manage to go back to their home country every year, which helps to establish a concrete cultural and linguistic base for the children.

Which Language to Educate the Children In?

The choice of school is an important one for the trilingual, because the child's most fluent language is likely to be that of the school. As table 12.5 shows, all of the families chose to educate their children in a school using the language of the country, as opposed to a school teaching only in a parental language.

It should be noted that being expected to become literate and pass examinations in a language not connected to a parent could be difficult for a child. Parents certainly need some knowledge of the other language to help with homework and to understand the school curriculum. Most of the families in my study send their children to local schools in countries such as Switzerland, Belgium, France, and Germany, and three families have children at European Schools (schools sponsored by the European Community, which are specifically tailored for multilingual children).

Table 12.5
Choice of Language for Trilingual Children's Education

Family	Country	School Language	Father's Language	Mother's Language
1	Belgium	French	English	German
2	Belgium	French	English	Spanish
3	Belgium	French/English	English	Swiss-German
4	France	French	English	Catalan
5	Switzerland	French	Hungarian	Bulgarian
6	Switzerland	Swiss-German	Dutch	English
7	Switzerland	Swiss-German	French	English
8	Germany	German	English	Polish
9	UK	English	Italian	Czech
10	Nepal	English	Dutch	French

Looking at the parental educational background, I found that only two of the twenty parents had had a bilingual education themselves, testifying to the recentness of this phenomenon. A typical family had both parents educated in their first language and university studies in a second language. I presume that they chose a local school because they live in a country where there is a good education system, or because they wished their children stay with the local peer group rather than be sent to a more exclusive (or expensive) private school.

Another factor could be that parents think the child can learn an "international" parental language, such as English or French, through the local school. However, a parental language learned at school will never be the same as if it was taught by native speakers or in the country itself. For example, English is taught as a foreign language in most schools. Parents were aware of this, and compensated by being teachers at home. They all reported extensive use of language aids for regular practice—books, videos, songs, and even the Internet!

I found that children attending the European Schools mixed languages more than those at a local school. Within the multilingual school the diversity of nationalities probably gives a sense of normalcy to mixing languages for communication. Modeling teachers and friends is a strong factor in language acquisition and usage. In contrast, the local schoolchildren will be exposed to one language, and children will be discouraged from mixing, especially with people who do not understand the trilingual child's other languages. Another possible factor could be that the locally schooled children have parents who are stricter about separation of languages and "proper" usage. It can also be hypothesized that children would be more prone to mixing if they lived in a country that has two or three official languages, such as Switzerland, because being surrounded by more than one language is a part of daily life.

Territorial Bilingualism

There were six families living in areas of "territorial bilingualism" or politically designated bilingualism—Switzerland (French, German, Italian, and Ro-

mansch) and Belgium (Flemish and French). A family living in an area of
territorial bilingualism would be indirectly exposed to the other country languages due to media or when traveling around the country. In Switzerland, for
example, supermarket packaging is usually in French, German, and Italian.

However, I did not find any children who fluently spoke two of the official
languages of the country. The territorial bilingual areas of Switzerland and
Belgium appear to be linguistically separate zones. In Switzerland, French, German, and Italian have very strong regional characteristics, and it could be hypothesized that the families are trying to fit in with the locals rather than take
advantage of a multilanguage system. Children attending local schools will
certainly have second or third language input, but this could remain passive
knowledge. In some situations a neutral language, such as English, is preferred.
A mixed language country could be an ideal environment for a trilingual, but
within Switzerland and Belgium some regional linguistic attitudes appear to
prevail.

One Parent, Two Languages (or More . . .): The Special Case of the Trilingual Family

Although trilingualism currently has relatively little research, it is evident
that trilingual families are a relevant group to study, and require further research. The fact that the children do not simply "pick up" three languages, but
acquire or learn them with great effort, assisted by parents, schools, and cultural
contexts, shows the link of languages to the environment. Trilingual families
offer an opportunity to study language use and social behavior beyond the
context of two languages or "alternating usage." The overlapping nature of the
languages, combined with the changing order of first through third language,
gives an insight into how acquisition works and how children evolve linguistically.

All of the parents in my study are trying to bring up their children trilingually, with varying degrees of success. The parents are extremely motivated
to keep their languages and cultures alive alongside the country language.
However, the families involved in the study are not representative of all trilingual families; the parents agreed to complete the questionnaire because they
are very interested in trilingualism. The study was mainly carried out in Switzerland, a trilingual country, and surrounding European countries where families use mostly European languages, which makes them a select group not
representative of trilingualism on a global scale. Other kinds of trilingual families should be included in future research: families who cannot enjoy the economic and educational opportunities of those in my study, parents using a third
language as their language of communication, and families who have permanently emigrated.

Some guidance is needed too, and a development from the one parent, one
language theory to a more appropriate one parent, two (or more) languages

approach, which is applicable to multilingual families. It is difficult to separate the languages because they frequently overlap; trilingualism is a more fluid and changeable state than bilingualism. Living with three languages and three cultures also demands different parenting attitudes. My research reveals that trilingual children need reassurance that each parent understands and speaks a good part of all three languages, as they are expected to do so. Parental efforts to "keep up" languages are important and so is the linking of a language to a culture. It seems that an appropriate role model is a parent who is linguistically flexible and can change languages to suit the current need.

Trilingualism is a growing phenomenon because the numbers of families living or working abroad and mixed marriages are increasing. Therefore trilingual acquisition patterns, education, attitudes within the family, and tricultural social aspects all require more research and investigation. I hope that trilingualism will become an academic discipline, a subject independent of bilingualism but connected by a theme of multiple language use.

REFERENCES

Abunuwara, E. (1992). "The Structure of the Trilingual Lexicon." *European Journal of Cognitive Psychology* 4, no. 4: 311–322.

Andersson, U. (1999). *Growing Up with Two Languages*. London: Routledge.

Arnberg, L. (1987). *Raising Children Bilingually: The Pre-school Years*. Clevedon, UK: Multilingual Matters.

Baetens-Beardsmore, H. (1982). *Bilingualism: Basic Principles*. Clevedon, UK: Multilingual Matters.

Baetens-Beardsmore, H. (ed.) (1993). *European Models of Education*. Clevedon, UK: Multilingual Matters.

Baker, C. (1996). *Foundations of Bilingual Education*. 2nd ed. Clevedon, UK: Multilingual Matters.

Baker, C. (2000). *A Parent's and Teacher's Guide to Bilingualism*. Clevedon, UK: Multilingual Matters.

Bloomfield, L. (1933). *Language*. New York: Holt Rinehart and Winston.

Byram, M. (1997). *Teaching and Assessing Intercultural Communicative Competence*. Clevedon, UK: Multilingual Matters.

Byram, M., and J. Leman (eds.) (1990). *Bicultural and Tricultural Education*. Clevedon, UK: Multilingual Matters.

Chick, K. (1999, August). *Teaching English in Multiethnic Schools in the Durban Area: The Promotion of Multilingualism or Monolingualism?* Paper presented at Annual Conference for Language Teachers, University of Natal, Durban.

Child, I.L. (1943). *Italian or American? The Second Generation in Conflict*. New York: Russell and Russell.

Clyne, M. (1982). *Multilingual Australia*. Melbourne: River Seine Publications.

Clyne, M. (1997). "Some of the Things Trilinguals Do." *International Journal of Bilingualism* 1, no. 2: 95–116.

De Jong, E. (1986). *The Bilingual Experience*. Cambridge: Cambridge University Press.

Elwert, W.T. (1959). *Das zweisprachige Individuum: Ein Selbstzeugnis*. Wiesbaden, Germany: Franz Steiner-Verlag.

Fantini, A.E. (1985). *Language Acquisition of a Bilingual Child*. Clevedon, UK: Multilingual Matters.

Gardner-Chloros, P. (1991). *Language Selection and Switching in Strasbourg*. Oxford, UK: Clarendon Press.

Gordon, A.I. (1966). *Intermarriage*. London: Beacon Press.

Grosjean, F. (1982). *Life with Two Languages: An Introduction to Bilingualism*. Cambridge, MA: Harvard University Press.

Hammarberg, B. (2001). "Roles of L1 and L2 in L3 Production and Acquistion." In J. Cenoz, B. Hufeison, and U. Jessner (eds.), *Crosslinguistic Influences in Third Language Acquistion: Psycholinguistic Perspective*. Clevedon, UK: Multilingual Matters.

Harding, E., and P. Riley (1986). *The Bilingual Family: A Handbook for Parents*. 9th printing. Cambridge: Cambridge University Press.

Hoffmann, C. (1985). "Language Acquisition in Two Trilingual Children." *Journal of Multilingual and Multicultural Development* 6, no. 6: 479–495.

Klein, E.C. (1995). "Second Versus Third Language Acquisition: Is There a Difference?" *Language Learning* 45, no. 3: 419–465.

Lambert, W.E. (1977). "The Effects of Bilingualism on the Individual: Cognitive and Socio-cultural Consequences." In P. Hornby (ed.), *Bilingualism: Psychological, Social and Educational Implications*. New York: Academic Press.

Mackay, W.F. (1968). "The Description of Bilingualism." In J.A. Fishman (ed.), *Readings in the Sociology of Language*. The Hague: Mouton.

McCarthy, T., and Watahomigie (1999). "Indigenous Community-Based Education in the U.S.A." In May, Stephen (ed.), *Indigenous Community-Based Education*. Clevedon, UK: Multilingual Matters.

McLaughlin, B., and R. Nation (1986). "Experts and Novices: An Information-processing Approach to the 'Good Language Learner' Problem." *Applied Psycholinguistics* 7: 41–56.

Magiste, E. (1986). "Selected Issues in Second and Third Language Learning." In Y. Vaid (ed.), *Language Processing in Bilinguals: Psycholinguistics and Neuropsychological Perspectives*. Hillsdale, NJ: Laurence Erlbaum.

May, S. (1994). "Making Multicultural Education Work." In *The Language and Education Library*. Vol. 7. London, UK: Taylor & Francis,

Milroy, L., and P. Muysken (eds.) (1995). *One Speaker, Two languages*. Cambridge: Cambridge University Press.

Nieto, S. (1996). *Affirming Diversity: The Sociopolitical Context of Multicultural Education*. New York: Longman.

Nullis, C. (2001). "Swiss-based Family Speaks in Many Tongues. Lessons for Learning?" AP news article. 7 January.

Oksaar, E. (1977). "On Being Trilingual." In C. Molony (ed.), *Deutsch im Kontakt mit andern Sprachen*. Kronberg, Germany: Scriptor Verlag.

Paradis, M. (1995). *Aspects of Bilingual Aphasia*. New York: Elsevier.

Pollock, D., and R. van Reken (1999). *The Third Culture Kid Experience: Growing Up Among Worlds*. Yarmouth, ME: Intercultural Press.

Romaine, S. (1995). *Bilingualism*. 2nd ed. Oxford: Blackwell.

Slobin, D.I. (ed.) (1985–1992). *The Cross-linguistic Study of Language Acquisition.* 3 vols. Hillsdale, NJ: Laurence Erlbaum Associates.

Tokuhama-Espinosa, T. (2001). *Raising Multilingual Children: Foreign Language Acquisition and Children.* Westport, CT: Bergin & Garvey.

Visser, J. (1997). *Multilingualism in a Pervasive Learning Environment.* New York: UNESCO.

Wei, L. (1998). "Language Maintenance and Loss in Ethnic Communities in Britain: What Schools Can and Cannot Do." Paper presented at the *Children and Multilingualism* conference, University of North London.

Wei, L., N. Miller, and B. Dodd (1997). "Distinguishing Communicative Difference from Language Disorder in Bilingual Children." *Bilingual Family Newsletter* 14, no. 1: 1–3.

Weinrich, U. (1953). *Languages in Contact.* New York: Linguistic Circle of New York.

Widdicombe, S. (1997). "Code-switching, Coining and Interference in Trilingual First Language Acquisition: A Case Study." M.Sc. thesis, Aston University, Birmingham, UK.

Woods, P. (1999). *Bilingual Education and Bilingualism,* no. 16. Clevedon, UK: Multilingual Matters.

13

What, You Speak Only One Language!?
A Trilingual Family's Story

Nicola Küpelikilinç

In the following case study I would like to illustrate how the environment plays a major role in the successful trilingual family and thus complement other essays in this book that emphasize the role of parents. This case is based on my own two children's upbringing in Turkish, German, and English in Germany at the turn of the millennium. It also offers an aspect rarely considered in German literature on multilingual language development: the language development of children with a minority first language, because the language development of ethnic minority children is often reduced to the issue of how to teach German to children from ethnic minorities as quickly and economically as possible. The question of *bilingual* development of ethnic minority children is rarely of interest.

I was born and brought up in England, the child of an English father and a German mother. Unfortunately, I grew up monolingual as a result of my mother's attempts to keep her mother-in-law happy (she valiantly read us *Winnie the Pooh* and learned all the "correct" nursery rhymes in English), and my father's attitude was that if someone did not understand English, one should just shout a bit louder. In the 1960s, German was still the language of the Nazis and the defeated enemy in the Second World War, a fact that did not increase my parents' motivation for my brother and me to learn German. My German grandmother often spent the summer holidays with us, which would have been a marvelous chance to learn German, but she was proud of her English and enjoyed the chance to be able to speak it. I learned German the hard way, as a foreign language in a British private school, where the German textbooks were dated 1932 and showed strong blond children rambling from youth hostel to youth hostel, singing all the way. Since I passed all my German exams with flying colors, I made the false assumption that I could speak the language. However, I found that when I arrived in the Rhineland-Palatinate, I could not understand a word because of the dialect spoken there.

At university I met my husband, who came from Turkey and was studying political science. He grew up in a village in southeastern Turkey in a mostly monolingual environment, the only contact with another language being through the Kurdish farmers in the area. At the time we met, German was our only language of communication. My husband learned English to help with his studies and spent six months at an English university. I learned Turkish and benefited from two long stays in Turkey, and now work as a child psychologist with many Turkish families. Despite the long waiting lists of patients, and the fact that Turks are the largest ethnic minority here, there are only a handful of Turkish-speaking psychologists in the Rhine-Main area.

WHICH LANGUAGES TO USE WITHIN THE GROWING FAMILY?

Our family quickly grew from just my husband and myself to one with a son and a daughter as well. Mahir is now ten years old and Ella is eight. When they were born, it was only natural that we each spoke our own first language with the children. German was a highly present language from birth, since Germany defines itself very much as a monolingual country (although there are indigenous language minorities). Our children both started in crèche (preschool) just after their first birthdays, and during this time, as well as in most subsequent schooling, German has been the only language granted any space, even if lip service was often paid to the attractions of bilingualism. German is also the language my husband and I speak together most of the time and the language of most of the surrounding media. Speaking German is also associated with high status. Command of German has become a very political issue and the ultimate measuring stick for dividing people into "good" and "bad" foreigners. People who cannot speak German are often described as "speechless."

English is a language that has a very high status. A good knowledge of English is considered to be essential for professional success and an important indicator of modernity. Parents will go to great lengths to ensure that their children learn English as early as possible, and English classes for preschool children and English in kindergarten are very popular in certain circles. It is also considered chic to use English phrases and expressions in everyday speech. However, in our everyday life, English is not a language with an extensive presence. There was never a sustained period of time when I was at home in England with the children, because I have been a working mother from the beginning. We have few friends for whom English is a first language, and it is unusual to hear people speaking English in the streets. English is present in popular music, as heard on the radio, and we now have a BBC cable channel on television. Otherwise the children's English language input comes from me; to a certain extent from their grandmother, with whom the children have a close contact; and the English-language media we have accumulated over the years.

With the Turkish language the situation is reversed. Turkish is a language with a very high presence in our everyday life. We live in a small town with a large ethnic minority population, the majority of which is Turkish. As in most towns in the area, there are many streets in which Turkish (and to a lesser extent, Berber) is the dominant language. Because many of the Turks come from the same village as my husband, and are often related somehow ("family" being a very elastic term of reference for the Turks), the children are accustomed to spending a lot of time in monolingual Turkish situations. Although my in-laws have always welcomed me with open arms, it has been under the premise that Turkish is the only natural means of communication within the family. Thus the children are used to hearing me speak Turkish. Furthermore, the children see my husband and me acting as interpreters at the doctor's, at parents' evenings, and at political events (we are both active in local politics). The children often stay with their aunt when my husband and I are busy. Her household is one of the central meeting points for the family and is nearly always full of people talking in Turkish. Turkish is also the language in the local shops, often the language of television programs, and of many friends in school. Thus Turkish is constantly present for the children.

However, Turkish is a language with a very low status in Germany. The general attitude is that Turkish is only for those who do not know any other language, a difficult language with few opportunities. German-Turkish projects for kindergartens or schools are often greeted by German parents with "What, is my child supposed to learn Turkish?" and by Turkish parents with "But I'm worried my child won't know enough German to be successful at school!" In particular young people of Turkish descent treat Turkish as an almost barbaric language of no use, and suggestions that they should include it as a skill on their curriculum vitae are met with scorn.

LANGUAGE DEVELOPMENT: MAHIR

In many bilingual families, including our own, the first child has an easier time gaining a foothold in the minority language because the influence of other children plays a smaller role in early language development. My husband spent the first year at home with Mahir, and when he was busy, his sister-in-law took over, and around his first birthday we spent a month in Turkey. Thus his first words were Turkish. When he started crèche at thirteen months, there was a period of a few months during which he learned few new words and successfully taught the whole group the Turkish word for water. Then his speech emerged in all three languages at once. Mahir separated his languages clearly from a very early age. He often told me something in English and repeated it to his father in Turkish. He would sometimes speak in a German/English mixture to me, then would repeat the same in clear German for somebody else in the room. At age two he would say, "Baba says *araba*, Mummy says 'car,' and Ansgar (his favorite person from crèche) says 'auto.' "

When he was three and a half, we visited England, and Mahir made two important discoveries. First, if he spoke to me in German, nobody else understood, a useful device for a rather shy child. Second, by speaking in German, he could save himself the effort of having to say everything to his parents twice. There then followed about nine months in which he refused to speak anything but German to his father and me. He also began a complicated process of sorting out who among the Turkish friends and relatives spoke German and who did not. Elderly, traditionally clothed Turks were nearly always addressed in Turkish, for example. One day he went to our neighbor's and heard the mother speaking German on the phone. He said "Aha, so you *do* know German after all!" and thereafter spoke no more Turkish in that household. Although I was careful not to put pressure on him to speak a particular language, I did rather despair, thinking that trilingualism was on the way out, and that German would become dominant. However, one day he accidentally discovered a home-made cassette with a few minutes of his voice in English. He reacted with amazement, and played this snippet over and over again, probably a hundred times within the next few days. Then one evening that same week I picked up his favorite nursery rhyme book to read it to him. He snatched the book from me and began reciting the nursery rhymes in English. From then on, his English has improved steadily. He speaks English to me a lot of the time, has no problem switching to English on holiday or with other English speakers, and is no longer so self-conscious about speaking it.

Turkish took longer to return, however. He often relied on us for translation while on holiday in Turkey. He was a solitary child between the ages of four and seven and did not mind playing on his own. He had no problems understanding the language, but spoke little. However since about the age of eight, he has begun to speak increasingly more, at least in family situations. He now automatically speaks Turkish on the phone as well as with relatives. Important factors seem to have been several journeys to Turkey without me, Turkish lessons at school, a closer identification with his father, and pride in being a member of an extended family. Mahir also has an increasing awareness of racist, xenophobic tendencies in Germany, which has given him a stronger affinity for his Turkish roots. German remains the dominant language, however, with respect to competence.

LANGUAGE DEVELOPMENT: ELLA

Ella had the second-child disadvantage: Her brother spoke German to her from the beginning, using the logic that children in the neighborhood all speak German. Because of her brother there were more children in the house, and the majority spoke German among themselves, whatever their origin. Ella's first language was German, and for a long time it was her only language, although she understood the others and listened to stories in English and Turkish with apparent comprehension and great pleasure. From her first to her third birthday we did not visit England. When we did, we realized that she had never met anybody who spoke English and who did not understand German. She behaved like the archetypal Englishman abroad, stamping her foot and speaking louder and louder whenever someone did not understand her (how dare they!). Soon after we returned to Germany, she began to speak English to me, or at least an English-German mixture. (The mixing never bothered me, because I knew she could speak all three languages without mixing in the presence of monolinguals.) Sometimes I would hear her "reading" a storybook to her dolls in English. Role-playing with her brother often involved the mother speaking (or more often scolding!) in English—Ella is a very good mimic and would often sabotage my attempts to tell her off by giving me a rundown of all my standard threats in perfect English ("I'll make mincemeat of you" being one of her favorites).

Turkish appeared in much the same way: The daughter of the family upstairs was monolingual Turkish until she started kindergarten. When she was about two and Ella nearly four, Ella realized that if she wanted to play properly with her, she would have to speak Turkish. Within two months she was fluent— even if this fluency was dependent on the presence of her friend. Without her, Ella became absolutely dumb in Turkish. Generally both Ella and her brother have been prepared to speak Turkish to small children. With her gift for mimicry, Ella was quick to pick up the village dialect while on holiday, while her brother tends to speak all his languages with a great emphasis on correctness in syntax. Thus Ella will open her mouth and spout forth whenever there is an adequate motive, while her brother waits until he is sure he knows how to say something.

THE ENVIRONMENT'S AMBIGUOUS ATTITUDE TO BILINGUALISM

The general attitude to our trilingual family in Germany is ambiguous. We are often greeted with certain incredulity, because trilingual families in Germany are a rarity, perhaps unlike the situation in Switzerland or the Netherlands. The second reaction is positive: "What a marvelous opportunity!" But this is quickly followed by certain skepticism: "Will the children be able to cope? Aren't they totally confused?" Unfortunately, this skeptical attitude tends to be the one that remains. I often wonder why Germans find it so difficult to listen to our children with an open ear and register that their German is perfect, without a trace of an accent and with a very good vocabulary. (Our daughter now attends an extra lesson for children with problems learning German as a second language, because school policy is to provide this instruction for all "foreigners." The fact that she continually corrects her mother's use of German gender words is something her teacher ignores, however, although this is a central learning goal in these lessons.) Fortunately, our children take very little notice of this attitude.

Among non–Germans living here the reaction is entirely positive. Turks, both here and in Turkey, generally have a very high opinion of people who can speak several languages, often quoting the aphorism "Iki dil, iki insan" (two languages, two people/personalities), which is understood as a positive increase in humanity and not, as is often the case in Germany, as a tendency to split personality. Many binational families with a minority status language find it difficult to maintain the minority language, and therefore take heart from our positive example. Our trilingual family is seen as being a good buffer against the generally skeptical attitude because my profession as a child psychologist and lecturer on language development carries a certain authority.

VALUE DIFFERENCES BETWEEN THE LANGUAGES

A major factor in our trilingual situation is the differing status accorded to the two minority languages. English is the world language: Everybody needs English, English is an important subject at school, and therefore it is a tremendous advantage for our children to learn English from birth. But who needs Turkish, a primitive, underdeveloped language in the eyes of many? Something I often find heartbreaking is the way in which young people of Turkish origin admire our children for growing up with more than one language. If you then point out to them that they also grew up bilingually, the answer is "Yes, but that was only Turkish, that doesn't count." Our children have always received a lot of praise and attention for their knowledge of English, but only rarely for their knowledge of Turkish. Their perfect command of German is also rarely a subject of attention, because German is considered to be as necessary to life as breathing or walking.

The difference in the reception of English and Turkish is something the children were aware of at a very early age, in spite of the fact that Turkish plays a more important role in our day-to-day life. When Mahir was about five, I overheard him arguing with one of his Turkish cousins. His claim for superiority was that he spoke better English, to which she countered that her Turkish was better. He retorted that no one learned Turkish in school, to which she said there were Turkish lessons in school. His trump card was then "Ah, but nobody pays to learn Turkish."

LANGUAGE AS A MEANS OF INCLUSION
AND EXCLUSION

English is a language that most people in Germany understand at least to a certain extent (and that few would admit to not understanding at least partially). Thus conversations between the children and me are often followed with interest, and when we are standing in a queue it is quite common for someone to add a few comments in English. With Turkish, however, the situation is different. Bystanders feel excluded, even threatened, by this language.

Even as someone of obvious European appearance, I have often been treated to hostile looks when talking to Turkish friends or when with Turkish children in the street. Sometimes reactions are condescending, in the sense of pity for someone who does not speak German. I have often heard from parents that their children did not want them to speak Turkish in public, and that younger brothers and sisters who had not yet learned German were a severe embarrassment.

In training sessions with kindergarten teachers, one important issue is addressing the feelings of exclusion that teachers experience when confronted by groups of children speaking in their mother tongue. At the same time it is necessary to create a sense of awareness in the teachers about what it means to a child to enter the world of kindergarten and have no means of making oneself understood, except possibly for a sympathetic older child with the same mother tongue. This underlying hostility to a language one does not understand is obviously a major obstacle in bringing up children confident in their ability to speak several languages.

EXPECTATIONS OF CHILDREN

Both adults and children can place a great sense of pressure on multilingual children by saying "Oh, do say something in . . ." or "What's that called in . . . ?" This is something to which my children have always taken great exception. It starts with well-meaning efforts to practice English on the children—both children have very sharp antennae for whether someone is a native English speaker or not, and shun nonnative speakers. Then come the testing questions to discover if the children really do speak the languages, and what child enjoys being put to the test? Then come the Turkish relations, for whom the question of whether the children speak Turkish or not is a one of family honor. Much as Germans sort foreigners into "good" and "bad" according to their knowledge of German, Turks will assess foreigners married to Turks according to their knowledge, and also their children's knowledge, of Turkish. I have often heard Turkish women arguing about whose daughter-in-law makes more effort to promote the Turkish language. This is to a certain extent understandable, because there is a great fear that in mixed marriages the majority language and culture will elbow out the minority language and culture. My children never believed in promoting their parents' standing in the family by demonstrating their knowledge of Turkish. (Only once, when two aunts were debating whether the children spoke Turkish or not, did my son turn round and say, in Turkish, "I can speak Turkish, but only when I want to." And that in the middle of his German-only phase!)

Requests to translate and help out when someone does not understand can be common, as when a teacher needs help to explain something to a Turkish mother. This seems to be something the children feel ambivalent about. I believe our children will help of their own accord when they sense that there are communication problems, but not when they are requested to take on the role of interpreter, because it is a type of "showing off" that creates great discomfort for them. Additionally, many teachers overestimate children's ability to translate, as opposed to explaining something in another language.

PRIDE IN A MULTILINGUAL WORLD

My children take great pride in their multilingual abilities and have always seen their languages as a source of self-esteem. Multilingualism is also something they see as normal. At an early age I remember them reporting in bewilderment that a certain friend could speak only one language. It is something that is an essential part of their self-perception, just as another child might emphasize his prowess in football. This is definitely helped by the approbation their parents receive when they act as intermediates. My children are used to being asked by teachers to take a notice home to be translated or by people coming round to have letters written (the downside of the coin is the time spent on such activities instead of on the children). Thus our children's situation is quite different from those of some of their Turkish friends whose parents are not in a position to support their children in the German-speaking environment. Teachers are often very blunt in their scorn for parents who do not speak sufficient German.

Although on the whole our children are proud of their trilingualism, the different statuses of their language also play a role here. English offers many more opportunities for one-upmanship. Ella's teacher often pays extra attention to her by speaking to her in English (usually in situations when she has not been paying attention and should actually be getting the cold shoulder). Our children can explain the meaning of English advertising slogans, or pop songs, and had the latest Harry Potter book long before it came out in Germany.

LANGUAGE AND IDENTITY

From a very early age both of my children have associated language with a sense of belonging. At four Mahir maintained he was German because he spoke German, his father Turkish because he spoke Turkish, and his mother was English by the same logic. Asked what his sister, who at that time was just beginning to talk, was, he gave it some thought and announced that actually she was nothing at all. Over the years the children's attitudes have changed, unfortunately influenced by the very racist undertones of some of the last election campaigns and increasing Neo-Nazi activities. As the children have become more and more aware of their "alien" status in Germany, they have developed a positive identity as dual nationals, and correspondingly have emphasized and developed their multilingual capacities. To put it bluntly, if I take the attitude that I am not dependent on Germany because I have alternative places to live, then I have to develop the linguistic abilities necessary for such an eventual transition. Again, this is a point in which the children find support in their parents' prominent role in the local community.

MULTILINGUALISM AS AN ENDLESS SOURCE OF POSSIBILITIES

Our children have always seen their multilingual life as quite varied. One does not actually have to put one's language abilities into practice to be able to show off being trilingual, but it is "cool" to have a way of communicating with one's parents without the whole world catching on. It's fun to be able to follow the secret conversations of your Turkish classmates. It's a great game to experiment with words, to see what things are called in other languages, and to create puns.

SUPPORTING MINORITY LANGUAGES

Had someone asked me ten years ago to predict my children's language development, I would have said that Turkish should be no problem, while English would suffer from the lack of input. I seriously underestimated the role that the status of the language would play. In spite of the times when monolingualism seemed to be gaining the upper hand, the minority languages have always surfaced again, though it has always been English that was quicker to recover. Turkish has always needed more active encouragement. To conclude this essay, I would like to summarize the factors I feel have been especially important in maintaining a minority-status language.

- *Contacts with the culture in which the language comes alive.* Our children have always had the advantage of seeing Turkish culture around them. Family gatherings, weddings, picnics, and religious festivals are an important part of our life. Additionally, there are the holidays in the mountain village my husband comes from, which is a child's paradise (especially for animal lovers like Mahir) and offers an important contrast to the ghetto situation in which the Turkish language in Germany lives. To be part of this life, contact with the Turkish language, at least passively, is essential. Thus the situation, for example, of a German-Ghanaian family living in Germany is much more difficult because the contact with the culture is often very limited.
- *Contacts with peers.* In my experience, wanting to make oneself understood by peers is the strongest motivation of all. Adults are not nearly so important to children, because they will go to endless trouble to try and understand what a child wants, and it is no disaster from the child's point of view if one needs an interpreter to communicate with an adult. However, parents should never make the mistake of assuming that they can determine which peers are interesting for their children, or which language the children will speak among themselves.
- *Presence of the language in schools.* One of the great boosts to our children's Turkish development was starting Turkish lessons in school (one of the few concessions German schools make to the presence of ethnic minority children is providing for in-

struction in the languages of those countries which were the primary countries of origin of migrant workers from the 1950s to the middle of the 1970s). These lessons elevated the status of Turkish in the eyes of our children a great deal. In Mahir's case, the fact that the teachers were men in the predominantly female world of German primary schools helped as well. However, this advantage can be lost when teachers pour scorn on the not-so-good language skills of children from multilingual families (something I have often heard but that, thankfully, does not apply to our teachers) and when the children have an extra burden, for example, having to go back to school in the afternoon when their friends are out playing.

- *Media.* The amount of time we have spent reading to our children in our first languages is definitely an important factor. Finding suitable and attractive books is no problem for high-status languages like English, French, and Spanish. Finding these in Turkish, Vietnamese, or Mandingo is another matter. In countries just a few decades away from illiteracy as the normal state, children's books tend to be few and far between, and often made to suit the ideals of a small, European-oriented upper class. From experience I find that the problems with the Turkish picture books, which are mostly made of thin paper and are physically unsuited to energetic two-year-olds, start with the physical quality. The contents often reflect the "Peter and Jane" standard of my early readers in the 1960s in England, and are about as un–Turkish as you can imagine, resulting in a very stilted text. In early years it is sufficient to tell stories in your language to accompany the pictures, but soon the connection between word and text becomes important. Reading the caption under an interesting photo in the newspaper, reading the labels on food products, and talking out loud while writing letters are activities that emphasize the importance of the language independent of the family. Films that can be enjoyed by the family also fill a function similar to reading material—the Turkish comic actor Saban is a great favorite with my husband and the children, and the ability to laugh together over his jokes and antics creates a linguistic joining and also an identification with the Turkish language far stronger than any originating from translated versions of Western media products.

- *Bilingual culture.* The growth of a Turkish immigrant culture is beginning to change the status of Turkish, at least in the eyes of people of Turkish origin. Although the disparaging attitude toward the Turkish language is still very prevalent among young Turks, there is another parallel trend: the development of a German-Turkish street language as a deliberate move to counter the sense of exclusion these people feel in *both* countries. There is a growing tendency among these groups to use the economic force they have on account of their numbers. This leads to Turkish songs being played on the radio and becoming hits, films with passages in Turkish (rather than having Germans play the roles of Turks, as was customary until a few years ago), and dual-language editions of newspapers. This has led to our children realizing that you can be "in" and trendy with a foot in both languages; now Ella can show off by singing pop songs in Turkish, not just in English! This is, however, a phenomenon closely associated with the history of migration in Germany and specific to the Turkish (and to a lesser extent the Berber) language, and thus not so relevant for the situation of other minorities, like the German-Ghanaians, although ethnic culture as a trend does rub off on all languages. This does not change the fact that there is a very long way to go until the prevailing attitude of German language supremacy begins to crack.

- *Fun, not pressure.* I am a great believer in not insisting that children must speak a particular language. But I have maintained that the opposite is also true, and the children could not force their father and me to speak one language. Making a game out of language has always been popular. A favorite game while riding in the car is saying one word and seeing who is the first to give the same word in the other two languages. Or English/Turkish speaking competitions: the first one to let a German word slip out has to pay a forfeit. Rhyming words or words with the same initial letter are just some of the many possibilities.

This is the incomplete story of our trilingual family. Just as I would have made different predictions ten years ago, so I am curious to see what the next ten years will bring. Although trilingualism was the natural solution for our family and not, as some people maintain, an experiment for my own curiosity, it has been fascinating to watch what the children have made of the situation and how different they are in dealing with their languages—and how the environment reacts. I hope this case study and others in this book encourage all multilingual families to find the solution that is right for them.

Part IV

Society and Languages

14

Third Culture Kids
A Special Case for Foreign Language Learning

Tracey Tokuhama-Espinosa

Third Culture Kids. Global nomads. Strangers in their own country. Natives in foreign lands. These are some of the many labels for the type of child who grows up in more than one country. What is a Third Culture Kid? While the term has become more and more familiar since the 1980s, it is still not a household word and needs clarification.

Third Culture Kids (TCK) spend at least part of their childhoods in countries and cultures other than their own. The term is used to describe a child who has parents of two different cultures, and they are "abroad" in a third. For example, Tom's mother is Haitian, his father is American, and the family lives in Mexico. Or it may apply to a child with parents from the same culture who lives in a country other than his or her own, and attends a school in a third culture, as does Mary; her parents are from the UK, the family lives in Thailand, and she attends an international school. Children are TCKs for many reasons: their parents work for international firms; their parents are diplomats; their parents are military personnel or missionaries; or there is civil unrest in the home country, causing the family to become refugees.

A Third Culture Kid (TCK) is a person who has spent a significant part of his or her development years outside the parents' culture. The TCK build relationships to all of the cultures, while not having full ownership in any. Although elements from each culture are assimilated into the TCK's life experience, the sense of belonging is in relationship to others of similar background. (Pollock and Van Reken 1999: 19)

The drawbacks of such an upbringing can be numerous, though they can be avoided with good guidance. There is a type of rootlessness, of not being able to answer the question "Where is home?" in all TCKs' lives. Is home where they are now, or where they were born, or where their family members reside? Other problems can be related to accustoming oneself to the transient lifestyle, finding it too difficult to formulate solid and lasting relationships because there is an internal desire or restlessness to "change the scene" every few years. While the downside to being a TCK is very real, the benefits can far outweigh the negative aspects.

THE BENEFITS OF A TCK UPBRINGING

. . . a child growing up abroad has great advantages. He [or she] learns, through no conscious act of learning, that thoughts can be transmitted in many languages, that skin color is unimportant. (Rachel Miller Schaetti, quoted in Pollock and Van Reken, 1999: 77)

There is a flip side to every coin. Some may see a move abroad as a devastation; others, as an opportunity. When faced with an inevitable move to another country—as thousands of families will do this year due to work alone—the best advice psychologically is to search for the rainbow.

Pollock and Van Reken outline some of the paradoxical thinking that TCKs experience when examining their lifestyle. Among the pairs of concepts in conflict are an "expanded world view versus confused loyalties," where TCKs may feel like traitors to their homeland if they adopt too many characteristics of the new culture. A "three-dimensional view of the world versus a painful view of reality," in which TCKs can see the world in more realistic terms, sometimes means being hit in the face with the poverty and lack of basic resources in many countries. "Cross-cultural enrichment versus ignorance of the home culture" means that while TCKs often try to learn all there is to know about the new host country, they should not do so at the risk of becoming "culturally illiterate" in their own country. Questions of character come into play as well. The conflict pair "adaptability versus lack of true cultural balance" occurs when a TCK decides to "be American" or "Indian" or "Japanese" because his family is living there, even if he is not from that country. TCKs need to be reminded not to do this at the expense of their home country culture. The conflict pair "blending in versus defining the differences" means balancing being part of the new culture and recognizing that differences *do* exist, and appreciating them for what they are. There is also a question of deep relationships versus superficial ones for protection ("less versus more"), and "the importance of Now versus the Delusion of Choice," making the most of the time one does have abroad and not wasting it in transition (Pollock and Van Reken 1999: 77–100).

Perhaps one of the greatest problems facing TCKs is in their multicultural existence. As one woman wrote on a multilingual family chat line:

I think it's very difficult, if not impossible, to truly belong completely to two (or more) different cultures, just because a normal part of any culture is NOT belonging to any other! Germans see my kids as Americans and Americans see them as German. We just spent three weeks in the U.S., and although my family is very supportive of our being bilingual and they all think it's wonderful, it's still a strange concept for them. (December 2000)

While questions of belonging to a culture, and the debate about whether or not an individual can actually be of two (or more) cultures, alarm parents of potential TCKs, many TCKs have written as adults to say that it is indeed possible. In response to this question, the Global Nomad Society was formed in 1984 by Norma M. Caig. This organization seeks to unify TCKs in their search for a common culture. Strangely enough, the commonality between members is the lack of attachment to a single culture. "Suddenly it came out . . . I am a global nomad. . . . I now have a culture. After three decades of learning other people's cultures and still being an outsider, I look to the future" (Nori Hsu in the *Global Nomad Quarterly*, quoted in Pollock and Van Reken 1999: xi–xii). Despite all of the questions and internal conflicts facing TCKs, many practical skills are born of such a lifestyle.

THE BENEFITS OF BEING A TCK

Some of the great benefits of being a TCK are cross-cultural skills, excellent observation skills (such a trait is necessary for survival out of one's known culture), social skills, and linguistic skills.

Heightened Linguistic Skills

The ability to speak more than one language is a valued skill, and is becoming more so with every passing year. In 1998, *USA Today* reported that the "top executives in the United States cited knowledge of a foreign language as the skill most lacking in their work forces" (Family.go.com 1999). "Bilingualism and multilingualism have advantages in addition to the obvious one of communicating with different groups of people. For instance, Dr. Jeannine Heny, an English professor, believes learning different languages early in life can sharpen thinking skills in general and can help children achieve academically above grade level" (Pollock and Van Reken 1999: 114).

Is this always the case? There is a possible negative side when the child loses the "mother tongue" because he or she spends formative years in a foreign language atmosphere and there is no attempt made at home to ensure that the child's native language develops as well. Observant parents who use a consistent strategy to support the home language skills while the family is abroad can remedy this.

Children who learn a language while steeped in its culture are far more likely to retain that knowledge. People who can use new language skills in meaningful situations on a daily basis have the opportunity to apply language to "real life," and they will develop a fluency that escapes most second language learners in a classroom setting in a monolingual culture. Individuals are more likely to develop a strong emotional link to a language that (hopefully) is positive. This enhances the possibility of retention and retrieval over the life span. Even if the child has only one or two years in the new language environment, if positive motivation to learn the language accompanies the third culture adventure, he or she has an excellent chance of learning the foreign language.

So it is with our lives as global nomads, as TCKs. During childhood and beyond, all of our experiences of mind, heart, body, and spirit—cultural, emotional, physical, geographical—all of the moves, the relationships, the places, the losses, the discoveries, the wonder of the world—are layered one upon another through time. (Norma M. Caig, Foreword to Pollock and Van Reken 1999: xv)

Questions about TCKs will continue to multiply as greater numbers of people live outside of their place of origin. Millions of people live in foreign countries, whether by choice or due to conflict, and this trend continues to grow. TCKs and their families can make the most of this situation by exploiting the benefits of this lifestyle and attempting to avoid the pitfalls. One of the greatest benefits is in the unique opportunity to learn a new language.

TCKs and their families face the challenge of making the most of their years outside their home country. One of the greatest long-term benefits of the time spent abroad can be the language of the host country. What can families do to ensure that they make the most of this opportunity? They can acknowledge the paradoxical pairs that Pollock and Van Reken defined (1999), by walking the fine line between the extremes of full integration and full retreat. Never minimize the home country language, values, and customs. A TCK should be proud of his or her origins. This means maintaining the family traditions or rituals that best reflect the family values. On the other hand, the TCK should never minimize the host country's language, values, and customs. Live with the saying "Equally logical but different." The TCK may find removing one's shoes before entering a house, eating with chopsticks instead of a fork, or sleeping on the floor not so easy to adjust to, but that does not make these practices wrong.

If the TCK can walk this path, foreign language learning becomes much easier. There are at least three ways of approaching the host country language:

1. *School*: Attend school in the host language. Depending on the age of the child, the school options available, and the linguistic relationship between the host and home languages, immersion in the local school could be the best option.

2. *Activities*: Find an extracurricular activity that the child enjoys, and do it in the host country language. Use something the child already loves (soccer, ballet, theater, ceramics, etc.) as the vehicle to deliver the new language.

3. *Friends*: There is no better teacher than a peer. If your child makes a friend from the host country, you can be sure his or her language abilities will flourish.

Other options exist, such as formal language classes, and can achieve similar success, especially with older children. But school, activities, and friends are particularly effective, mainly because they develop an internal, positive motivation and positive emotional links.

The TCK has a special opportunity that children who do not travel abroad never have: exposure to quality native language input over a prolonged period of time, which can be delivered through a school, activities, or friends. While the positive aspects of being a TCK are numerous none is more so than language, which opens even further opportunities in the realms of culture.

Through language, TCKs open doors to new cultures and, with guidance, can learn to see themselves better through the eyes of others.

REFERENCES

Bell, L.G. (1997). *Hidden Immigrants: Legacies of Growing Up Abroad.* Yarmouth, ME: Intercultural Press.

Larson, A. (1997). *Dads at a Distance: An Activities Handbook for Strengthening Long Distance Relationships.* Provo, UT: A&E Family Publishing.

Pollock, D., and R.E. Van Reken (1999). *The Third Culture Kid Experience: Growing Up Among Worlds.* Yarmouth, ME: Intercultural Press.

Roman, B.D. (1999). *Let's Move Overseas: The International Edition of Let's Make a Move!* Wilmington, NC: BR Anchor.

Schaetti, B.F. (1995). "Families on the Move: Working Together to Meet the Challenge." In B.F. Schaetti (ed.), *Moving On: Strategies for the Homeward Bound.* London: FOCUS, 1995.

Shepard, S. (1997). *Managing Cross-cultural Transition: A Handbook for Corporations, Employees, and Their Families.* New York: Aletheia.

Smith, C.D. (1996). *Strangers at Home: Essays on the Effects of Living Overseas and Coming "Home" to a Strange Land.* New York: Aletheia.

Storti, C. (1997). *The Art of Crossing Cultures.* Yarmouth, ME: Intercultural Press.

WEB REFERENCE

Family.go.com. *Widening Horizons: Parent Advice for Bilinguals.* www.family.go.com/ Features/family_1999_08/penn/penn891language/penn89language3.htm/

15

The Yellow Streetcar
Shaping a Polyphonic Identity

Cristina Allemann-Ghionda

A MULTILINGUAL CHILDHOOD . . .

"Da oggi parlo italiano"

In my bedroom at my Swiss "home" in Basel, a silver frame surrounds an enlarged snapshot taken in 1952 on one of those huge ocean liners that used to cross the Atlantic when it was still uncommon to fly from Rio de Janeiro to Naples. An Italian sailor holds in his arms a three-and-a-half-year-old girl with fair bobbed hair and plump cheeks, arms, and legs, an apple core in her hand. The sailor wears a white T-shirt and a broad smile showing all his beautiful teeth—looking as you would expect an Italian sailor to do on such a ship. Another photo shows the little girl at the bar, a frown on her face, concentrating on her job of washing dishes and espresso cups. The family chronicle tells that after one week (the journey was long in those days) she declared: "From today on, I am going to speak Italian."

Before that first linguistic turn, for three years the family language had been Brazilian Portuguese—more precisely, the Carioca version spoken in Rio de Janeiro. My "teacher" had been my *tata*, the nanny who took care of me from my sixth month for about three years. My parents spoke Italian when they were talking to each other, just as they had done in Rome before. This must have been quite a task for my mother, whose native language was German: a language she apparently did not like to speak at that time because of her traumatic experiences during the war in Berlin and the still vivid memories that the German language evoked in her mind. But when the three of us were together or when the *tata* was with us, the common language was Portuguese. This language arrangement was due to a fundamental decision that my parents had made when my father, strongly supported by my mother, had chosen to join the Italian foreign service. In each country, the language had to be learned as fast as possible, and the new culture was to be considered a new world full of surprises, some of them certainly more pleasant than others, that were worthwhile discovering.

There was no question about considering Italian food and customs as the only and best. On the contrary: Such an attitude, when detected in other people, was invariably and intolerantly labeled "provincial," which was almost a four-letter word in the family lexicon. The intercultural confrontation between father (Italian) and mother (German) had been taking place since they had met in Berlin during the war, and there was no doubt, at home, about one thing: All cultures are equally interesting and include elements that are neither good nor bad in absolute terms, but that you may personally like or dislike. In order to like or dislike something, however, you must try to get to know it; this is no sacrifice, but a very interesting activity. The language of the place you move to (or any other language) is the main key to discovery and communication, and to a certain amount of practical relativism.

After returning from South America, the family settled in Rome again for two years, as was customary in the foreign service. Italian was now the family language, and contacts with relatives, friends, and shopkeepers enlarged the number of speakers around us. Again, a *tata* contributed to my language learning. She made pasta at home, and with my help she violently and repeatedly flung the dough on the marble table until it had the required elasticity. While she prepared pasta or cooked *baccalà*, salted fish that had been soaking for three days, we talked. I stayed at home, since a one-day visit to a kindergarten in the neighborhood apparently was not attractive enough for me to insist on going there, and my mother did not insist either. So I played by myself at home or with acquaintances in the Villa Glori, a beautiful park where my mother took me every day. By the time I was fluent in Italian, the next move was announced to us: Liège, in the French-speaking region of Belgium. Most of our relatives came to say good-bye to us at the port of Naples, where—again—we embarked on an Italian ship.

"Mademoiselle, la lettre "m" a-t-elle deux ou trois pattes?"

My memories of the Belgian period are strongly connected to what I experienced in kindergarten and school. Kindergarten was seen as a necessity. My parents thought it was the best way to get in touch with peers and with native speakers, in order to get ready for school. What I very clearly remember about my first contact with kindergarten is a sense of anxiety. Would I be able to paint the edge of that chestnut leaf with green watercolor just as Mademoiselle wanted me to do—I, who had never held a paintbrush in my hand until the age of five, and who did not understand a word of French? How to tell whether what I was supposed to write was "m" or "n," whether it has two or three "legs"? How to ask Mademoiselle about the correct thing to do, if I could not speak a word of French? How to let her know that I badly needed to go to the toilet? Altogether, this meant lots of emotions so unpleasant that once, going home, my mother holding my hand, I suddenly had wet pants.

Had Mademoiselle been too impatient, had her body language transmitted her negative feelings, was she unaware of the fact that a bilingual child learning her third language at the age of five might need more support and encouragement than blame or punishment? This anxiety has never quite left me. In such cases, I try hard, so hard that I get a stiff neck. I recognize the same physical and mental pang every time I have to face a new major challenge—for example a new job, a separation, or moving to a new city, as I had to do recently for my job in Cologne.

After a couple of months, my family moved from a house in the countryside, a house with a wild garden. There were beautiful, big, deep-blue hydrangeas, and the gardener explained to me how to make them blue: by sticking an iron nail into the ground. We moved to an apartment in town. A little brother had joined us by then. I attended a new kindergarten, which was around the corner. I remember a spacious classroom with a very large group of children and a teacher who managed to keep us completely still and concentrated, painting tiny dwarfs made of clay, then practicing how to brush our teeth. Whether this silent, soldierlike discipline was a reality or is merely an idealized picture in my memory, supported by later readings about Belgian specialized pedagogy and child psychology, I am not completely sure. What I am sure about is that I tried hard to adapt, and that this cost me lots of energy, and my appetite.

Surely, albeit slowly, my French was beginning to materialize. Once, only once, they took the class to a music room where each of us was assigned an instrument. Since I was a foreigner and my French was still very poor (I suppose this was the reason), I had to play the triangle. But I was content with that; after all, I had found a role in a group and I enjoyed the music we made. This period was very short, because the time came for entering school. Madame M., my teacher in the first grade, seemed to be aware of the challenge: Not only did I understand and speak very little French, but I had to learn how to read and write and count and draw and socialize . . . all at one time and in a country that was entirely new to me. This was the method some people call "sink or swim." One day we had to compose pictures using round stickers of brilliantly colored, shiny paper of different sizes that I found very pleasant to look at and to touch. We were allowed to chose our colors. Delighted by the new game, which meant that school was not just a place where you had to suffer doing very difficult things that seem to be far beyond your range, I decided to compose something in royal blue and pale pink. Madame said, "How beautiful, you are using the shades of Italian Renaissance painters!" I felt understood and appreciated, although I obviously had no idea about "Renaissance" or Raffaello, whose colors I now find so fascinating. Madame M. coached me through this hard apprenticeship, and the progress was as fast as it was satisfying for both of us. I was fluent in French after a few months, though Italian continued to be the family language.

During that period, which lasted three years, my grandmother came from Berlin two or three times to stay with us and to help look after my baby brother. She slept in my room, so how to communicate? In German, of course! Following the recipes she knew by heart, she baked wonderfully big, rich, yellow cakes. Luxurious chocolate was added if she decided it had to be a marble cake. I was allowed to "clean" the bowl that had been used to mix the batter, and regularly had a bittersweet stomachache. But that was part of the game. Every morning at eleven, my grandmother had her second breakfast: dark rye bread with cottage cheese and apricot jam, a combination that I rediscovered many years later as my favorite breakfast. My kitchen and household German vocabulary owes very much to that happy time with my grandmother, who also came to see us years later in Rome. Through our conversations about cakes, knitting (she taught me that, too), and fairy tales, she gave me a playful and loving opportunity to add a fourth language to the three I had already assimilated.

Once the language problem was mastered—once French was the key that allowed me to discover friends, what school had to offer me, and all the pleasant sides of daily life—Belgium presented itself to me as a place of extraordinary gastronomic wonders. I had regained my appetite. But I also began to realize that the world was made of more than chocolate and lobster, *gaufres* (waffles), *moules* (mussels), and *frites* (french fries). In the area of Liège, much of the wealth was built on the profits of coal mines. Most miners were from southern Italy, especially appreciated because they were hardworking and of small stature. Through my father's job, I learned that hundreds of thousands of people did not change countries under privileged circumstances, but to escape misery, often risking their lives. That was the first perception of work migration, a subject that was to become central to my professional life some twenty years later. I realized that people lived under very different material conditions, depending upon where life's circumstances had placed them.

Spanish Grammar and Boiled Potatos

Our own migration took a new direction. From Europe, we headed for Latin America again, this time by plane. The destination was Bogotá, Colombia. From the language and culture point of view, this was to be a challenge of a special kind. One of the bilingual schools was chosen for me (my brother was still too young for school). Because French was by then like a native language for me, it was a school with a French-Spanish curriculum. The learning process was now quite short (Spanish could install itself on four other languages), but lots of hard work was involved all the same. A Spanish teacher, an elderly lady with doll-like fair hair, gave me private lessons every other day early in the afternoon. Her method was as old-fashioned as it was effective. She taught me Spanish grammar, dictating the rules in a very systematic order. Each time she estimated that a paragraph was finished, she said: "Renglón de por medio"

(Skip a line). Then came the next subject. There was a simple and precise structure in her archaic procedures. The verbs and rules had to be learned by heart, and the beginning of each lesson was dedicated to checking if I had done so. No communication-based or theme-centered language learning, no indulgence of bad spelling. Just total immersion based on the grammar rules. There was no explanation in French, since this teacher spoke only Spanish. It worked, and I worked with pleasure thanks to her friendly and firm ways.

On the other two days, I got private math classes from a French teacher, whom I found very elegant in her Parisian (or so I thought) New Look skirts and stiletto shoes. She used to boast about how smart and precocious young students were in France, suggesting that of course it was not the case where we were, at the cultural periphery. I listened to her every word as if it were the absolute truth. Her job was to give me a crash course in order to help me catch up with what I had missed by changing school systems and by skipping one year due to the different schedule. This worked, too.

I had a lunch break alone in the school yard, where I ate a picnic brought from home: usually boiled potatoes with salt (still one of my favorite dishes), some fruit, and milk. That time alone was spent eating, playing with grass and stones (no games were available), meditating, and studying the lessons for the next day when necessary. Lots of learning by heart was involved. I suppose this is where I learned to be on my own without missing anything or anybody: I had to fill the time as best I could; the only resource was myself, and it never occurred to me to rebel against that imposition. That was life.

The curriculum of that school was equitably distributed between the French and Colombian Spanish, and distinct syllabi were used. The history classes told us, in French, about "nos ancêtres les Gaulois," (our ancestors the Gauls), and in Spanish, about the pre–Columbian civilizations and the independence wars of the different countries, under the leadership of Simón Bolívar. The pre–Columbian peoples were presented to us as what they were: highly elaborate civilizations that had been destroyed by the Spanish conquerors, and then restored. In my forties, I happened to revisit this very subject—in more general terms, the encounter with the "other"—thanks to a book by the French sociologist and historian Tzvetan Todorov (1982), an analysis based on authentic chronicles, some of them painted hieroglyphs by the indios, in which the author depicts the encounter between the Aztec civilization and the Spanish destroyers. As I now see, the bilingual school in Bogotá, by assembling those pieces into a curriculum, proposed a "double original perspective" just as it is proposed today by educators who criticize ethnocentric views of culture in school programs.

While my Spanish got more and more fluent, I asked my father to teach me some basic rules of spelling and grammar in Italian. This informal learning was natural and playful. Never did I hear a word at home about how hard it might be to learn several languages. The playfulness of our multilingual life was supported by our listening to the latest Italian songs on the hit parade (sometimes it was opera) and reading the lyrics, which we soon knew by heart and sang.

Focusing on Italian Culture

The Colombia period was over after only twenty-two months, and the next destination was Peru. Here, a bilingual school was found for both of us (my brother was then old enough to attend school). The classes were taught in Spanish for some subjects and in Italian for others. My knowledge of the Spanish language became more articulated, and I was proud of learning so much about the local culture. Italian, which had been spoken only at home until then (but my brother and I spoke Spanish together), now became a more complex instrument of communication, oral and written. At the same time, the school introduced English and Latin classes into the curriculum. But even more important than the language development was the fact that aspects of Italian culture became more and more distinct to me. I knew Italian food as very good among many other tasty foods that I had eaten and appreciated. Then, as a teenager, I discovered Italian fashion, which everybody considered as the *ne plus ultra* of glamour. The history and geography of the country in which I was born, but which was a foreign country to me, became more and more concrete. I wished I could go back to Rome very soon, to see and touch all the things I knew from books and records (television was not as developed and global as it is today). I wished I could swim in the lukewarm Mediterranean, which I imagined to be as smooth as a lagoon of turquoise-blue transparent oil, after I had enjoyed some very wild and exciting swimming in the gray, ice-cold, house-high waves of the Pacific near Lima.

The Designated Center of a Multicultural Life

After three years in Lima, we kids were told that in three month we would leave for Rome. Never did I look forward so strongly to going to a place. I kept counting the days and figuring out what I would do. At last I would be able to enjoy all the things and places that peopled my imagination. At last I could integrate that piece of my identity. As a thirteen-year-old, I knew enough to perceive the psychological side of it all, although I lacked the appropriate concepts and vocabulary. But the joy of that Roman perspective, of meeting the center of my multicultural life, was mixed with sorrow you are not allowed to feel, very much as described by Pollock and Van Reken (1999: 167 ff.). I had formed a few very deep friendships with girls of my age. One of them I told just the day before I was to leave. I had not been able to tell her before, so deep was the grief about that departure. My classmates organized a very sympathetic *despedida* (farewell) party for me. Our family's journey back "home" included a short stop in New York, during which my brother and I got two transistor radios. That was the ultimate technological gadget in 1962. We kept listening night and day for months, and we were thrilled with the "strange" radio stations you could catch with those tiny radios.

Our arrival in Rome was akin to Christmas or Easter. Some of our relatives came from Naples to welcome us. There was a big family gathering at my grandfather's house. All the aunts, uncles, and cousins were there, which for me was the very symbol of my being "at home." I was happy, curious about discovering how my relatives lived, yet aware of the differences between us. My way of speaking Italian was correct. I had attended a good school, and the language was well spoken at home. But I did not have any regional nuances in my speech, and the juvenile jargon of the time was totally unknown to me, because my friends had been South Americans or second-generation Italians with whom I spoke Spanish. My relatives, among whom were four aunts who were teachers and school principals, admired the number of languages I was able to speak and read and write, but every now and then they gently made me notice that I was not a "real" Italian, and that Latin was more important than modern languages anyway. My Latin was poor indeed. In a way, I felt foreign "at home."

While this feeling was only faint and absolutely bearable during my contacts with my extended family, it became a problem during my first contacts with young people in the neighborhood where we lived in Rome. It was also difficult to place me in an Italian state school, because I had not reached the required level in Latin. Latin and Greek were considered to be far more important than modern languages, just as my four aunts had told me. Hours and hours of private lessons instead of a lunch break would have been necessary to catch up. What I had to offer was not required by the school system. Another solution was found: a private "international" school, in which the curriculum placed much emphasis on modern languages, in my case German and English, with Italian as a main language. This proved later to be a sensible decision. Psychologically speaking, this choice helped me to strengthen my positive feelings about being a multilingual person with a cultural identity composed of experiences in several settings. However, during my whole teenage years and for several years afterward, cultural identity was an important issue, and it required hard work to develop emotional stability about it. I remember telling a dear friend, who was to become my husband: "I always feel like I'm sitting between two chairs." I was twenty or so.

"Spaghetti" Meets the Barbarians

The first sixteen years of my life were determined by Latin ways of life and languages with a sprinkling of German culture and language. My mother had devoted herself to a complete adaptation to Italian and then Latin American customs, while keeping alive values and traditions like being punctual and effective and celebrating Christmas the German way.

After this, a new era began, in which the dominant surrounding was German, but the Latin element did not disappear. The new era began when my parents moved us to Bonn, Germany. The impact was preceded by tearful good-byes. We had been in Rome, the best of places in spite of all intercultural relativism, for three years. We kids did not want to leave, yet we had to. What followed was an adaptation to a new life in which the language had to be studied more thoroughly, the weather was mostly cold, and the communication with people less easy than in Italy or South America, not only for language reasons, but also due to cultural differences. As I entered my classroom in my new school (a German state high school that claimed to be more "international" than others), the school principal presented me, the new Italian classmate, in a Roman outfit yet not a tunic, rather a dainty, British winter coat in the fashion of the sixties, and a voice from the back of the classroom hissed at me: "Spaghetti!" Teenagers are so charming when it comes to accepting someone who looks and speaks differently.

Now, from the ages of fifteen and a half to eighteen, problems of adaptation were more complex than they had been before. They were a mixture of seeking my identity as a girl and a woman, learning to express myself in a language I knew quite well from the grammar point of view but had not yet mastered, adapting to the weather, fitting into a culture that I perceived in many respects to be opposite to the one I had experienced in Rome and Naples, and before that, in South America. Cold weather and snow (which I had hardly seen before) kept me permanently chilled, and it was not easy for me to feel comfortable in the vaguely military unisex topcoats called parkas that were in fashion among youngsters at that time in Germany. I wore such clothing in order to be somewhat less different in my appearance, but I did not feel "myself." Youngsters did not then dress the same way all over the world, so if you changed countries, adaptation was needed.

I perceived the German character as rigid, sometimes too precise (for example, when you lent someone ten pfennig, less than a dime, you were assured that you would be repaid very soon), and also rough if not rude, free from all that decorative embellishment you find in Latin communication and cultures. Altogether, a shocking contrast to my increasingly idealized memory of the Roman soul, which I liked to remember as always joking, ironic, generous, tolerant, capable of enjoying all the pleasant things life has to offer, encouraged by the wonderful climate in which even the rain has a different, sensuous smell. When it rains in Rome in October, there is a smell of pine in the air. Never before had I seen such opposition between my "home" culture and the new culture I found myself in. This is particularly strange because the German culture was not unknown to me: my mother and grandmother had shown me some elements of it.

Most of my friends in Germany were "third culture kids" like me: India, the Philippines, Turkey, and Spain were their countries of origin. It was easy to make friends with people who were facing the same kind of problems (i.e., coping with a different climate, food, school system, ways of spending leisure time, and of making friends). Again, as during every other change I had gone through, I had to cope with stress. I survived, thanks to good friends and, again, to a couple of intelligent and compassionate teachers. They neutralized the mass of school professionals who seemed barely able to tolerate foreign students as an inevitable nuisance. Why had these kids with poor German skills and an uncertain school past (if any) not stayed home? It was obvious to those diligent pedagogues that all other school systems were inferior to the German one; did other countries have any schools at all? I eventually had to learn Latin, which turned out to be very enjoyable. My multilingual skills helped me greatly at that stage.

After three years of hard work, I was done. I passed my school-leaving examinations, the German *Abitur*. My school time was completed. I could look back on seven school changes, seven language acquisition processes, and numerous experiences of being exposed to cultural patterns that first astonished me but to which I always developed a close relationship, so close that they became part of me. I had to come to terms with different ways of transmitting knowledge in the education system, roughly speaking the Latin way and the German way, the former more deductive and the latter more inductive, each of them presenting positive and negative sides. Those naive comparisons were to shape my understanding of research on education in later years. Comparative education became my approach in the profession I am immersed in now.

Migration and Political Awareness

The next cultural shock came soon after my school time was over. My father was appointed to Basel, Switzerland, and there was no way for me to stay in Germany, as I would have preferred. My sweetheart (or so I thought he was) was a good reason for me to stay, and so was my longing to remain in the same education and cultural system, attending the University of Bonn, but family circumstances were not favorable for my personal autonomy. So I followed my parents, as did my brother, both of us less than willingly.

Basel is in the German part of Switzerland and borders Germany and France. One might think that moving only 480 kilometers south along the Rhine would be a change so small that it is not worth mentioning. This was not the case. First of all, there was the impact of a language we had not even suspected to exist until then: the Swiss-German dialect, which is used as a vernacular language in all spoken interaction. It took months for me to be able to understand what people were saying. My use of German (a language I spoke like a native speaker by then) often provoked impatient or even aggressive reactions. This had to do with the tense relationship the German-speaking Swiss have with Germans. Moreover, since the end of the 1960s, certain political parties in Switzerland have repeatedly tried to convince the voting population to drastically reduce the percentage of foreigners in the country. They have regularly missed their target, but foreigners have had a hard time with xenophobia and racism. In addition, foreigners have been expected and urged to assimilate, to completely give up their culture of origin. Integration was the alternative concept proposed by many foreigners and by political groups that saw foreigners (most of whom were immigrants) as valuable contributors to the Swiss economy. In this view, a foreigner was expected to adapt, and he or she was to be given the opportunity to participate in the structures of society while being allowed to keep strong links to the culture of origin. It is clear that the integration option was the only one I could accept.

My university years in Basel were essential for my integration into Swiss society. They opened my mind to social and economic problems, which had been mostly concealed during my life in a privileged milieu. And, most important, the subjects I chose to study were exactly what I needed to stabilize and to develop my compound cultural identity: the German, Italian, and English languages and literatures. Spending three months with families in the United States was an enriching way to learn a new culture and to practice a language I knew only from college and from living two months with Irish families as a teenager. Surfing between those worlds was like continuing, on another scale and using more sophisticated tools, what I had been doing for the first nineteen years of my life.

A MULTICULTURAL PROFESSION AND LIFESTYLE

Toward the end of my studies, in 1972, the dominant issue in my mind, nearly an obsession, had two sides: How could I achieve a cultural identity without feeling like some kind of patchwork or undefined person? How could I use my multilingual competencies in a society and a labor market that obviously were not ready to appreciate them? My studies had helped to amalgamate my different cultural and linguistic selves, but the journey was not complete. One central problem remained unsolved: What could I do with that beautiful theoretical knowledge I had acquired, and that appeared to me as an adornment for cultivated conversations (which I did not disdain) that was of no practical use whatsoever? What role could I play in life? That was a deep crisis in which anger and a sense of powerlessness worried me so much that I saw a psychologist for two months. It helped: She saw the point, enhanced my skills and potential, and that gave me oxygen to let me go on.

The practical solution to my aim-in-life problem came thanks to my friendship with a fellow student who was the son of Italian immigrants. Through his life experience and some research he was doing, he showed me the problems of migrants, often functional illiterates, facing the task of surviving in a complicated language situation. The Swiss-German dialect was the generally spoken language, standard German was written, the immigrants spoke their own dialect, and their countries' authorities spoke and wrote their standard language. After studying these problems, giving German classes to adult Italian migrants, and publishing some papers and a book with my friend (a handbook designed to teach Italian immigrants the German language), then teaching migrant children for some time, I discovered my first real profession: organizing education and training for adult migrants in order to facilitate their integration. It was a way of putting into practice what I had learned from books about linguistics and what I had learned in practice about intercultural communication.

That work experience allowed me to find a place in society while doing something socially useful, as opposed to the kind of life I had observed in the foreign service. I felt that kind of life in privileged settings contained too many futilities, forcing people to live too many superficial relationships, and it had little meaningful content. This was the perception I had as a daughter, knowing too little about the real content of my father's job. I wanted to be a person with distinctly different aims in life compared to my parents. I wanted to invest my skills, especially my language skills, in a relevant project that not only would bring me personal satisfaction but also would contribute to a better life for other people. Moreover—and this is probably the deeper reason why I slipped into it—that work experience as an adult education manager was an appropriate arena where I could fight all my battles about cultural identity, about juggling social classes, about the affirmation of minority languages in a country that has four national languages and is officially multilingual but profoundly parochial in many sectors of daily life (which resulted in the militant use of Swiss-German dialects), about integration in a society where the migration issue was and is paramount, about feminine emancipation in a country that gave women the right to vote only in 1972. In a few words, it was the central period for sorting out the person I wanted to be.

At the same time, my parents moved to El Salvador for their last post before they finally retired to Rome. Just after we got married, my husband and I traveled to El Salvador, Guatemala, and Mexico, which was a way for me to revisit and expand my Latin American experience. I then felt the freedom and the burden to reinvent myself while staying in the same city where I lived for six years with my family of origin.

From Practice to Theory to Practice

The "social" period, defined by my commitment to migrant education and more generally to migration issues, lasted fifteen years. But my research interests had only temporarily been put to sleep. They gradually emerged again and became a support to my further educational projects. Several papers and a second book, the latter about migrant women in Switzerland, were published. After a period of self-directed studying and publishing that formed a sort of transition from practice to theory, I embarked on (or, rather, was pushed onto) the path of an academic career. My own experiences with language and culture transition; the comparisons between education systems related to those passages; my work as a teacher of migrant children and then as a manager of adult education; my anger about the migration and refugee policies, and the integration and citizenship un-policies in the country that was first my host country and then the country of which I became a citizen by marriage; the frustration about the "lack of purpose" of some types of ivory tower research—all these blended to shape my second profession, the one I have been practicing since 1990.

In my work as a professor and researcher, it is my aim to show my students (many of them will become teachers) some of the many facets of transitions between languages and cultures in education. Theoretical concepts and research results are blended with personal experiences. The former make the latter plausible, and vice versa. The comparison among all the teachers I came across (some of whom were understanding and supportive, while others merely reacted to what they felt was a bothersome extra workload) shows how powerful teachers are in motivating or demotivating students. Schools—not only private international schools but also state schools—are attended by more and more "third culture kids," many of whom cannot count on materially and educationally rich family backgrounds. Reasonable teachers are necessary in any case. If, additionally, they are sensitive to intercultural, multilingual, and international issues, it will help the students and themselves.

In my personal life, the theme of linguistic variety and cultural transition, as well as intercultural communication, is pervasive. In spite of all language transitions, subtractions, and additions, or perhaps as a necessary complement, Italian has remained a main pillar in family interaction. My son and I (his father died when our child was less than three years old) made Italian our language, while German and French are what we speak with most of the people surrounding us. French has become one of our daily languages since I began a "privileged friendship" with a man from the French-speaking part of Switzerland. By working one year in Geneva, I enlarged and deepened my contacts in French Switzerland. This arrangement is most enjoyable and enriching, and no disadvantage whatsoever has appeared in my son's language or social development or in his school achievement. Probably encouraged by his parents', his grandparents', and his uncle's liking for languages and traveling, he has developed strong interests in the discovery of cultures, but he changed the geographical direction: it is Eastern Europe that has caught his mind.

THE OCEAN, THE STREETCAR, AND THE HOUSE

A recurrent memory and two recurrent dreams contain the essence of my multilingual and multicultural experience and the coping strategies involved. The memory concerns a terrifying and delightful day swimming at a beach near Lima. I was about thirteen, and the family was spending the Sunday at the seaside with friends. One of these friends, who was in the Belgian foreign service, and I were the only ones who decided to swim in that ice-cold water (caused by the Humboldt Current, I was told in school) and to defy the nearly irresistible force (the *resaca*) that dragged you away from the shore before you even grasped what was happening. We were soon underwater most of the time, with very little control over our movements, not knowing the difference between top and bottom, prisoners of the powerful whirls and waves thickened by plankton and inhabited by an impressive collection of fauna: jellyfish, flying fish, and some dolphins. For a time that seemed interminably long, we could not reach the shore, but we eventually did after a very strenuous struggle. Exhausted, we walked out of the waves that resolved themselves in thick, cream-shaded foam, and we were very happy to be able to breathe the crab-smelling wind instead of swallowing liters (or so it seemed) of very salty and bitter water. My parents and his wife scolded us for that most imprudent adventure. Actually, the wife was especially angry at me, the naughty teenager, guilty in her eyes of the crazy idea of going into the water and of pushing her husband, a grown man, into that perilous enterprise. Since then, many times, in critical situations, those images came, and still come, to my mind. They mean that no matter how turbulent the waters, I will finally emerge.

Every time I am in some agitation due to my mobile lifestyle, which is almost permanently the case, I have the following dream: I am taking a trip in a bus or streetcar, sometimes a train or a plane, and the route is very complicated. I have to change, and I don't know when or where, so I may end up in some strange, unexpected village (in Central America?), often after a tortuous ride on muddy or stony roads. Or I hold several purses with currencies from different countries, and have a hard time choosing the right money to pay for my ticket. Once, I was standing, lost, at a crossroad. It was my husband as a young man who helped me to sort out the appropriate currency. Or I miss the plane I am supposed to catch, because I can't find my way to the check-in area. Sometimes, the vehicle "tells me the direction." Recently, a yellow streetcar, very much like those in Lisbon (were they yellow in Rio de Janeiro, too?), bore the destination sign "Wettstein." This is the name of the neighborhood where I live when I am in Basel. This is the main "home," the place where I most enjoy being, where I feel totally relaxed.

In the third recurrent image, the main feature is an apartment or a house. Sometimes it is completely deserted, perhaps with a long balcony of gray cement, not a flower or any other decoration to make it more comfortable or aesthetically pleasing. Sometimes the house has a garden with bright green grass and many multicolored flowers that seem to live without much initiative on my part; or there may be a veranda full of luxuriant plants that need water. In between, there is a range of intermediate versions: more or less sunlight, flowers or not, nice furniture or a camplike improvisation. Needless to say, the comfortable scenarios reflect a serene state of mind, one that implies "I have found my place, I am in the right place, my place has a very pleasant atmosphere." In other words, "I am on the whole satisfied with my inner life." The house dream in the well-furnished version has become increasingly frequent during the past years.

At this point, the following question might be discussed: When a person has grown up in so many different places and, after becoming an adult, has continued to expand her references, so that her past is multilingual and multicultural, and her present is polycentric culturally, linguistically, and geographically, then, what is "home"?

One possible answer is the one the yellow streetcar suggested: the place where one most enjoys being. Or the place one misses most when away from it, because it is related to the people who most matter to you, because of the whole atmosphere, the sense of *gemütlichkeit* it gives to you. But what if you have several places where you feel comfortable to a great extent, because you are fluent in the language, you quite understand the culture, and you have important relationships with people that mean a great deal to you? In that case, one might say that "home" is any place where you feel at ease, where you don't feel like a "stranger," and where you want or like to return regularly. This can be more than a single place. At least for a multilingual and multicultural person, "home" is not necessarily, and/or not only, the place of birth or the place of the parents' origin. It may be the place of birth, plus the place you have lived in for the longest time, plus (maybe) the place in which you find some kind of fulfillment, be it professionally or emotionally. If life circumstances gave you the opportunity to feel at ease in several countries and cultures and their languages, you carry something of those places and forms of expression in yourself. Your own way of seeing things, of shaping your life, is then influenced by the different cultural processes you underwent.

This observation leads to the next question: Can a person have a compound cultural identity? During a seminar I organized in the 1990s at the University of Bern for teachers and other professionals interested in migration issues, I had the pleasure of discussing with a psychiatrist (an orthodox one as she turned out to be) the question of identity. I asserted that, for example, in a migration context it is possible to have a compound identity. A bilingual child can *feel*, and therefore *be*, Turkish and Swiss, if she or he "identifies" with both the culture of the parents and the culture of the country or region in which she or he has been raised. This "double" identity can very well be a normal (i.e., not pathological) state. If there is a disorder, I said, then it might most probably be the result of the behaviors of monolingual and monocultural persons (especially persons in authority, like teachers or school psychologists) who, out of lack of experience and knowledge in that field, could not understand the normality of a double, or even multiple, cultural reference system, and therefore stigmatize a bilingual and bicultural child. The psychiatrist firmly rejected this view, arguing that the very word "identity" implied the notion of "unity," as the Latin etymology unmistakably proved. As a medical doctor, she was adamant about her monopoly on judgments regarding who is normal and sane and who is not, so that the argument was very short. And, of course, both parties remained firm in their position, much to the irritation of the participants who had come to hear about "solutions."

Years later, I found this same discussion in a book on multiple identities in the era of the Internet (Turkle 1995). For the author, an MIT psychology researcher with a psychoanalytic approach, the exclusive views on identity are a legacy of the Freud-based, still dominant theory of identity as a unity. But even within psychoanalysis, there are theories that explain identity as something composed of several elements. In a postmodern philosophical view, as Shirley Turkle writes, and in a world where more and more people grow up and live with various cultural references—even more so after the expansion of the Internet—it is meaningless to stick to the monistic concept of identity. Identity can be multiple, it can be plural. Such a compound identity should not be confused with the pathology of fragmented personalities. While Turkle develops her arguments mainly by reflecting on people's virtual experiments with multiple identities in the Internet, I would apply the same view of the identity issue to the situation of people exposed to more than one culture in "real life." There is no reason why a person who participates in two or more cultures and their languages should be (considered as) a pathological case. If particular problems do manifest themselves, one should bear in mind that people with a monocultural identity also can have all sorts of problems or even pathologies. The real question is how the environment interacts with a personality that has a polyphonic identity (i.e., one with several voices and with a compound voice). And how does the polyphonic individual interact with his or her environment, especially with monocultural people?

How Fragments Become Facets

Going back to the multicultural life experience I am recollecting here, there is a great potential for conflict in the way people with polyphonic identities live their lives. First of all, the process of becoming a "positively thinking" person who enjoys her or his multiple identity can be a tortuous one. Becoming an adult and at the same time sorting out one's life view and lifestyle, while changing contexts several times, requires hard physical and mental work. This is made fascinatingly clear in Elias Canetti's novel *The Tongue Set Free* (1977), in which he describes his efforts to learn German (incidentally the language that made him earn the Nobel Prize) essentially to please his mother while enduring the mental cruelties inflicted on him by an obtuse teacher. The multilayered search for an identity as an individual, as a member of a social group, and as a linguistic-cultural person can be psychologically exhausting, and it can contain several sources of disorientation. The manufacturing of the final product—the adult with a personal, a social, and a cultural identity—may take longer than under monolingual and monocultural circumstances, as has been described in recent literature on "third culture kids."

Second, even when you have become a person with a polyphonic identity and do not feel awkward about this anymore, there is still the continuous task of communicating with a society composed of individuals, many of whom are monocultural and very often ethnocentric. When I registered in Cologne, my latest new "home," I had a hard time convincing the city hall authorities that there was nothing illegal about having two passports (Italian and Swiss) in which the data were slightly different. In the Italian passport, the place of birth is relevant, and only the maiden name is mentioned. In the Swiss passport, what counts is the place of "origin" (and this can even be twofold), which in my case means the places of origin of my late husband and of his father, who in his turn inherited the places of origin from *his* father, and so on. This custom originated some generations ago when people were less mobile. Also, the Swiss passport contains the maiden name and the name acquired by marriage; you can decide in which sequence you wish them to be printed, but then you are supposed to stick to that version. The Swiss passport is written in four languages (German, French, Italian, and English), while the Italian passport bears the most relevant entries in the twelve languages of the European Union, including German, so it was readable. I had two different names, my place of birth and of origin were not the same, my passports were multilingual. What the hell was happening? Some new type of crime? What drugs was I trying to smuggle into Cologne?

This situation was utterly puzzling for the young woman in the city hall, so she eventually stood up behind her desk and yelled at me: "If I were you, I would have denounced the Swiss government a long time ago for those mistakes in your passport! Put some order in your personal situation! We are in Germany here, and we have to act according to the German law! I'll check with the Italian consulate if what you are telling me is the truth!" And, after a short break that allowed her to recover her breath, and twenty decibels louder: "You have two identities!" Like an earthquake, my bizarre and contradictory documents had shaken her most fundamental beliefs about what identity *is* and what it *ought to be*. Since I remained calm (although I was boiling inside), she calmed down and realized that there was no mistake whatsoever: There simply were different views and different laws in different countries. This is an extreme example of bureaucracy, and fortunately, such incidents are rare.

But then there is the wider field of social relationships. The following is a reality that can be observed: The dominant attitude in people is inspired by the belief that each person has *one* cultural origin, and that people with two or more cultures of references *lack* unity. Persons with multiple references have a hard time developing the inner strength that will enable them to act naturally about their being "different" from others, and to persuade others that they are not so different from everybody else, but simply (although it is not so simple) have a special way of looking at life: with a multiplicity of facets and perspectives.

The repeated exposure to diverse languages and cultures may also affect multicultural persons in their communicative behavior, both verbal and non-verbal. No matter what language one is speaking, even fluently or like a native, the other languages may have left their mark on one's pronunciation. It may happen that a person with particularly sharp ears, like Shaw's Professor Higgins, detects a trace of a Latin American accent in my Italian speech a few seconds after meeting me, and without knowing anything about my past. Once, after a presentation I made in English at an international conference on educational research, an Australian colleague from Hong Kong came up to me, smiled, and said: "Your way of speaking and moving has something French." He did not seem irritated at all; it was just a observation. I told him that, indeed, I had attended French-speaking primary schools for five years. One may enjoy making cross-cultural language jokes that are not transparent to persons who do not share the same vocabulary and the experience that is behind and inside it. One's body language may include disparate elements, so that one may appear hard to classify: not typically Italian or German. It is precisely this multiplicity of layers, perspectives, and signs (in the semiotic sense) that can make one appear strange to other people, until one learns to deal with it in social interactions.

What makes a person successful in finding her or his way, converging several linguistic and cultural paths into a multicultural highway? From a subjective point of view (shaped by my professional and private experience), I would name the following factors:

- Parents with a positive, accepting attitude toward languages and cultures, who naturally live by the relativist principle that everything is interesting and worth knowing
- Teachers who are informed about, and trained to react positively to, the issues of migration and mobility, whether dealing with socially privileged or deprived conditions of bilingualism, cultural difference, intercultural communication, and the consequences of these issues for classroom work
- Institutions (school is definitely the most important one) that encourage acceptance and integration of "foreign" people (Allemann-Ghionda 1999)
- Friends
- A personal curiosity and commitment to affirm one's own view of things, using all the tools and resources that one has been able to discover and to incorporate.

It greatly helps if, among these tools, you cultivate some hobby or passion, some means of self-expression in which the verbal aspect of communication is not foremost, and which is, therefore, transcultural: dancing, painting, playing an instrument, sport. Perhaps it takes a touch of stubbornness, in the sense of that eloquent expression in German, "jemandem die Stirn bieten," literally "to present one's forehead to someone," in order to find in you, and to defend, the person you have become under multilingual and multicultural circumstances, and the person you *like* to be.

REFERENCES

Allemann-Ghionda, C. (1999). *Schule, Bildung und Pluralität: Sechs Fallstudien im europäischen Vergleich*. Bern: Peter Lang.

Canetti, Elias (1977, 1999). *Die gerettete Zunge*. Munich: Hanser. Translated as *The Tongue Set Free: Remembrance of a European Childhood*. New York: Farrar, Straus and Giroux.

Pollock, D.C., and R.E. Van Reken (1999). *The Third Culture Kid Experience: Growing Up Among Worlds*. Yarmouth, ME: Intercultural Press.

Todorov, T. (1982). *La conquête de l'Amérique: La Question de l'autre*. Paris: Seuil.

Turkle, S. (1995). *Life on the Screen*. New York: Simon and Schuster.

16

Linguistic Hegemony
Is There a Superior Language?

Tracey Tokuhama-Espinosa

Is there such a thing as a "superior" language? One could use various criteria and get different answers: Is one language more dominant today in commercial and diplomatic ventures than any other? Is any one language more beautiful than another? Is any one language richer in vocabulary and expression than the others? Is any one language more dominant in terms of literary wealth? Is one language older, and therefore more established, than any other? Is any one language more intricate in its writing system than others? Is any one language more logically based than another? Or, similarly, we could ask, Does the sheer number of native speakers make a language superior? Does ease of learning make any one language superior to another? If a language's "popular" version is very close to its "correct" usage, does that make it superior? Is a dynamic language superior or inferior to a static, standardized language?

If answering the superiority question seems initially daunting, how about approaching the question from the opposite angle? Is there such a thing as an inferior language? A "barbarous tongue"? "No language . . . has been shown to be more accurate, logical or capable of expression than another," writes J.R. Edwards in Grillo (1989: 73). And "A basic premise of modern linguistics is . . . that all languages are equal." Just as anthropologists refuse to judge the relative worth of cultures, so linguists believe that one language is as good and adequate as any other (Trudgill 1992).

While this may seem generous on the part of linguists, the fact of the matter is that subordinate languages are "despised" languages (Grillo 1989: 174), though this must be viewed in historical context. In the sixteenth century, the Italians described the French language as "barbarous," whereas modern-day Italians would probably find such a statement politically incorrect. Confining ourselves to the general discussion of language and perceived superiority, with-

out going into the details of the written versus the spoken language, we move
to the realm of the individual speaker.

ON A WORLD SCALE

When geography, political borders, religious ethnicity and language all coincide, there
is generally very little conflict over language policy, and the minority groups whose
political aspirations and language practices differ from the monolingual majority often
find very little room to make a claim for pluralism. When, however, categories such as
geography, ethnicity and religion cut across language and literacy, the potential for
controversy and even conflict multiply. (Halemariam, Kroon, and Walters 1999: 475)

   Language policy and the use of language as a political tool to wield power
over minority groups is well documented. The above statement was made about
the situation in Eritrea, and the use of native languages in the school was
considered "a victory" in South Africa that "made headlines in academic circles," (Kamwangamalu 1998). Robert Early's "Double Trouble, and Three Is a
Crowd: Languages in Education and Official Languages in Vanuatu" (1999)
shows that the question of language policy is ever on the minds of those search-
ing for the correct balance of power within their nations.
   While these examples may seem far from home, statistics about the American language situation are also interesting. An article in the *Houston Chronicle*
states that one in five school-age children in the United States has a foreign-
born parent (23 March 2001); the statistic is similar for Germany, where just
over 20 percent of all children have a parent with a different nationality (1998
census). Such figures indicate that if there is not yet a strong language policy
in these countries, there may soon be one. While always proud of being a
multicultural nation, consciously or accidentally, the United States is fast becoming a multilingual nation. Americans and Germans will soon have to choose
between espousing a nationalistic view of languages and proclaiming a single
language policy, or embracing the multilingualism encroaching on their mono-
linguistic states.
   Ironically, whereas America is becoming multilingual more quickly than
policy is being developed, Japan has a different problem: English is overwhelming the system. Recently former Primer Minister Obuchi Keizo recommended
that Japan consider adopting English as a second official language sometime in
the near future (Asia Week.com 2000). His proposal sparked a debate in which
many Japanese stated that Japan must boost its "global literacy," meaning its
ability to share information and ideas in the world, by using English. Opponents say this would accelerate the decline of Japanese in the world even further. Technological dominance exists as well: 90 percent of Internet hosts are
in English-speaking countries today (Henderson 2001). Given the boom in
technology, "no language has ever been so widely taught, read, or spoken as
English is today" (Henderson 2001).

WHAT ARE THE MOST WIDELY SPOKEN LANGUAGES IN THE WORLD?

The sheer number of speakers can add to the argument about "dominant languages." What language is most spoken in the world? Two languages reached approximately 1 billion speakers by the end of the twentieth century. *Puntongha* (literally "commonly understood language," in Chinese), which we know as Mandarin Chinese, is the official language of the most populous nation on earth. English is its counterpart, now the most widely used and studied language of the world (Linguasphere Page 2000). English has a tolerance that other languages lack, adding new words at a faster rate than any other, which is perhaps the reason it is so widely used today. David Graddol of The English Company UK spoke of a "fusion between English and other languages" (Wallraff 2000) because English incorporates borrowed words from other languages easily, and creates nouns and adjectives to suit itself.

The Linguasphere Page categorizes language groups according to the number of speakers. The next group of languages includes pairs which are mutually intelligible when spoken and which total over half a billion speakers. Among these are Hindi-Urdu and Spanish-Portuguese. Three additional languages, Russian, Bengali, and Arabic, have more than 200 million speakers each. "Megalanguages" have more than 100 million speakers. These include Japanese, Malay, Indonesian, German, and French (French is the official language of more nation-states than any other language, apart from English).

Why is English the popular second language for so many people? Many argue that due to political, military, and economic strength, monolingual Americans (and their British, Australian, and to some extent Canadian counterparts) have "forced" English into its present role. "The general pattern of language use follows geopolitics: national language + English in Western Europe. English has the de facto status of language of contact . . . English is given a superior status" (Treanor 2000). Geoffrey Nunberg wrote, "In 1898, when Otto von Bismarck was an old man, a journalist asked him what he took to be the decisive factor in modern history. He answered, 'The fact that the North Americans speak English.' In retrospect, he was spot on the mark about the political and economic developments of the twentieth century" (Nunberg 2000).

What happens in the political area has a direct impact on the individual. While reasoning behind language policy choices may be influenced by religion, colonialism, and education, language as it relates to identity issues is on a very personal level.

ON AN INDIVIDUAL SCALE

"Language and Identity . . . emphasizes the inherent emotional and spiritual connection between a person and his/her natural language (or in some cases the language of his/her immediate ancestors)," writes John Myhill (1999: 34–35). There must be a balance between using a language that is practical (as English is viewed today) and preserving national identity. The French are some of the most concerned with this last question. "To combat the creep of English, a commission on terminology regularly turns out alternatives to the English computer and business terms like 'startup,' 'think tank,' 'World Wide Web,' and even 'CD-ROM.' The government is obliged to use these new terms, many of them clunky even to the French ear. Everyone else is free to be amused. The suggested terms rarely catch on" (Daley 2001: A1). Eckart Wetheback is a conservative German politician sponsoring a "language purification bill" which would impose fines on those caught using Anglicisms in the language (Daley 2001).

Social attitudes toward language are the key influencing factors in any relationship between class and educational failure, writes Trudgill (1975). Problems such as insecurity in the new language, how the child feels his native or home language is perceived by the teacher, and the perceived sociolinguistic barriers that are created by the general school atmosphere have an influence on a child's success in a foreign language, or different accent or dialect language environment. No one would blame the child for the subculture he or she comes from before attending school, but few efforts have been made to raise children to the school standards without labeling them "deficient." Children who come from countries with lower socioeconomic standards are labeled, and often separated from "normal" children when they initially come to a new country as immigrants or refugees. This has a huge impact on children's self-perceptions.

Self-perception plays a key role in determining language hegemony. It was found in a Swiss study that immigrants who had a low self-image believed their own language was inferior to French, and subsequently learned French in school much quicker than those with a high self-image. Cristina Allemann-Ghionda, Claire de Goumoëns, and Christiane Perregaux found that immigrants from unpopular countries (Kosovo, the former Yugoslavia, Albania) learned French quickly and shed their old national identities with the new language skills (1999). Conversely, Americans and British who are fiercely proud of English were very slow to learn French.

Professor Yukio Tsuda of the Graduate School of International Development in Nagoya, Japan, discussed the question of self-perception in great detail (1996). In his paper he acknowledges that "English is the de facto international language of international communication today, but it is also evident that the dominance of English today causes not only linguistic and communicative inequality but also the feelings of anxiety and insecurity especially on the part of the non-English-speaking people in a rapidly globalizing world in which English dominates extensively" (1996: 1). Tsuda points to the work of Ngugi (1981), who believes that linguistic domination leads to mental control. This type of linguistic colonization can be resolved, says Tsuda, through a new linguistic paradigm where cultural pluralism will be secured. Tsuda is not alone in his view of English dominance; the Russian director of an Internet service provider described the Web as "the ultimate act of intellectual colonialism" (quoted in Nunberg 2000). At its core, this paradigm assumes that language is culture, and a source of personal identity.

How, then, is language introduced and cultivated by society? And where are the gaps in this process with children whose linguistic levels do not reach those required by the school system? Fundamental differences between the common language that is spoken, and the "standard" or "correct" language that is written in the schools, exists in all cultures. And this is deepened through compulsory language education from the primary level to advanced secondary education, not to mention the differences in countries where compulsory education is erratic at best.

The British, notes Grillo in his book *Dominant Languages*, are obsessed with "class" and the belief that "we signal class by grammar, vocabulary and perhaps above all accent" (1989: 151). The Dutch, Grillo relates, believe there are only two ways of speaking, based on regions and not on class, and they are employed depending on the situation. The French, since the Revolution, seem not so concerned about regional differences as they are with the status of the national language compared with other languages or dialects in France and abroad. The Americans approach English on an egalitarian scale, but are obsessed with issues of language and ethnicity, according to Grillo (1989: 152).

PRESTIGE LANGUAGES

Such separation spills over into the realm of linguistics. Diglossia is said to exist where there are two varieties of language with distinct functions—a prestige (high) form used in formal setting and in writing, and a nonprestige (low) form used in everyday information communications. An example can be seen in Switzerland, where German is the prestige form of language (what is taught in the schools) and Swiss-German is the colloquial version (what is spoken with your friends). This is similar to Haiti, where French is the prestige form and Haitian Creole is the language of the people. In Greece *katharevusa* is the formal language, and *dhimotiki* is the informal language. Different activities utilize either the prestige or the nonprestige form. The prestige language is used for religious services, personal letters, university lectures, news broadcasts, editorials, news stories, poetry and literature, and speech in government settings. The lower forms are used when speaking to servants, family conversations, tutorial discussion, soap operas, political cartoon captions, and folk literature (Centre for Linguistics 1998).

CHANGING TIMES

Non-English speakers are the fastest growing group of new Internet users, and it is assumed that "Internet traffic in languages other than English will outstrip English language traffic within the next few years (Henderson 2001). Whereas in 1998, 85 percent of the Web pages on the Internet were in English, in 1999 this figure dropped to 72 percent. It is sure to continue this decline.

Even though English appears to be ahead in the polls, the world trend is toward multilingualism. In a recent European Union survey, 70 percent of those questioned agreed that "everyone should speak English," but nearly as many said that his or her own national language "needed to be protected" (Daley 2001). What does this imply? Learn English *and* preserve the home language. The Britons are the last of the monolinguals in Europe; everyone else has adopted at least one other language and recognizes all of the official European tongues.

But how to increase multilingualism (and move away from English dominance if that is, indeed, what is desired)? Treanor makes several useful suggestions within the European context: multilingualism should be a condition of access to tertiary education; product information should be available in a maximum number of languages; all research funded by the EU should result in multilingual publications; newspapers and magazines should be multilingual; no person should be refused a job simply because he or she doesn't speak English; and no person competent in four European languages should be refused employment on the grounds of language, even if those languages are Polish, Russian, German, and French, not all of which carry the "prestige" tag of approval.

CONCLUSIONS

It appears that English has won the popularity contest, at least for the moment. Perhaps it is not the most beautiful language, but it is spoken by more people than any other language in the world. Perhaps it is not the most prestigious, but it is the most practical. Perhaps it is not the language of the greatest literary wealth (though Shakespeare, Faulkner, and Whitman fans would argue otherwise), but it is the one used most in diplomacy and economics. Perhaps English is not the oldest language, but it is one of the most flexible in terms of adopting words from other sources. And English is not the most logical language linguistically, but more people choose to learn it as a second language than any other. On balance, English is the language of choice, at least for this generation.

How can English avoid the negative description of "intellectual colonialism," and not threaten minority languages? Perhaps by adopting some of Tsuda's criteria, English speakers can learn to balance the enjoyable status as the dominant language and still show a responsibility toward multiculturalism. By respecting a general human rights perspective, equality in communication, multilingualism, maintenance of languages and cultures, protection of national sovereignties, and the promotion of foreign language education, English speakers can show a healthy respect for other languages, even as they retain their seat at the helm.

REFERENCES

Allemann-Ghionda, C., C. Goumoëns, and C. Perregaux (1999). *Pluralité et culturelle dans la formation des enseignants.* Programme National de Recherche 33. Bern: Presses Universitaires de Fribourg, 1999.

AsiaWeek.com magazine editorial (2000). "English 'Imperialism': The Japanese Have More to Gain Than Lose by Learning the Language." *Asia Week* 26, no. 13 (7 April 2000). www.asiaweek.com.asiaweek/magazine/2000/0407/ed.english .html.

Baker, C. (1992). *Attitudes and Language.* Clevedon, UK: Multilingual Matters.

Bruner, J. (1996). *The Culture of Education.* Cambridge, MA: Harvard University Press.

Centre for Linguistics, University of Western Australia (1998). "Diglossia and Multilingualism." Language, Brain and Culture, Linguistics 102, Index to L-102 notes. October.

Clavet, L.-J. (ed.) (1987). *La Guerre des langues.* Paris: Payot.

Daley, Suzanne (2001). "In Europe, Some Fear National Languages Are Endangered." *New York Times*, 16 April, A1.

Early, R. (1999). "Double Trouble, and Three Is a Crowd: Languages in Education and Official Languages in Vanuatu." *Journal of Multilingual and Multicultural Development* 20, no. 1: 13–33.

Geller, E. (1994). *Encounters with Nationalism.* Oxford and Cambridge, MA: Blackwell.

Goetschy, H., and A.-L. Sanguin (1995). *Langues régionales et relations transfrontalières en Europe.* Paris: L'Harmattan.

Grillo, R.D. (1989). *Dominant Languages: Language and Hierarchy in Britain and France.* Cambridge: Cambridge University Press.

Halemariam, C., S. Kroon, and J. Walters (1999). "Multilingualism and Nation Building: Language and Education in Eritrea." *Journal of Multilingual and Multicultural Development* 20, no. 6.

Henderson, A. (2001). "Has Internet Spelt the End of the English Language?" 9 April. www.smh.com.au/news/0104/09/features/features2.html.

Kamwangamalu, N.K. (ed.) (1998). *Aspects of Multilingualism in Post-Apartheid South Africa.* Berlin: Mouton de Gruyter.

Linguasphere (2000). "What Languages Are Most Spoken in the World." 25 February. www.linguasphere.org/language.html.

Myhill, J. (1999). "Identity, Territoriality and Minority Language Survival." *Journal of Multilingualism and Multicultural Development* 20, no. 1: 34–50.

Ngugi, T. (1981). *Decolonizing the Mind: The Politics of Language in African Culture.* London: James Carey.

Nunberg, G. (2000). "Will the Internet Always Speak English." *The American Prospect* 11, no. 10. Available: www.prospect.org/vii/10/nunberg-g.html.

Osborn, T.A. (2000). *Critical Reflection and the Foreign Language Classroom.* Westport, CT: Bergin & Garvey.

Treanor, P. (2000). *Making Europe Multilingual.* Hanover: Verlag Heinz Heise, 24 November. www.heise.de/tp/english/inhalt/te/1155/1.html.

Trudgill, P. (1975). *Accent, Dialect and the School*. London: Open University.

Trudgill, P. (1992). "Sociolingustics." In T. McArthur (Ed.), *The Oxford Companion to the English language*. Oxford: Oxford University Press.

Tsuda, Y. (1994). "The Diffusion of English: Its Impact on Culture and Communication." *Keio Communication Review* 16: 48–61.

Tsuda, Y. (1996). *Shinryaku-suru Eigo, Hangeki-suru Nihongo* (The Invading English, the Counterattacking Japanese). Tokyo: PHP.

Wallraff, Barbara (2000). "What Global Language?" *The Atlantic Monthly*, November. Available: www.theatlantic.com/issues/2000/11/wallraff.htm.

Watts, R.J., and J.J. Smolicz (eds.) (1997). *Cultural Democracy and Ethnic Pluralism: Multicultural and Multilingual Policies in Education*. New York and Frankfurt: Peter Lang.

Wodak, R. (ed.) (1989). *Language, Power and Ideology: Studies in Political Discourse*. Amsterdam: John Benjamin's Publishing Co.

17

Foreign Adoption and Bilingualism

Nicola Küpelikilinç

Is a child born in India who is adopted by a German couple at the age of seven months bilingual, or can he become bilingual? Or what about a Bolivian child who does not come to Germany until she is adopted at the age of seven? What is the actual "mother tongue" of these children? The adoptive parents are often under the impression that their children have no relationship to the language of their country of origin. Is this impression correct, or is the first language still slumbering in a hidden place? Is it important for adopted children to maintain ties to their first language? These are some of the questions I will address in this essay.

On the one hand, there has been a great deal of research on language and bilingualism in early childhood, but on the other hand, the situation of adopted children who lose touch with their first language to a great degree is rarely discussed in the literature on bilingualism. This essay seeks to marry the two areas of research in a more complete view of foreign adoption. The first section addresses general issues of bilingualism as applied to adoptive children, who have to adapt to a new language within the course of adoption; the second section is addressed directly to (prospective) adoptive parents, and offers practical advice concerning the child's language development.

Before I address the meaning of language in early childhood development, a question arises: What should this language of early childhood be called? In most of the literature it is simply called the "native language" or "mother tongue," but the definition of a native language is not as simple as it appears. Polyglots are often asked what their native language is, but for many it is difficult to answer this question because they feel at home in more than one language. Is a *mother* tongue qualitatively different from a *father* tongue or a *grandparent* tongue or a *nanny* tongue? What if the mother spoke different languages with the child? Can someone have two native languages, or can the native language change during the course of one's lifetime? Due to this problem of definition, and since the term "mother tongue" can be associated with the biological as well as the adoptive mother in the case of adopted children, I have decided to use the term *first language* here in order to make it clear that the earliest childhood experiences with language are meant.

PSYCHOLOGICAL RELEVANCE OF THE FIRST LANGUAGE

When asked about the beginning of language development, many people will say that it starts around the first birthday. Lately, however, scientific research has increasingly focused on what a child can learn before birth. For example, newborns will react to music that was played to them frequently during the pregnancy (see chapter 9). Further tests have shown that four-day-old newborns can distinguish their mother's language from others: it is primarily the melody and intonation of the speech that is important, because they are perceived by the infant through the abdominal wall during pregnancy. At the age of six months, infants can still differentiate all sounds, even if they do not exist in their mother tongue. In the months thereafter, the child will be mostly interested in sound combinations that exist in his first language, and at the age of ten months, can distinguish only the sounds of the first language (but not those which are irrelevant for that language). When children begin to "babble," they still produce all sounds, independent of the language of their environment; but at the age of six months they primarily use the sounds of the language of their surroundings, and from their first birthday on, they produce many "nonsensical words" that clearly follow the rules of the first language with regard to intonation and sounds. Thus, it is obvious that the child has gained much experience with the language of his or her surroundings within the first year of life.

The first language that we learn is the one in which the formation of concepts takes place. Within the framework of concept formation, the young child must determine, for example, what characteristics an object must have so that one can call it "table." The formation of concepts includes sensory perception, intellectual processing, and linguistic formulation of experiences. This process is a productive, and not merely a reproductive, act, as one can recognize when children use words of the adult language in their own way and create new words. When acquiring a second language, this process is not necessary to the same extent: if one hears that a table is called *Tisch*, one assumes that *Tisch* has the same characteristics as "table." That means that words in the first language are more closely tied to one's sensory experiences. If the first language is lost, access to the roots of one's own language development is also lost.

The language is shared by parents (or other caregivers), and is a very individual and private matter. Even those who are not bilingual can comprehend the psychological importance of key words from childhood. Language differs, for example, even within monolingual arenas. Greetings in Germany can range from *Guten Tag* to *Grüß Gott* and the northern German *Moin* used at any time of the day. If a native of Munich is addressed with *Grüß Gott* in Hamburg, this will lead to psychological reactions that can vary from a positive "we" feeling to deep dislike because someone wants to deny his origin. Whether the reaction is positive or negative, the person so greeted will not be indifferent. The same applies to the names of objects used in daily life, from *Brötchen* (roll) to *Hähnchen* (roast chicken), and days of the week or festivals like *Fasching* (which is also known as *Karneval*). Language is also used to demonstrate that one belongs to a certain group, a delineation that is particularly important to youths. Among Turkish teenagers in Germany, one can currently observe a special Turkish-German language developing in order to emphasize their independent cultural identity. Concepts from childhood often trigger feelings of security and familiarity. If this effect is already created in one language area, how much greater the effect must be when one is totally cut off from one's childhood and family language, when hardly anyone in the environment speaks this language. In *Out of Egypt: A Memoir*, André Aciman describes how his two grandmothers, Jews who had emigrated from Istanbul to Alexandria, got to know each other through their common language (Ladino):

To the two who had discovered one another, Ladino spoke of their homesickness for Constantinople. To them, it was the language of loosened ties, unbuttoned shirts, and overused slippers, a language as intimate, as natural, and as necessary as the smell of one's sheets, of one's cupboards, of one's cooking. They returned to it after speaking French with the gratified relief of left-handed people who, once in private, are no longer forced to do things with their right. (1996: 45)

As a rule, different languages have different functions for bilinguals. A truly emotional statement is often easier to make in one of the two languages. A Finn who had been living in Sweden for many years, working as an interpreter, reported that when he hurts himself, he can curse in Swedish twenty times and still not feel better, but if he curses once in Finnish, he feels relief. The same man said that he could easily say the words "I love you" in Swedish, but in Finnish, he could express them only in very intimate situations. A German woman who was living in England and spoke English fluently, called the doctor in panic because her infant was having a febrile seizure. Afterward, the doctor told her that she had spoken only German on the telephone, a fact of which she was not aware. There are many such anecdotes demonstrating that particularly in emotionally charged situations, one language or the other is extremely important, and often this is the language of early childhood.

If one changes languages, not only the words but also gestures and facial expressions, intonation and posture, change. It is often possible to tell from afar, without hearing any words, what language bilingual acquaintances are currently speaking. Bilinguals report that their behavior changes with the language. For example, very direct demands can be made in German in a manner that one would not dare employ in Turkish, Arabic, or English. A certain culture is tied to a certain style of communication, and thus influences the language. Even one and the same language can be influenced differently by different cultures, as is the case with American and British English.

SOCIAL RELEVANCE OF THE FIRST LANGUAGE

Language is the carrier of societal knowledge. Fairy tales, stories, and songs provide access to the collective knowledge of a society. If language skills do not develop appropriately with age, it is difficult to find one's way in social relationships. There have been studies in the United States of third- and fourth-generation immigrants who demonstrate a heightened interest in their ethnic origin and describe how this search is made more difficult because they do not know the language used in their place of origin. In the case of adopted children, the questions "Who am I?" and "Where do I belong?" are very important issues in the development of identity. For children who were born abroad and have little contact with persons from their culture of origin, these questions are even more complex.

Tove Skutnabb-Kangas, one of the leading researchers on the topic of bilingualism, and the product of a bilingual upbringing, draws a comparison to a water lily: When we hear a child speak, we see only what lies above the water's surface, the water lily itself. But the roots of the language and their associated semantic complexes lie below the water's surface. When a child learns a second language, he or she quickly acquires the everyday language and good pronunciation, so that the new water lily blooms on the water's surface just the same, but for a long time the water lily remains a language without roots, swimming on the water's surface (Skutnabb-Kangas 1981).

BILINGUALISM AND ADOPTED CHILDREN OF FOREIGN EXTRACTION

I would like to address two central points: settling in the new family and the process of acquiring the new family language, and monolingualism or bilingualism as a part of the adopted child's identity.

Language and Settling In

With regard to settling in, we must never forget how much strength is required of the child who comes through adoption to Germany to settle into a new family. In addition to the demands made on the child in a monocultural adoption, a foreign adoption is a long journey to an unknown world. In light of the often very poor conditions under which many children live prior to adoption, the new world lies beyond the realm of the child's imagination. Add a different climate, different eating habits, different furnishings in the home, and a different language. As the previous discussion clearly shows, language is important to the infant who does not yet speak a word of the first or second language. The first language that surrounded him or her as familiar background music has disappeared, and even the manner of nonverbal communication has changed. Anyone who has traveled to a foreign country alone, having only rudimentary skills in the language spoken there, knows the feeling: "One more word, and my head will burst." Children who can talk already are put in a severe state of uncertainty when every object, every expression of feeling, every animal, and every request suddenly has a different name. From the egocentric viewpoint of a child up to the age of six or seven years, his or her language is the only correct one. Not until children are older and can understand the concept of a country where a foreign language is spoken, can they at least partially prepare themselves for the change. To understand the dimensions of this change, let us consider the situation of children in Germany who start kindergarten or school without knowing German. Although these children return to their familiar language environment after only a few hours, most of them initially react with uncertainty and withdrawal, even if they acquire the community language very quickly after a settling-in phase. Adopted children usually do not have the opportunity to return to their first language in the evening, and many of these children have already had difficult experiences, so that a move to a foreign country is a further uncertainty added to the weak sense of trust in their surroundings.

What can be done to make the transition easier on the children? First, it is important to determine, as closely as possible, what languages the child previously heard or spoke on a regular basis. It is estimated that India, for example, has 200 to 700 different languages from four unrelated language families. But one frequently hears people refer to the "Indian" language. Many Latin American countries have an official language (usually Spanish or Portuguese) as well as many different native languages. It is generally necessary, in the case of a foreign adoption, to learn as much as possible about the family and heritage of the child at the time of the adoption, because it can be very difficult to obtain this information later on. Which language(s) did the parents and/or caregivers speak with the child, and until what age? How much can the child speak at the time of adoption, and in what languages?

A good tip is to take a cassette recorder and blank cassettes when you journey to meet your new child. Use the opportunity to record the caregivers talking to the children, to record children playing together and people chatting. Perhaps there is an opportunity to record people singing songs or telling stories. Perhaps your child is prepared to say a few words for the cassette recorder. The child may refuse to listen to these cassettes, but don't be disappointed. Your child will need time to discover what role his languages play in different circumstances. The chances are that these recordings will help to build the bridge back to the culture of origin when your child is ready for this journey.

Further, it is important to maintain at least small bits of the first language. This includes, most of all, the child's name, since adoptive parents often want to give the child a new name. This is an understandable desire, but one's own name forms a particular cornerstone for answering the question "Who am I?" Perhaps it would be possible to learn a few words in the first language, such as names of objects that the child brings along, or words used frequently by the persons to whom the child related previously. The idea is not that these words are necessary for daily communication, but that the child can bring something from his previous life, and thus can make his own contribution to the family language.

However, it is important not to inundate the child with your good ideas for promoting both the first and the new language. When learning the new family language, it is essential to give the child time. Watch your child carefully, and observe when he or she is curious about the new language, and when he or she is cautious. Language should be linked to actions, especially everyday actions such as getting dressed or having a meal. Linguistic rituals such as rhymes to begin a meal, a special nursery rhyme that is sung on the way to the shops, or a bedtime lullaby offer the child a sense of security and orientation. In difficult situations it is important to reduce the amount of verbal communication and rely more on nonverbal communication through body language and tone of voice. If you observe that the child is confused, remove the child from the situation and avoid too many people trying to help at the same time. It is vital to try to maintain visual and physical contact at all times.

Factors Affecting Language Development after Adoption

Age at Adoption

Children up to the age of two to two and a half years tend to regard language as a private code between themselves and their caregivers. Children who are bilingual from birth do not yet distinguish between two separate language systems. If a child of this age changes language owing to adoption, it normally only takes a short time for the child to start producing the first utterances in the new language, often embedded within the first language. With older children up to the age of about six, the situation is somewhat different. These children find it confusing that their caregivers do not understand their language and are not sure how to react. Only after the age of about five or six does a child have the metalinguistic abilities to understand that different people in different countries speak different languages, and that it is not a matter of somebody not wanting to understand.

The strategies employed by children are very individual, and linked to personality and previous experiences. Some children remain silent for a long time, then begin talking quite suddenly and in complete sentences. Others are eager to fit in, and will adopt the linguistic models presented by the adoptive parents faithfully and literally. Some are eager to avoid making a mistake and prefer to wait until they are quite sure that a particular reaction (verbal or otherwise) is correct.

Language Development Before Adoption

As mentioned above, many of the children adopted from another country grow up under very poor conditions, which often means developmental delay owing to general health problems and malnutrition or to a lack of personal contact and sensory and verbal stimulation (for example, in orphanages). Generally speaking, language is a very sensitive area of development, and language delay is often the consequence of general developmental problems. Furthermore, language development can be disturbed by emotional trauma caused by abuse, separation from trusted caregivers, or other events. A common reaction to trauma is the refusal to speak (general or partial mutism).

It is advisable to try to collect information about the child's level of language development at the time of adoption. Obviously a detailed report by a speech therapist is absolutely unrealistic, but even a little information is useful. As a rough guide, children generally produce their first words around their first birthday, combine two words to form short sentences around their second birthday, and speak fairly fluently, although not in grammatically correct form, around their third birthday. It is important to ask caregivers if they can easily understand the child's speech.

Language Delay After Adoption

What can you do if you feel an adoptive child is making little progress in the new language? It is important to abolish two myths. First, language delay is not caused by bilingualism. Both bilingual and monolingual children can show signs of language delay for a multitude of reasons. Second, the fact that your adopted child is learning the new language more slowly than you expected, or than other adopted children, does not mean you are making a mistake. Adopted children are as individual as children who grow up in their families of origin. A major issue is the question of whether the child grew up under emotionally deprived conditions from birth or was able to establish stable bonds in the family of origin before being exposed to deprivation (for example, by the death of the parents). The answer to this question is not always easy to establish and is often a matter of guesswork.

If you are worried, it is important to watch your child carefully to observe how he establishes contact. Does he avoid all contact or only verbal contact? Does he attempt to make himself understood through language? As a rough guide, children who attempt to make themselves understood but have difficulties are more likely to be showing signs of language delay, while children who avoid communication, especially verbal communication, are more likely to be showing signs of emotional disturbance.

It is advisable to gain the advice of a speech therapist or other expert who has experience with multilingual children. Otherwise, there is a great danger of being told the child is bilingual and therefore delayed in speech. However, extensive diagnostic sessions should be avoided within the period of adapting to the new home environment. The only exception is qualified hearing tests to exclude the possibility of speech delay owing to impaired hearing, a common diagnosis among children with a history of health problems.

IDENTITY AND BILINGUALISM

In the first section it was explained how bilingualism can be an important part of one's identity and personal communication structure. Adoptive parents often ask, "Can our child, adopted in another country, grow up bilingual?" There is no general answer to this question, because the answer depends on various conditions. First of all, I would like to emphasize that despite all of the advantages of bilingualism, one cannot force it. It is rarely realistic to expect that adoptive parents will learn their child's first language in order to use it as a family language. Learning the first language does have other advantages, however, such as getting to know the child's heritage better, intensifying contacts with the country of origin through vacations, or showing the child and others that the linguistic and cultural background is valuable. But the family language after the adoption will in most cases be the majority language in the new country. (There can be exceptions where a binational family adopts from one spouse's country of origin or one parent already has good proficiency in the child's first language, through extended stays in that language environment.)

What experiences do you, the adoptive parents, have with language learning? Is it something that fascinates you and that you regard yourselves to be good at? Or does learning another language bring back bad memories of boring school instruction? Do you regret not having grown up with two languages, and do you want to maintain the child's contact with his or her first language at all costs? Take the time to think about situations in which you were the one who didn't understand what was going on, who missed out on the jokes or wondered why everyone was shouting. Perhaps you spent time in another country on a school exchange or as a student.

As adoptive parents it is necessary to reflect on your own attitude toward bilingualism and to consider your motivation for choosing the language strategy used in your family. In Germany and in other overtly monolingual countries there is often an ambivalent feeling toward bilingualism. On the one hand, a person who is seen to switch effortlessly back and forth between languages is admired. On the other hand, this admiration is usually limited to proficiency in a few European languages, while persons who are bilingual in German and Turkish, or German and Urdu, are hardly recognized as bilinguals.

In addition, numerous myths about childhood bilingualism remain in the backs of people's minds, such as "Bilingual children do not learn any language properly" or "Bilingualism fosters a lack of identity." These myths are without any scientific basis, and it is worthwhile to acquire information on the subject to be able to counter such prejudices more effectively. Adoptive parents, like all people who live in bicultural relationships, have to take a good look at what it means to be different, and to reflect on the attitudes toward foreign things that they themselves acquired during their upbringing. Only then will a supportive, affirmative attitude toward bilingualism become a reality.

Adoptive parents often ask whether their child's first language disappears altogether, or if it might return later. There is little definite evidence, but it would seem that at least after the age of about a year and a half to two years, certain traces remain and relearning the language is easier. There are also ample case studies of children who at first have only passive contact with a language but can't or won't speak it, then later begin almost spontaneously to speak the language. It is quite normal for adopted children to go through a phase when they refuse to have any contact with their first language. As explained in the first section, language can be used as an important marker of identity, and at times it may be necessary for an adopted child to emphasize his belonging to the adopted culture, either for reasons of personal security or to demonstrate belonging to the outside world. It is important not to force a language on the child at such times, because such efforts are often counterproductive. Instead, the opportunity to be in contact with the first language should be kept open, combined with the message to the child that he or she can choose to make the most of this opportunity when and how it is right for him or her.

Of course, the age of the child at the time of the adoption plays a crucial role in the question of whether the child will grow up bilingual or not. Independent of that, there are ways to maintain access to the first language, even if this does not necessarily lead to active bilingualism. Contact with people who share the same first language with the child is of prime importance. If one looks at a listing of clubs and associations in urban centers, one will find that almost all nationalities and cultures are represented. In Germany, at festivals and other social events, the child can discover that for some people his first language is nothing exotic, but a part of everyday life. Songs and music can be means of access—try cultural associations for suggestions on how to obtain suitable cassettes. Anyone who has contacts in Great Britain or the United States will find a large selection of child-appropriate materials for the speakers of minority languages who live there. The Internet is another valuable source for books and cassettes in less common languages (see chapter 18). In addition, one can get in contact with other parents of adopted children or binational families with members from the same country. This way, the child will learn that his or her first language is normal, and that competence in it will be recognized and will be appreciated and respected, at least in certain circles. If the adopted child wants to learn about his or her country of origin later, he or she will have an important bridge to do so if the first language is maintained at least on a passive level, and is not torn out by the roots at a young age.

REFERENCES

Aciman, A. (1996). *Out of Egypt: A Memoir*. New York: Harvill Press.
Skutnabb-Kangas, T. (1981). *Bilingualism or Not: The Education of Minorities*. Clevedon, UK: Multilingual Matters.

18

Bringing Up Bilingual Children in Scarce Language Environments
How the Internet Can Help

Maria Johnson

I always knew that I would raise my children to speak both Italian and English, but I never knew what a challenge it would be to accomplish. I was in the United States, the superpower of the world, the economic leader. I should have been able to find anything I was looking for, but there was nothing that would help me teach my future children Italian. Sadly, from where I stood, I was in what I now know to be a "scarce language environment."

I continued hunting for information that might help me find insight as to how I should raise a multilingual child. I went through many parenting books. Occasionally I would come across a paragraph or two about language development and children, but none were very informative and even fewer were supportive of the idea. I was able to find only one book in our local library specifically about raising a child with more than one language. The author was able to travel often, and when not traveling to countries where the language that she was teaching her children was the native language, she would bring in an *au pair*. Neither of these was a reasonable option for me.

When I contacted the local schools to see if they had any advice for me, I found that although the National Standards in Foreign Language Education, issued by the American Council on the Teaching of Foreign Languages, along with the American Association of Teachers of French, the American Association of Teachers of German, and the American Association of Teachers of Spanish and Portuguese, recommended introducing a foreign language in elementary schools (http://www.accesseric.org/resources/ericreview/vol6no1/standard.html), none of the schools in my area had even started planning to add a foreign language, nor did they intend to do so any time soon. They were more concerned about figuring out how to teach English to their nonnative English-speaking students.

Everywhere I turned the attitude was "You are in America, and Americans speak English." People didn't see the value of speaking more than one language, especially if the language was not Spanish. With the influx of Spanish-speaking individuals from Mexico, many people believed that if I felt it necessary to teach my children a second language, then the only one that might have any value was Spanish. But finding quality materials for children even in Spanish seemed nearly impossible.

Not giving up on the concept of teaching my children Italian, I questioned one of my colleagues who traveled quite often. Thinking that he might have taken the time to learn at least some key tourist phrases for one or two of the countries he had traveled to, I asked him if he had any suggestions for me. I was surprised at his response that he had never tried to learn even two words in another language. His feelings were that if he needed to communicate with the locals, they would have to figure out his English, especially if they wanted his business. At this point I was quite discouraged.

THE INTERNET

It seemed that I had nowhere else to turn, so I decided to try the Internet. I was thrilled to see all the material that was out there to help me, much more than I had thought. The Internet had many layers, and each one held numerous and wonderful treasures. These tools would help me achieve my goal of raising my children with both Italian and English, even if the scarce language environment I was living in would not.

The World Wide Web

On the World Wide Web my geography no longer mattered; I found a network overflowing with information. I could travel all over the world by using my browser, keyboard, and mouse. This wonderful piece of technology, originally designed for professors and academics, and later infamous as a military tool, was going to help me obtain what I needed to give the gift of Italian to my children.

Search Engines

The key to being able to pinpoint the information I was looking for amid the millions of dotcoms on the Web was to learn to use a number of search engines and directories. Although search engines and directories have some differences, they are not usually evident to the user, so for the purposes of this essay I will refer to both of them as search engines. Basically, search engines are used to find Web sites about a particular subject. A topic is typed in—a single word, multiple words, or even a phrase—and the search engine hunts through the millions of pages in its index to find matches. Almost instantly, I was presented with a list of sites, ranked on the relevance that the engine had assigned. A search engine's ranking system can be based on several things, from the number of times a word appears on the Web page to how a site was reviewed by one of the search engine's staff. Different search engines produce different results, so it is always a good idea to use a variety of search engines. Some of the larger search engines are Yahoo, Lycos, Altavista, Google, and Mamma. There are even search engines that will search multiple search engines for you at the same time. A few examples of these are Dogpile and Gogettem. The trick to getting the best results while using a search engine is to come up with different terms to submit. I was able to make my search as specific as putting in an author's name and book title, which could lead to a few results, or as general as putting in the word "bilingual" or "parenting," which could give me thousands of results. I also could do searches in different languages, so knowing key terms in my target language was quite helpful. As I learned more about my subject matter, I was able to fine-tune my searches.

The first thing I wanted to do was read what the experts had to say about teaching children more than one language. I was looking for some sort of reading list. I hoped to find a review or two so that I wouldn't pick an author who had been proven wrong. I wanted to know that what I was planning to do was not going to cause problems for my children. My first search was "books on raising bilingual children." With those few words I started my journey. The search engine I was using came up with many matches, one of which really pointed me in the right direction. It was Cindy Kandolf's "The Bilingual Families Web Page" (http://www.nethelp.no/cindy/biling-fam.html). This Web site was great, full of information. The first thing I took from it was the reading list, and contacted our local university, looking for the books mentioned or any books by the authors listed. I read through the books as quickly as I could. I found out I wasn't going to do damage to my future children by teaching them Italian. On the contrary, I was doing them a great service that could help them in different aspects of their lives. The books also helped me build my bilingual parenting vocabulary. I would go on to do many more searches based on the terminology I was learning, and found many other wonderful sites. Before going much further, I thought I would go back to Cindy's site to see what else I could find there.

Mailing Lists

Another great item on "The Bilingual Family Web Page" was the Bilingual Family Mailing List, also known as Biling-fam. This was my connection to other families who were raising their children to speak two or more languages. These families communicated with each other through E-mails. I read through the Frequently Used Terms area on the site so I wouldn't get too lost while following the conversations. I lurked for quite a while, only reading through the numerous E-mails that were distributed, before jumping in. Some of the members were seasoned veterans and were very vocal, while others were less informed than I was. Many of the new members were looking for resources and guidance. No matter the experience level, we were all there because we shared a common interest: language and our children. Other book titles were brought up on the list, and a few authors actually were members. This led to more reading and more knowledge.

E-commerce

All of these books included brief guidelines for a parent raising a multilingual child. Both the members of the list and the books I read suggested that I should purchase music, videos, and, most important, books in Italian. Although the mailing list had mentioned many sites to purchase items in other languages, Italian had never seemed to come up. I went back to the search engines to find places to buy the items I needed.

Now I was off and running, trying to find Web sites that sold Italian items. For books I started in the large online book chains like Amazon and Barnes and Noble. They had items that would be good for teaching Italian as a foreign language, the way kids learn Spanish or French at school, but I was looking for materials that would help me teach it to them as more of a second language. I wanted my children to learn Italian as Italian children do, or at least as close to that as possible. I wanted books that mothers in Italy were reading to their children. I also wanted books that were originally written by Italian authors. I believe that different countries have different ways of thinking about things; there are concepts and ways to express feelings in one language that you don't necessarily find in other languages. I think that the books originally written in Italian would help my children become familiar with those unique concepts and expressions.

I found a few smaller on-line bookstores that had books from Italy, but their prices seemed very high and I wanted to be able to buy more than one book. Most of the books were Disney products that had been translated into Italian, defeating my purpose of finding books by Italian authors. At the time the news was full of tidbits about on-line auctions. E-Bay seemed to be the hottest one around. I decided to take a look and see what I could find. There were a wide variety of foreign language books. A few of them were written in Italian. I bid and I won, but quite a few times, after the shipping and handling costs, I ended up paying more than I intended. And I was not always happy with what I received. I did, however, purchase a series of videos that taught Italian while telling a captivating story. I paid less than half its retail price, and found it worth double its price in learning for my children.

Nowadays, there are even reverse auctions that let buyers list what they are looking for and people who have items that match the requests place bids for the buyer. Overall, I think auctions can be very helpful. The trick, though, is to set a spending limit and not go beyond it. You should also make sure you really want the product and ask the seller any questions you may have before placing a bid. Retracting a bid is not looked upon favorably. The auctions brought me a little closer, but, still not satisfied with what I had found, I continued my search.

A Web site kept coming up in discussions in Biling-Fam and in my searches. This site was www.eleaston.com. The Web master, or organizer, of this site was a member of the mailing list, and she often brought up different resources she had to offer, especially when others asked for materials in the language they were trying to share with their children. At first glance, I thought this site was going to be only geared only toward foreign language teachers rather than parents. I decided to try the link about Italian. After a bit of hunting, I found what I was looking for: an Italian on-line bookstore, www.internetbookshop.it. This was an Italian bookstore that would ship books to other countries.

I immediately found many children's books that I wanted to order. Other bilingual parents had warned me that ordering books from overseas could be very expensive. They indicated that the shipping costs had a tendency to be excessive. Being aware of this, I read all the information on shipping and handling costs and on the currency exchange policy. I determined that it would actually be quite a bit less in comparison to what the U.S. sites were offering, mostly because of the exchange rate. It was quite surprising that the shipping cost included two-day shipping, giving me my product virtually right away, direct from Italy. It is highly recommended that you check the exchange rates before placing orders.

Video purchases are also possible, but the problem with ordering them is that they are in a different television format and DVDs are set to different regions. Here in the United States our televisions and VCRs are in NTSC format and we are region 1 for DVD players, whereas Italy runs on PAL and is in region 2. Although we can purchase VCRs and DVD players on the Internet to take care of these issues, they are very costly. Looking around some more, I found out that American Web sites will sometimes sell PAL Italian videos without necessarily making it clear that is the case. These videos won't work on the NTSC TVs or players, so the only thing to do is pay to have them converted, another costly procedure. As far as the DVD issue, there are many Web sites that go into great detail to explain how to deal with it, but I'll leave it to you to do a search on. I was able to obtain many pieces of Italian children's music in MP3 format and downloaded them off the Web. The most difficult part of finding the music was coming up with titles and artists. After digging, E-mailing people on the list, and even seeing an Italian children's concert on television, I tracked them down. I had the information I needed to order full CDs from the on-line bookstore.

With everything I had found, even without the videos, when my son was born, I felt I was prepared to raise him as a bilingual child. His arrival led me on to the second category of items on the list of musts for raising a multilingual child. It was time for me to start coordinating myself with others in the real world. That meant play groups. I started asking for advice from members of Biling-Fam, and they all agreed that second-language play groups were great. Some of them had formed their own, but most of them were in Europe, where there seems to be more support for multilingual children. One thing I also found was that many were interested in putting them together but didn't know how to find others with the same languages and in their area. Seeing a need, I offered to put together a database. Individuals could E-mail pertinent information, and I would match them with others who had already registered. Thus, the Multilingual Playgroup/Playmate Database was formed. Hundreds of individuals have submitted their names, and matches are made very regularly.

That still didn't help me find individuals in my area who spoke Italian. I tried putting up ads and contacting local universities, but with no luck. I decided to do the next best thing. I formed a play group of multilingual children with a wide variety of languages. At least this way the kids were exposed to other languages and cultures, and realized that speaking more than one language did not make them strange; rather it made them special and able to be a part of this group, Multilingual Munchkins.

Though my son is still too young to participate, I have found sites for international pen pals. Some are handled through Chats, real-time conversations, and others are bulletin boards, where he will be able to post items and wait for responses. All claim to be set up with tight security to protect participating children from predators.

With all of the information I had gathered from my many searches, and now with the database, I thought I would put together my own Web site, www.multilingualmunchkins.com. I thought that it would be easier for parents to find everything they were looking for in one place. It has its own mailing list, and I add items to the site daily. The never-ending process of finding new items to add leads me back to where I started the original quest: the search engines on the World Wide Web.

Now I am trying to help other parents who want to raise their children with more than one language. Not only are my three children benefiting from all the information I have collected among the millions of Web pages I have found through the search engines, but so are the children of hundreds of parents every week. The Internet is helping them, just as it helped me, to make their geographic location less of a "scarce language environment."

19

Multilingualism and Cosmopolitanism

Konrad Gunesch

This essay focuses on the relationship between multilingualism and cosmopolitanism. The research has two aspects: a synthesis of a conceptual framework, and an empirical investigation building on this theoretical conceptualization based on studies conducted with European postgraduate social science students. First, a working definition of multilingualism will be developed and put in the context of functions and virtues of foreign language learning. Second, a matrix of what constitutes a "cosmopolitan person" or what makes a "cosmopolitan cultural identity" will be presented, as synthesized from the relevant literature. For reasons discussed below, both the multilingual and the cosmopolitan aspect will be presented within a Western European geographical and linguistic context.

The definition of "multilingualism" and the matrix of "cosmopolitanism" have both been developed through a conceptual synthesis based on an exhaustive literature review; they did not previously exist in this form. The empirical part of my research—the analysis of which is currently in progress—will find out whether and how this cosmopolitan matrix "fits" a group of multilingual people, expressed in terms of their perceptions about issues of and arising from the matrix.

MULTILINGUALISM AND COSMOPOLITANISM

Multilingualism is investigated from the aspect of how learning multiple foreign languages and mastery of a language shapes the identity of the individual. *Cosmopolitanism* is understood as a form of cultural identity, in contrast to mainly politically oriented concepts, such as cosmopolitan citizenship, cosmopolitan democracy, cosmopolitan law, cosmopolitan intervention, or development aid. (For an overview, see Brennan 2001: 76ff.) Thus while political aspects may form part of the cultural notion of cosmopolitanism, they are not the main focus of this research.

Motivation for the Research

The main reason for investigating "multilingualism" and "cosmopolitanism" together is that on a popular level there appears to be a broad, established relationship between "language(s)" and "world significance" (in the sense of cosmopolitanism) almost as a matter of course. But when it comes to applying "world significance" to "a number of languages" (in the sense of multilingualism), research and scholarship are extremely scarce. That is, a stated relationship between multilingualism and cosmopolitanism is lacking, though its existence in the literature, and to a certain extent in common social understanding, is clearly apparent. This is surprising for several reasons.

- In *fictional literature*, the link between individual "knowledge of many languages" and "world significance" of the main characters has been described in some well-known novels.

- Several rather well-known *aphorisms* hint at the cosmopolitan nature or "world significance" of language as such or of foreign language learning in particular. An example of the former is Wittgenstein's "the limits of my language mean the limits of my world." An example of the latter is the popular saying that "learning a new language is taking on a new world."

- There are accounts of *historic figures* reporting on the "world significance" of their personal multitude of languages. Examples are the Victorian explorer Sir Richard Francis Burton (1821–1890) and the German archaeologist Heinrich Schliemann (1822–1890). Other well-known writers have made plain statements on the value of foreign languages for "worldly experiences"—for instance, Ralph Waldo Emerson: "No man should travel until he [sic] has learned the language of the country he visits" (Crystal 2000: 44).

- On a *popular* and on a scientific level, the general helpfulness of languages has long been recognized, as seen in the examples of Wittgenstein or Emerson, a recognition gaining particular weight in today's global society (Lantolf and Sunderman 2001: 23).

- On a *scientific level*, the relationship of the broader fields within which multilingualism and cosmopolitanism are located—language and culture—has been extensively researched (Wierzbicka 1986: 368), yielding the presumed relationship alluded to earlier.

- And on *a psychological and linguistic level*, the concept that one's world is shaped by the words with which one has to reflect on one's surroundings is embodied in the Sapir-Whorf hypothesis (see Seidl 1998: 102).

A review of the literature reveals only one work that treats the two concepts in the same text (Bruckner 1996). While Bruckner focuses mainly on cosmopolitanism, there are passages that directly link his notion of "cosmopolitanism" with his description of "authors writing in foreign languages."

It is presumed that one of the reasons for this lack of research is the multidisciplinary character of the question at hand, which requires the exploration and synthesis of literature from the fields of education, linguistics, politics, psychology, cultural studies, and anthropology. The dearth of concrete literature in the multilingual-cosmopolitan field is so great that the scientific literature often refers to popular literature to explain its own concepts.

Research Question

Due to the exploratory character of the research, a causal link between multilingualism and cosmopolitanism will not be investigated. In view of this, the question that I focus on can be seen on two different levels. On a general level, relevant to the overall research, the question is: Is there a relationship between multilingualism (as a form of multiple foreign language learning and mastery) and cosmopolitanism (as a form of cultural identity)? And if there is, how can that relationship be described? On a specific level, which connects the conceptual framework and the subsequent empirical research, the question is: How do multilingual individuals, in their perceptions, relate to the categories and issues of the developed conceptual framework of "cosmopolitan cultural identity"?

Focusing on Western Europe and the European Union

I have chosen to focus on Western Europe rather than the whole world in my research for reasons of practicality, a certain comparability of the languages involved, and personal interest. From a geographical viewpoint within Europe, the focus of "multilingualism" is on nation-state languages because it does not seem useful to address regional languages within one or several nation-states; considering all regional languages would be impossible, and any choice would necessarily be arbitrary. Furthermore, without prejudice to the research question, cosmopolitanism is commonly understood as transcending nation-states: The dictionary defines 'cosmopolitan' as "with features of different countries: composed of or containing people from different countries" (*Encarta World English Dictionary* 1999: 427).

The European Union (EU) currently is comprised of fifteen nation-states with eleven official nation-state (Community) languages: German, French, English, Italian, Spanish, Dutch, Portuguese, Greek, Swedish, Danish, and Finnish. According to Crystal (2000: 134), "it is perhaps not surprising to see European support these days for multilingualism, given that the European Union has affirmed the national language principle in its affairs."

The Conceptualization of Multilingualism

Before defining "multilingualism," a summary of the functions and the virtues of foreign language learning can provide the theoretical foundation on which a relationship to cosmopolitan cultural identity may be investigated within the European context.

Language learning as providing different viewpoints and worldviews

According to what is described as "the relativist theory," the acquisition of several foreign languages leads to the adoption of different viewpoints: "Whenever we learn a foreign language and want to understand another culture, it is not enough to come to terms with another lexical or grammatical code. We need to view the world from another perspective. In short . . . speaking another language means adopting another point of view" (Seidl 1998: 102; see also Kellman 2000: 81). A number of writers reiterate this viewpoint aspect in a variety of contexts and mention that language learning leads to the adoption of different worldviews (Buttjes 1991: 8; Edwards 1994: 5).

Language as a cornerstone of one's own culture

The literature on the link between language and culture is vast (Wierzbicka 1986: 368). There are two main tendencies. Some critics endorse an indissoluble relationship between language and culture, arguing that they are synonyms or that the two are hardly distinguishable (Andrews 1998: 106; Strevens 1987: 170–171). Some authors are somewhat more skeptical, but still endorse a decisive relationship—which, however, they do not see as shutting out other possibilities (Crystal 2000: 12, 122; Wierzbicka 1997: 21).

Language learning as a cornerstone of cultural awareness

Many authors comment on the relationship between language learning and cultural learning. According to them, language learning provides a key to other cultures. This "key function" is conceptualized in terms of "access," "understanding," "competence," "insight," "knowledge," and "inseparability and domination with respect to the cultural dimension" (Coleman 1996: 66; Coleman 1998: 45–46; King 2000: 3; Lambert 1993: 317; Seidl 1998: 102).

Some who take a more critical stance maintain that in the context of pupils, language learning as an isolated process does not lead per se to cultural learning, or cultural proficiency and attitude. Hence cultural learning has to be deliberately integrated into language learning (Byram et al. 1994: 5, 39–40; Hinkel 1999: 7). However, one can assume that the cultural learning element is addressed in the case of learners beyond the school age. Hence, in the empirical part with multilingual adult students, I was able to concentrate on cultural learning, with language learning as part of a cosmopolitan cultural identity.

THE VIRTUES OF FOREIGN LANGUAGE LEARNING

As was seen with the three functions of foreign language learning named above (language learning as providing different viewpoints and worldviews, language as a cornerstone of one's own culture, and language learning as a cornerstone of cultural awareness), the literature does not refer to cosmopolitanism. Similarly, within the *virtues*—the perceived general advantages of foreign languages for individuals within the European context—cosmopolitanism is again ignored. Many writers generally endorse foreign language learning within Europe (King 2000: 3; Quist 2000: 138). Others explicitly endorse multilingualism without defining it (Lüdi 1996: 233–234; Werlen 1997: 308–309). Others mention multilingualism in terms of professional and cultural key competencies (Apeltauer 1993: 281; Graddol 1998: 146). Of all these, only Apeltauer provides a definition of multilingualism, which is discussed below.

The Definition of Multilingualism

There are two basic areas that need attention in a definition of multilingualism: the quantity (number) and quality (mastery) of the languages that individuals are required to speak. These two factors are not independent, since the definition of mastery is a prerequisite for counting. Christ uses the image of a continuum: "Si l'on veut parler de degrés de plurilinguisme, il faudra les imaginer comme des continuums, représentés sur une échelle ouverte" (1996: 502), which I translate as "talking about degrees of multilingualism, one should imagine them like continua, represented on an open scale." From a theoretical viewpoint, these two factors will be described separately in order to define multilingualism more precisely.

Quantity

When I was setting up research on multilingualism and cosmopolitanism, I needed to establish robust definitions for these two concepts. The *Framework* of the Council of Europe (1998) offers an argument for demanding more than one foreign language for the concept of multilingualism and nonethnocentrism. The Council maintains that "while the knowledge of one foreign language and culture does not always lead to going beyond what may be ethnocentric in relation to the 'native' language and culture, and may even have the opposite effect (it is not uncommon for the learning of *one* language and contact with *one* foreign culture to reinforce stereotypes and preconceived ideas rather than reduce them), a knowledge of several languages is more likely to achieve this, while at the same time enriching the potential for learning" (1998: 97).

In terms of considering what the term "multilingual" means, one could suggest knowledge of two or more foreign languages. Recent literature on "trilingualism" (meaning mother tongue plus two foreign languages) names this as one form of "multilingualism" (Cenoz, Hufeisen, and Jessner 2001: 1ff.; Cummins 2001: 61; Griessler 2001: 50ff.). The European Commission's *White Paper on Education and Training*, in its fourth General Objective, "Proficiency in Three Community Languages," states, "It is becoming necessary for everyone, irrespective of training and education chosen, to be able to acquire and keep up their ability to communicate in at least two Community languages in addition to their mother tongue" (1996: 47).

To make the research on *multi* linguals as meaningful as possible, I chose individuals who spoke as many languages as possible. To be on the safe side with regard to the toughest literature definition as provided by Apeltauer (1993: 275), I thus opted for three foreign languages as a minimum. These were to be nation-state languages, according to my focus. This brings up the question of how well the persons would have to speak the languages.

Quality

The positions in the literature vary considerably in their required degree of language mastery for "multilinguals." At one end are those who demand almost native mastery. For instance, Quist compares the linguistic requirements of British university language degrees and nonlinguist degrees where the language is applied or combined with other degrees. She maintains: "In all these courses the eventual aim will be to achieve a competence in the foreign language to allow the graduates to engage with the target society at a level of communication which is comparable to some extent to that of an educated native speaker" (2000: 124).

At the other end of this scale are the overwhelming majority, who see this requirement as not necessary. Apeltauer opts for an open definition regarding the competence in each of these: "When does multilingualism begin, and where does it end? . . . For the sake of simplicity I am going to adopt [a] definition [that] presupposes productive abilities in all three languages but does not attempt to define the level of mastery of each of these languages" (1993: 275).

The majority of recent literature makes it clear that "a very important aspect that has emerged from . . . writing about multilingualism is that it is inappropriate to expect near-native speaker competence. . . . Instead it is suggested that a limited mastery in several languages can suffice . . . what is emphasised is a richness of linguistic and cultural understanding" (Morgan 2001: 46; similarly Gnutzmann 1997: 163). Some substantiate this as a "different profile of competences in one language as compared with others" (Council of Europe 1998: 96), and in general "as forming part of a *multiple* competence which it [partial competence in any one language] enriches" (Coste 1997: 91).

In my own research, I set quite rigid standards on quality of multilingualism, again to be on the safe side and to make the study on multilinguals as meaningful as possible. On the one hand, I tried to come as close as possible to Quist's "[comparable] to some extent to that of an educated native speaker" by giving preference to candidates with advanced knowledge levels. On the other hand, bearing the reasonable and realistic arguments of the majority of the literature in mind, working knowledge was regarded as sufficient as well, and elementary knowledge was allowed as long as it did not occur in all languages of a candidate and in not more than two of the four skills (speaking, writing, reading, and listening). To that end, I provided a table defining all these categories more closely within a self-reporting scheme of a questionnaire. This procedure was backed up by literature that dismisses proficiency tests (Naiman et al. 1996: 9), and regards self-reporting as quite reliable among adult students (Coleman 1996: 53; Steel and Alderson 1995: 100), such as those who made up my target group.

The Multilingual Identity

The literature treating the identity of multilingual persons is scarce and unrelated to cosmopolitan cultural identity. The two main sources found to exemplify this are George Steiner (1998) and Susan Bassnett (2000).

George Steiner, who describes himself as a perfectly balanced native trilingual, asks numerous questions about the relationship between the different languages of a multilingual person and the relationship between identity and the language set in *After Babel* (1998: 120–127). The ones that come closest to my research question are: "Does a polyglot mentality operate differently from one that uses a single language or whose other languages have been acquired by subsequent learning?" and "In what language am I, suis-*je*, bin *ich*, when I am inmost? What is the tone of self?" Steiner himself gives vast evidence of his conclusion that "one finds few answers to these questions in the literature."

Bassnett comes to the same conclusion when she quotes some of Steiner's questions, especially his last one: "He [Steiner] raises question after question, culminating in the most profound question of all: In what language am I?" (2000: 66–67). Bassnett then describes her own experience of having learned numerous languages, and compares Steiner's identity perception with her own: "George Steiner asks what is the tone of the self. . . . I have never asked myself that question, because I have always seen the various languages in my head as rather like the skins of an onion: peel them away and you have nothing left. . . . At different times in my life, different languages have been important, sometimes because I spoke them, at other times because I desired to learn them, at still other times because my life led me into contact with them" (Bassnett 2000: 67).

What seems to be crucial in these examples is that there are different perceptions of the multilingual self according to the language learning history and personality of the writer, exemplified by Steiner and Bassnett, who are arguably both exceptionally gifted multilinguals. Second, Steiner's remark that one finds few answers to his questions in the literature directly acknowledges the considerable gap in the literature. This statement then applies all the more to the investigated relationship between multilingualism and cosmopolitan cultural identity. My research proposes to fill this part of the gap.

THE CONCEPTUALIZATION
OF COSMOPOLITANISM

In view of the complex issues involved, cosmopolitan cultural identity can be defined by the catchword phrase "feeling at home in the world," as seen, for instance, in the title of Brennan's 1997 book *Feeling at Home in the World: Cosmopolitanism Now*. Feeling at home in the world can be defined as straddling certain cultural aspects of "the global" and "the local" within the individual in terms of thinking and identity perception. "Straddling" in this sense means combining both aspects by having one foot on each side, the global and the local, and finding a balance in which the global is decisive without necessarily dominating all the time. Thinking and identity perception were taken as verbalized perceptions of an individual's "cultural identity" in the empirical phase of my research.

The Straddling of "the Global" and "the Local"

Part of the literature distinguishes between cosmopolitanism and localism, or between cosmopolitans and locals, with Hannerz's work (1990, 1992, 1996) having a central position in this and several other issues of cosmopolitanism. For Hannerz both the global and the local are part of what he calls "world culture," by which he means not a replication of uniformity but an organization of diversity. This world culture is "created through the increasing interconnectedness of varied local cultures, as well as through the development of cultures without a clear anchorage in any one territory" (1990: 237; 1996: 102). Central to Hannerz's writing is the interdependence between "cosmopolitan globalism" and "localism." Hannerz (1990) suggests that both cosmopolitans and locals "have common interests in the survival of cultural identity" (249–250). They are biased toward different extremes, thereby complementing each other and in the end depending on each other as in an ecosystem, in which the cosmopolitan is interested in the survival of diverse cultural identities.

This exclusive existence of cosmopolitans and locals does not, however, seem to be unanimously shared in the literature, part of which criticizes the opposition between cosmopolitan and local. Rather, such critics see a network of interdependencies and a possibility of constructing one's life in between, or of a "balancing act" between the global and the local (Anderson 1998: 273; Clifford 1992: 108; Friedman 1995: 78).

Cosmopolitan "Competence" or "Mastery"

Taking into account interest in and simulation of local knowledge, Hannerz describes different grades of expertise within a cosmopolitan mind-set:

Cosmopolitanism tends also to be a matter of competence, of both a generalised and a more specialised kind. There is the aspect of a state of readiness, a personal ability to make one's way into other cultures, through listening, looking, intuiting, and reflecting, and there is cultural competence in the stricter sense of the terms, a built-up skill in manoeuvring more or less expertly with a particular system of meanings. In its concern with the Other, cosmopolitanism thus becomes a matter of varieties and levels. Cosmopolitans can be dilettantes as well as connoisseurs, and are often both, at different times. Competence with regard to alien cultures for the cosmopolitan entails a sense of mastery. (1990: 239–240; 1992: 252–253)

Hannerz defines the dilettante as "'one who delights'; someone whose curiosity takes him a bit beyond ordinary knowledge, although in a gentlemanly way [sic] he refrains from becoming a specialist" (1990: 250; 1992: 301). In view of the number and differentiation of alien cultures, this suggests that the cosmopolitan is a connoisseur regarding some of them, and a dilettante regarding probably the great majority of them. One could think of a continuum here, from the state of dilettantism to the state of mastery, so that a development process can also be taken into account.

The Question of Mobility or Travel

Part of the literature seems to put the mobility aspect, especially the travel experience, at center stage (Appadurai and Breckenridge 1998: 5; Brennan 1997: 19; Clifford 1992: 103). However, Hannerz contrasts "simply moving around in the world" with a "metacultural position": "Often the term [cosmopolitan] is used loosely, to describe just about anybody who moves about in the world. But of such people, some would seem more cosmopolitan than others, and others again hardly cosmopolitan at all. A more genuine cosmopolitanism entails a certain metacultural position. There is, first of all, a willingness to engage with the Other." Hannerz (1992: 252; 1996: 102–103) compares cosmopolitans with other groups of people who also can be described as mobile, footloose, or "on the move in the world"—for example, tourists, exiles, expatriates, transnational employees, and labor migrants. He makes clear that mobility alone is no guarantee of cosmopolitanism, but rather the (sole) characteristic of the "typical tourist" (1990: 240; 1992: 247; 1996: 104).

The Relationship Between Cosmopolitanism and Tourism

The literature unanimously excludes the tourist from the "connoisseur" status and from feeling at home in any one place and with the locals (Baumann 1996: 29; Featherstone 1993: 182; Hannerz 1990: 240ff., 1992: 247ff.; Rée 1998: 81; Shore 2000: 229; Theroux 1986: 133). But it does not say whether this applies to all tourists or if there may be different kinds of tourism. After all, it is difficult to imagine that a cosmopolitan cannot be a tourist as well, at least from time to time. Indeed, Appiah says cultural tourism is something "which the cosmopolitan admits to enjoying" (1998: 91). Hence one can conclude that the literature has the image of the "typical tourist" in mind. Appiah's statement indicates that some might see the difference between the cosmopolitan and the tourist as different, or maybe less clear-cut, with shades of gray in between, which offers yet another point for empirical research.

"Home" for the Cosmopolitan

Hannerz explores the classical sense of home, since this can now be located anywhere within or between his spheres of "the local" and "the global." What is evident is that home is not any more, at least not exclusively, the "home culture," because the cosmopolitan person can easily disengage from the culture of origin (1990: 240; 1992: 253). He then presents an open definition of home: One possibility is that cosmopolitans "are never quite home again, in the way real locals can be," since there is no more "taken-for-grantedness." Or "the cosmopolitan makes 'home' as well one of his several sources of personal meaning," or "he is pleased with his ability both to surrender to and master this one as well." Or, last but not least, home could be "a comfortable place of familiar faces, where one's competence is undisputed . . . but where for much the same reason there is some risk of boredom" (1990: 248; 1992: 253–254; 1996: 110).

One could see this last possibility of the "comfortable place of familiar faces" as antithetical to the one mentioned above, where cosmopolitans "are never quite home again like locals." This seems to emphasize that there is a range of possibilities, some of which may well be contradictory. While Hannerz makes it clear that home is no longer exclusively the culture of origin (home culture), in the end the question of where "home" is for the cosmopolitan remains literally wide open.

The Relation between Cosmopolitanism and the Nation-State

A recurring aspect of cosmopolitanism is a critical attitude toward the nation-state. This discussion can be seen as a special aspect of straddling "the global" and "the local," since the nation-state, as it is probably fair to generalize, is usually smaller than "the global" and bigger than "the local."

Models that Dismiss the Existence of Nation-States

Sarup searched for "a new form of world citizenship" (1996: 142) and, with Rée, considered the categories of the nation-state and of internationality to be inadequate for their cosmopolitan models (1998: 88). Nussbaum (1996: 4) explicitly puts forward a model of cosmopolitan identity as "world citizenship," based on the Greek Stoics after Diogenes. "He [Diogenes] meant by this . . . that he refused to be defined by his local origins and local group memberships . . . he insisted on defining himself in terms of more universal aspirations and concerns. The Stoics who followed his lead developed his image of the kosmou politês or world citizen" (1996: 4).

Examples of similar aversions against nation-states can be found in fictional literature, mirrored by scientific literature. Robbins sees Michael Ondaatje's best-selling novel *The English Patient* (1992) as a literary description of cosmopolitanism as "an eroticising of bonds not just across different races within one nation but across different nations" (1999: 164–168). Robbins quotes most of the passages in the novel relating to the main character, Almásy, that contain his clear denial, and even hatred, of any national attachment, and Robbins explicitly characterizes Almásy as "cosmopolitan" (1999: 165). While in the novel the nationality of "the English patient" is not entirely clear until the end, highly interestingly from the viewpoint of this research is the description of Almásy by another character, David Caravaggio, as follows: "He knew all about the desert. He knew all about dialects" (Ondaatje 1992: 163).

Models that Try to Reconcile Cosmopolitanism and the Nation-State

A number of authors comment on what they perceive as an interdependency between the attachment of the cosmopolitan to the nation-state and to larger units of loyalty. Some of them advocate a model of a "rooted cosmopolitanism" (Appiah 1998; Malcomson 1998).

Some American authors have criticized Nussbaum's model of cosmopolitanism as world citizenship. The first argument is that such an exclusive world citizenship would be emotionally too weak in comparison with smaller units of loyalty as expressed in patriotism (McConnell 1996: 81; Pinsky 1996: 89; Putnam 1996: 96). Countering this critique, Nussbaum and others dispute the alleged affective weakness of cosmopolitanism as something that could be invoked against patriotism in the same way (Nussbaum 1996: 17; Robbins 1995: 174ff.). As the second main argument against Nussbaum's model, some criticize what they perceive as a forced exclusive choice between nation-state and cosmopolitan attachments (Gutmann 1996: 71; Putnam 1996: 97; Walzer 1996: 127).

In an attempt to solve this dilemma, several writers put forward a "rooted cosmopolitanism" (Appiah 1998: 91; Malcomson 1998: 234ff.). "The cosmopolitan patriot can entertain the possibility of a world in which everyone is a rooted cosmopolitan, attached to a home of his or her own, with its own cultural particularities, but taking pleasure from the presence of other, different, places that are home to other, different, people. The cosmopolitan also imagines that in such a world not everyone will find it best to stay in a natal patria, so that [there will be] circulation of people among different localities" (Appiah 1998: 91).

In sum, even for the models that try to reconcile cosmopolitanism and the nation-state, the identity forms *beyond* the nation-state are taken for granted. The discussion centers on the desirability of forms of attachment and identity *toward* the nation-state. This suggests that even here cosmopolitanism retains more of its Greek meaning of being a "world citizen" than of being a "country citizen."

Bruckner's Notion of Cosmopolitanism and its Relationship to Foreign Languages

Bruckner's notion of individual cosmopolitanism expressed in his article "The Edge of Babel" (1996) comes closest to my research question. His position is closely linked to the linguistic development of the individual. This is central to the research, since no other position in the literature seems to have tackled the issue in a similar way. Furthermore, his position gives deep value to individual cosmopolitanism within the European context.

One of Bruckner's main points is that cosmopolitanism is a state deliberately and voluntarily chosen by the individual, and it is pursued in an intense and arduous, even painful, process.

In this context, Bruckner describes mainly the cases of the poets Elias Canetti, Vladimir Nabokov, and Agota Kristof, and includes references to the arduous process of their foreign language learning and the use of foreign languages in their works instead of their mother tongue (1996: 247). This establishes exactly the kind of relationship between multilingualism (especially foreign language learning) and the special process of forging a cosmopolitan personality that my research project is investigating. Bruckner appears to be one of the few writers to tackle the link between "foreign languages" and "cosmopolitanism."

Bruckner explicitly links his examples of poets who use foreign languages to the making of a truly cosmopolitan person: "In short, one is not born cosmopolitan, but becomes so in an act of unlimited devotion and respect and by taking on an endless debt to a foreign reality. The elation of playing in several keys, on several keyboards requires the incorporation of another world's structure . . ." (1996: 247–248). The difference of Bruckner's target group from my research sample has to be acknowledged, since he describes a very elitist group of famous authors.

Cosmopolitan Elitism

Elitism is a key element in Bruckner's writing as well: "Cosmopolitanism involves suffering. It is a trial that superior beings choose, finding joy and strength in overcoming habitual limits" (Bruckner 1996: 247). But others also suggest that a cosmopolitan person is always to some extent "outside" or "aloof" from the natives of any culture, and this carries with it notions of superiority and hierarchy (Brennan 1997: 19; Friedman 1995: 78–79; Tomlinson 1999: 185–186). Some see "intellectualism" as one of the most characteristic traits of cosmopolitanism (Cheah 1998: 312; Robbins 1998: 254). However, some are skeptical about the elitist notion due to "the cosmopolitan identification with the larger sphere of the world" (Anderson 1998: 268), and one could see this sphere, for instance, in the societies of the various local cultures in Hannerz's sense. Some hold that there are material explanations for a favorable intellectual disposition of the cosmopolitans, such as access to knowledge, connections, or time, rather than reasons within the character of cosmopolitans (Polan 1996: 282).

What seems to be missing in all this literature is the point of view of the local. If one assumes that cosmopolitans may never completely have "local-equivalent" cultural or linguistic competence, then in relation to any local culture or language the cosmopolitan must be judged inferior.

Cosmopolitan Effort

There may be an aspect of elitism in cosmopolitanism that involves considerable personal effort. The "effort" aspect is mentioned by some as an element of cosmopolitanism (Ferguson 1999: 100), but without Bruckner's "suffering." Yet in Rabindranath Tagore's novel *The Home and the World* (1921), the central figure of Nikhil, which several writers (Nussbaum 1996: 5; Robbins 1999: 161–162) explicitly name as an example of a cosmopolitan, reflects that "suffering there must be" in the context of his "narrow domestic world" (Tagore 1921:85). This notion of suffering comes up again in the context of his distinct aversion to any kind of "bondage"—for instance, in a national sense (Tagore 1921: 208, 309).

SUMMARY OF THE CONCEPTUAL FRAMEWORK

According to the synthesized literature, multilingualism has been characterized in two ways.

- *Quantitatively*: three or more foreign languages, in order to make the research into multilingualism as meaningful as possible and to fulfill even the toughest literature requirements
- *Qualitatively*: a relatively open definition that takes into account varying levels of competence and purposes. Again, to make the research as meaningful as possible, I have substantiated this on the tough side by requiring, if possible, advanced level or at least a good working knowledge in each language.

The following are the main areas of personal concern or engagement for a cosmopolitan person, according to the literature review. Special consideration is given to the points where the literature itself does not present a clear picture, so that empirical research with multilingual persons can shed new light on the existing body of knowledge:

- *A straddling of the "global" and the "local" spheres*, with a decisive impact of the global or "world" citizen (a focus on Western Europe is directed by feasibility). Hannerz's rather black-and-white conception of "cosmopolitan globals" and "locals" is contrasted with literature that takes into account spaces in between, shades of gray, and especially the "balancing act between the global and the local" (Anderson 1998; Clifford 1992; Friedman 1995).

- *A "connaissance" with respect to (local) cultural diversity* wherever possible, otherwise an interested "dilettantism."

- *The mobility to travel,* with a discussion about whether this is sufficient.

- An *attitude* not of the "typical tourist," while the "occasional tourist" accommodates fewer concerns.

- *A notion of "home"* that can be extremely varied; while it is no longer undisputedly the "home culture," it also is not "everywhere."

- *A critical attitude toward one's (own) nation-state,* which can range between "rooted" and "unrooted" identity expressions of cosmopolitanism.

- *A sense of elitism,* which is not an undisputed requirement.

- *A sense of "personal effort"* with respect to the realization of a cosmopolitan cultural identity, which may or may not involve "suffering."

PROJECTION OF THE FINDINGS

The exploration of these and other issues is ongoing within the analysis of the empirical work. Though final conclusions have yet to be drawn, certain preliminary interpretations of the data will be given here; they may, of course, be subject to modifications or even substantial changes, depending on the final results.

The multilingual students selected for this research were questioned about the issues of the cosmopolitan matrix in individual, open-ended, and in-depth interview sessions before letting them have group discussions about my interpretations of these interviews. In the individual sessions, they were explicitly told that in order to receive their spontaneous and unbiased statements and thoughts, the working title of the research, "Language and Identity," did not give away the real topic (which was, of course, the relationship between multilingualism and cosmopolitanism). The real topic would be revealed in the group discussions.

In view of this, one of the most interesting and astonishing results at first sight was that several of the students independently and in a surprisingly detailed manner brought up the concept of "cosmopolitanism" while discussing the importance of multilingualism in their lives or in abstract terms. Given the dearth of research linking the two fields, these unforced statements are deemed to be very meaningful and revelatory. This is a direct example of how a presupposed relationship between "language" and "world significance," as expressed in Wittgenstein's "The limits of my language are the limits of my world," has been considerably substantiated through this research. Of course, the number of students interviewed was too small for statistically generalizable interpretations.

Another very interesting point was that the majority of the students seemed to hold remarkably strong critical opinions about nation-states and nationalism in general, and their home country in particular. Some were explicitly expressing an "internationalist" standpoint. This point is strengthened through statements about the place they perceive as "home"; it was hardly ever the "home country" in a predominant or exclusive role. On the whole, the group seemed to be closer to the model of "rooted cosmopolitanism" than of "unrooted cosmopolitanism."

Relatively few of the students attached special importance to their multilingual status *in terms of multiple linguistic identities*. For example, hardly anybody saw his or her identity as being composed of the linguistic domains he or she possessed—for example, feeling French when speaking French, Hispanic when speaking Spanish, and so on. This seemed to be an issue they had not thought very much about. But even in the scientific literature only two sources (Steiner 1998; Bassnett 2000) asked about the composition of the multilingual identity at all, only to leave it open in the end.

But the students brought up a number of points that the literature has obviously not thought of yet, or hardly at all, especially regarding cosmopolitanism. So here the investigation had a chance to make original contributions. Remarkably, almost all of the students saw open-mindedness as the most decisive characteristic of a cosmopolitan, and set out to define it in several dimensions. Only one writer, Hannerz, has touched upon open-mindedness—in a single instance.

The literature treats what has been synthesized as the two sides of the cultural experience: mobility/traveling and residence/roots. Here, the interviews shed light on the relation between these two aspects. For instance, several students defined time periods for each of them, or defined mobility as "not only physical but also mental mobility."

Several students spoke of a continuum of cosmopolitanism as "a scale with an open end." Some mentioned that cosmopolitanism "is an age/lifestyle thing." It also would "diminish without exposure." Some said "cosmopolitanism cuts across topics or issues within every individual." One person stressed that she would not be afraid of the unfamiliar because she would face it prepared, a view not mentioned in the literature. Some students stated that they did not yet feel ready to feel or to call themselves "cosmopolitans." However, the majority seemed to embrace the concept.

Regarding the overall importance of foreign languages and foreign language learning for a cosmopolitan cultural identity, the students' opinions can be put in a nutshell more or less like this: Languages may or may not be essential for being or becoming a cosmopolitan. But they surely help a lot, and arguably there are limits to an individual's cosmopolitan development if he or she does not have a set of foreign languages to start with. Overall, the seemingly pre-established relationship between multilingualism and cosmopolitanism is now substantiated, and seems to be quite strong as far as my research is generalizable.

Conclusive and detailed findings will be shared later. The results of this research should enhance our knowledge about the identity of multilingual persons with respect to the cultural identity notion of cosmopolitanism. Multilingualism and cosmopolitanism receive more and more interest and treatment, which reflects their present currency. The exploration of their relationship thus addresses a very interesting and relevant, yet hitherto largely neglected, research area. It does so through the eyes of multilinguals (both myself as a researcher and the cohort of respondents). It is thus of interest for both multilinguals and those striving for multilingualism.

REFERENCES

Anderson, A. (1998). "Cosmopolitanism, Universalism, and the Divided Legacies of Modernity." In P. Cheah and B. Robbins (eds.), *Cosmopolitics: Thinking and Feeling Beyond the Nation.* Minneapolis: University of Minnesota Press.

Andrews, L. (1998). *Language Exploration and Awareness: A Resource Book for Teachers.* 2nd ed. London: Lawrence Erlbaum Associates.

Apeltauer, E. (1993). "Multilingualism in a society of the future?" *European Journal of Education* 28, no. 3: 273–294.

Appadurai, A., and C. Breckenridge (1998). "Why Public Culture?" *Public Culture Bulletin* 1, no. 1: 5–9.

Appiah, K.A. (1998). "Cosmopolitan Patriots." In P. Cheah and B. Robbins (eds.), *Cosmopolitics: Thinking and Feeling Beyond the Nation.* Minneapolis: University of Minnesota Press.

Bassnett, S. (2000). "Language and Identity." *The Linguist* 39, no. 3: 66–71.

Baumann, Z. (1996). "From Pilgrim to Tourist—or a Short History of Identity." In S. Hall and P. du Gay (eds.), *Questions of Cultural Identity.* London: Sage.

Brennan, T. (1997). *At Home in the World: Cosmopolitanism Now.* Cambridge, MA: Harvard University Press.

Brennan, T. (2001). "Cosmopolitanism and Internationalism." *New Left Review* 2, no. 7: 75–84.

Bruckner, P. (1996). "The Edge of Babel." *Partisan Review* 63, no. 2: 242–254.

Buttjes, D. (1991). "Mediating Languages and Cultures: The Social and Intercultural Dimension Restored." In D. Buttjes and M. Byram (eds.), *Mediating Languages and Cultures: Towards an Intercultural Theory of Foreign Language Education.* Clevedon, UK: Multilingual Matters.

Byram, M., C. Morgan, et al. (1994). *Teaching-and-Learning Language-and-Culture.* Clevedon, UK: Multilingual Matters.

Cenoz, J., B. Hufeisen, and U. Jessner (2001). "Towards Trilingual Education." *International Journal of Bilingual Education and Bilingualism* 4, no. 1: 1–10.

Cheah, P. (1998). "Given Culture: Rethinking Cosmopolitical Freedom in Transnationalism." In P. Cheah and B. Robbins (eds.), *Cosmopolitics: Thinking and Feeling Beyond the Nation.* Minneapolis: University of Minnesota Press.

Christ, H. (1996). "Tests de plurilinguisme." In H. Goebl et al. (eds.), *Contact Linguistics: An International Handbook of Contemporary Research*. Vol. 1. Berlin and New York: Walter de Gruyter.

Clifford, J. (1992). "Travelling Cultures." In L. Grossberg, C. Nelson, and P. A. Treichler (eds.), *Cultural Studies*. New York: Routledge.

Coleman, J.A. (1996). *Studying Languages: A Survey of British and European Students. The Proficiency, Background, Attitudes and Motivations of Students of Foreign Languages in the United Kingdom and Europe*. London: Centre for Information on Language Teaching and Research.

Coleman, J.A. (1998). "Evolving Intercultural Perceptions Among University Language Learners in Europe." In M. Byram and M. Fleming (eds.), *Language Learning in Intercultural Perspective: Approaches Through Drama and Ethnography*. Cambridge: Cambridge University Press.

Coste, D. (1997). "Multilingual and Multicultural Competence and the Role of School." *Language Teaching* 30, no. 2: 90–93.

Council of Europe (1998). *Modern Languages: Learning, Teaching, Assessment. A Common European Framework of Reference*. Strasbourg: Council of Europe, Council for Cultural Co-operation, Education Committee.

Crystal, D. (2000). *Language Death*. Cambridge: Cambridge University Press.

Cummins, J. (2001). "Instructional Conditions for Trilingual Development." *International Journal of Bilingual Education and Bilingualism* 4, no. 1: 61–75.

Edwards, J. (1994). *Multilingualism*. London: Routledge.

European Commission (1996). *White Paper on Education and Training. Teaching and Learning: Towards the Learning Society*. Brussels: European Commission.

Featherstone, M. (1993). "Global and Local Cultures." In J. Bird et al., *Mapping the Futures: Local Cultures, Global Change*. London: Routledge.

Ferguson, J. (1999). *Expectations of Modernity: Myths and Meanings of Urban Life on the Zambian Copperbelt*. Berkeley: University of California Press.

Friedman, J. (1995). "Global Systems, Globalisation and the Parameters of Modernity." In M. Featherstone, S. Lash, and R. Robertson (eds.), *Global Modernities*. London: Sage.

Gnutzmann, C. (1997). "Multilingualism and Language Teaching: Some Pedagogical Implications with Reference to Language Awareness." *Fremdsprachen Lehren und Lernen* 26: 156–166.

Graddol, D. (1998). "What's the Future for Languages?" *The Linguist* 37, no. 5: 144–146.

Griessler, M. (2001). "The Effects of Third Language Learning on Second Language Proficiency: An Austrian Example." *International Journal of Bilingual Education and Bilingualism* 4, no. 1: 50–60.

Gutmann, A. (1996). "Democratic Citizenship." In J. Cohen (ed.), *For Love of Country: Debating the Limits of Patriotism*. Boston: Beacon Press.

Hannerz, U. (1990). "Cosmopolitans and Locals in World Culture." In M. Featherstone (ed.), *Global Culture: Nationalism, Globalization and Modernity*. London: Sage.

Hannerz, U. (1992). *Cultural Complexity: Studies in the Social Organization of Meaning*. New York: Columbia University Press.

Hannerz, U. (1996). *Transnational Connections: Culture, People, Places*. London: Routledge.

Hinkel, E. (1999). "Introduction: Culture in Research and Second Language Pedagogy." In E. Hinkel, *Culture in Second Language Teaching and Learning*. Cambridge: Cambridge University Press.

Kellman, S.G. (2000). *The Translingual Imagination*. Lincoln: University of Nebraska Press.

King, L. (2000). "Preface." In A. King (ed.), *Languages and the Transfer of Skills: The Relevance of Language Learning for 21st Century Graduates in the World of Work*. London: Centre for Information on Language Teaching and Research.

Lambert, R.D. (1993). "International Education and International Competence in the United States." *European Journal of Education* 28, no. 3: 309–325.

Lantolf, J.P., and G. Sunderman (2001). "The Struggle for a Place in the Sun: Rationalising Foreign Language Study in the Twentieth Century." *Modern Language Journal* 85, no. 1: 5–25.

Lüdi, G. (1996). "Mehrsprachigkeit." In H. Goebl et al. (eds.), *Contact Linguistics: An International Handbook of Contemporary Research*. Vol. 1. Berlin and New York: Walter de Gruyter.

Malcomson, S.L. (1998). "The Varieties of Cosmopolitan Experience." In P. Cheah and B. Robbins (eds.), *Cosmopolitics: Thinking and Feeling Beyond the Nation*. Minneapolis: University of Minnesota Press.

McConnell, M.W. (1996). "Don't Neglect the Little Platoons." In J. Cohen (ed.), *For Love of Country: Debating the Limits of Patriotism*. Boston: Beacon Press.

McCullough, C. (1977). *The Thorn Birds*. London: Warner Books.

Morgan, C. (2001). "Multilingualism and Multilingual Language Learning." In W. Weidinger (ed.), *Bilingualität und Schule? Ausbildung, wissenschaftliche Perspektiven und empirische Befunde*. Vienna: Öbv & Hpt (Österreichischer Bundesverlag & Verlag Hölder-Pichler-Tempsky).

Naiman, N., et al. (1996). *The Good Language Learner*. 2nd ed. Clevedon, UK: Multilingual Matters.

Nussbaum, M.C. (1996). "Patriotism and Cosmopolitanism." In J. Cohen (ed.), *For Love of Country: Debating the Limits of Patriotism*. Boston: Beacon Press.

Ondaatje, M. (1992). *The English Patient*. London: Macmillan.

Pinsky, R. (1996). "Eros Against Esperanto." In J. Cohen (ed.), *For Love of Country: Debating the Limits of Patriotism*. Boston: Beacon Press.

Polan, D. (1996). "Globalism's Localism." In R. Wilson and W. Dissanayake (eds.), *Global/Local: Cultural Production and the Transnational Imaginary*. Durham, NC: Duke University Press.

Putnam, H. (1996). "Must We Choose Between Patriotism and Universal Reason?" In J. Cohen (ed.), *For Love of Country: Debating the Limits of Patriotism*. Boston: Beacon Press.

Quist, G. (2000). "Language Teaching at University: A Clash of Cultures." *Language and Education* 14: 2, 123–139.

Rée, J. (1998). "Cosmopolitanism and the Experience of Nationality." In P. Cheah and B. Robbins (eds.), *Cosmopolitics: Thinking and Feeling Beyond the Nation*. Minneapolis: University of Minnesota Press.

Robbins, B. (1995). "The Weird Heights: On Cosmopolitanism, Feeling, and Power." *Differences* 7, no. 1: 165–187.

Robbins, B. (1998). "Comparative Cosmopolitanisms." In P. Cheah and B. Robbins (eds.), *Cosmopolitics: Thinking and Feeling Beyond the Nation*. Minneapolis: University of Minnesota Press.

Robbins, B. (1999). *Feeling Global: Internationalism in Distress.* New York: New York University Press.

Rooney, K., et al. (eds.) (1999). *Encarta World English Dictionary.* London: Bloomsbury.

Sarup, M. (1996). *Identity, Culture and the Postmodern World.* Edinburgh: Edinburgh University Press.

Seidl, M. (1998). "Language and Culture: Towards a Transcultural Competence in Language Learning." *Forum for Modern Language Studies* 34, no. 2: 101–113.

Shore, C. (2000). *Building Europe: The Cultural Politics of European Integration.* London: Routledge.

Steel, D., and J.C. Alderson (1995). "Metalinguistic Knowledge, Language Aptitude and Language Proficiency." In D. Graddol and S. Thomas (eds.), *Language in a Changing Europe: Papers from the Annual Meeting of the British Association for Applied Linguistics, Held at the University of Salford, September 1993.* Clevedon: British Association of Applied Linguistics/Multilingual Matters.

Steiner, G. (1998). *After Babel: Aspects of Language and Translation.* 3rd ed. Oxford: Oxford University Press.

Strevens, P. (1987). "Cultural Barriers to Language Learning." In L.E. Smith (ed.), *Discourse Across Cultures: Strategies in World Englishes.* London and New York: Prentice-Hall.

Tagore, R. (1921). *The Home and the World.* London: Macmillan.

Theroux, P. (1986). *Sunrise with Seamonsters.* Harmondsworth, UK: Penguin.

Tomlinson, J. (1999). *Globalisation and Culture.* Cambridge: Polity Press.

Trim, J. (1999). "Language Education Policies for the Twenty-first Century." In A. Tosi and C. Leung (eds.), *Rethinking Language Education: From a Monolingual to a Multilingual Perspective.* London: Centre of Information on Language Teaching and Research.

Walzer, M. (1996). "Spheres of Affection." In J. Cohen (ed.), *For Love of Country: Debating the Limits of Patriotism.* Boston: Beacon Press.

Werlen, I. (1997). "Mehrsprachigkeit und Europa." In C. Allemann-Ghionda (ed.), *Multikultur und Bildung in Europa. Multiculture et Éducation en Europe.* 2nd ed. Bern: Peter Lang.

West, M.L. (1991). *The Ringmaster.* London and Melbourne: William Heinemann.

Wierzbicka, A. (1986). "Does Language Reflect Culture? Evidence from Australian English." *Language in Society* 15: 349–374.

Wierzbicka, A. (1997). *Understanding Cultures Through Their Key Words: English, Russian, Polish, German, and Japanese.* Oxford: Oxford University Press.

Part V

Individual Differences

20

A Voice within a Voice
Federman Translating / Translating Federman

Raymond Federman

Sometimes I confuse myself with my shadow and sometimes don't.

Samuel Beckett

A voice within a voice speaks in me, double-talks in me bilingually, in French and in English, separately or, at times, simultaneously. That voice constantly plays hide-and-seek with its shadow. Now there is nothing unusual about that. Many people nowadays, in many parts of the world, speak two or three or even several languages. Whether or not I speak French and English well is another question that is not for me to answer. But the fact remains that I am a bilingual being, a double-headed mumbler, one could say, and as such also a bicultural being. I spent the first twenty years of my life in France, therefore inside the French language and the French culture, and spent (more or less) the last forty years in America, therefore inside the American language and culture. My social and cultural activities reflect this.

But I am also a bilingual writer. That is to say, I write both in French and in English, and that is perhaps less common. Furthermore, I also, at times, translate my own work either from English into French or vice versa. That self-translating activity is certainly not very common in creative writing. In that sense, then, I am somewhat of a phenomenon. The French would say: Federman, *c'est un drôle de phénomène!* Indeed, I have often wondered, as a bilingual writer and a self-translator, whether I am blessed because of this phenomenon or cursed because of it.

The fact that I am, that I became, a bilingual writer may be an accident—an accident of history as well as an accident of my own personal experience. In any case, I am often asked if I think in French or in English, if I dream in French or in English. And I usually answer (at cocktail parties, on the golf course, at various intellectual gatherings), because one must always answer such questions, if only for the sake of answering something and not being bothered any further with an unanswerable question: I think and I dream both in French and in English, and very often simultaneously.

That, in fact, is what it means to have a voice within a voice. It means that you can never separate your linguistic self from its shadow.

There seems to be a lot of interest these days in bilingualism and multilingualism, related of course to the current concern with multiculturalism. Recently a friend of mine who is writing a book on the subject of bilingual writers—such as Vladimir Nabokov, Joseph Conrad, Elsa Triolet, Samuel Beckett, myself, and others—asked me in a letter to reflect on my own bilingual condition, and answer some questions.

Though I exist bilingually, in my life as well as in my work as a poet and a fiction writer, I have never really tried to articulate a theory of my bilingualism. It was, therefore, interesting and provoking for me to answer my friend Elizabeth's questions having to do with what she calls the location of bilingualism, the space between the two languages, the verticality versus the horizontality of bilingualism, the periodicities of alternation, the horror of self-translation, and so on.

This is what I wrote to Elizabeth in my reply:

I do not normally question or analyze my schizophrenic bilingualism. I just let it be, let it happen in me and outside of me. I have no idea in which side of my brain each language is located. I have a vague feeling that the two languages in me fornicate in the same cell. But since you are probing into my ambivalent (my ambidextrous) psyche, I can tell you that I believe I am left-handed in French and right-handed in English. I am not kidding. You see, I was born left-handed (in Paris, some years ago), but when I broke my left wrist at the age of nine or ten (I forget exactly when now), I was forced to become right-handed. You might say that I am a converted lefty, just as I am a converted Frenchman who became an American. However, there are certain things, certain gestures and motions which I cannot do with my right hand (like brushing my teeth or throwing a ball), and others which I can only do with my right hand (like writing or playing tennis). Could this have something to do with my bilingualism? It is also true that there are certain texts which I can only write in English, and others only in French, even though eventually I feel a need to translate these texts from one language into the other.

What amazes me, but perhaps it should not, is how true I am to the patterns you describe in your essay. [Elizabeth had enclosed with her letter a copy of an essay she had just published, titled "Prolegomena to a Study of Bilingual Writers," in which she delineates certain patterns of behavior for bilingual writers, such as periods of rejection of one language in favor of the other, or a need bilingual writers seem to have to return to their native tongue in the later years of their life.] Considering myself just beyond the mid-course of my literary career, I find that I am more comfortable these days writing in English than in French. This does not mean, however, that I have rejected the French language—my native tongue. I have merely placed it (temporarily) in parentheses. Though it seems that whenever I begin a new book there is a quarrel inside of me between the two languages to decide which I should use.

Knowing that I have written extensively on the work of Samuel Beckett, Elizabeth asked, "How do you compare yourself to Beckett? And should the case of Beckett be examined? He was such a classical and backward case."

In terms of his bilingualism and the act of self-translating, Beckett was a superman, an angel. He came from above. I am a mere mortal. I come from below, from the cave. Yes, of course, Beckett's case should be examined, carefully examined. In my opinion, Beckett was a most unique, a most extraordinary case of a bilingual writer, for he had, at least since 1945 until his death in 1989, sustained his work in French and English to the point that for him language one and language two became totally interchangeable. Therefore, when reading Beckett it is absolutely irrelevant to ask which text was written first. His twin-texts—whether French/English or English/French—are not to be read as translations or as substitutes for one another. They are always complementary to one another. In many ways, I consider my own work, my bilingual work, to be some-what the same. Whether written in English or in French first, the two texts complement and complete one another.

"Is there anything familiar to you in what I am saying in my essay?" Eliz-abeth asked.

Yes, most of it, especially the problem of periodicities of alternation (I seem to be constantly vacillating between the two languages), and also what you call "the horror of self-translation." (It scares the hell out of me whenever I begin to translate myself, though lately, in spite of the horror, and even the boredom at times, of translating my own work, I also find a constant temptation to do so, as if there were a profound need in me to see everything I write exist immediately in the other language.) There are, however, a few things in your essay with which I seem to differ, but then this may have to do with my own idiosyncratic mind.

For instance, I do not seem to feel, as some of the bilingual writers you discuss (Nabokov and Elsa Triolet in particular), that there is a space between the two languages in me that keeps them apart. On the contrary, for me French and English always seem to overlap, to want to merge, to want to come together, to want to embrace one another, to mesh one into the other. Or if you prefer, they want to spoil and corrupt one another. Therefore, I do not feel that one language is vertical in me, and the other horizontal, as you suggest. If anything, they seem to be standing or lying in the same direction—sometimes vertically and other times horizontally, depending on their moods or their desires. Though the French and the English in me occasionally compete with one an-other in some vague region of my brain, more often they play with one another, es-pecially when I put them on paper. Yes, I think that the two languages in me love each other, and I have, on occasion, caught them having wild intercourse behind my back. However, I cannot tell you which is feminine and which is masculine, perhaps they are androgynous.

To tell you the truth, Elizabeth, there is perversity in my bilingualism. Usually when I finish a novel (as you know I have written seven or eight now, either in English or in French), I am immediately tempted to write (rewrite, adapt, transform, transact, trans-create—I am not sure what term I should use here, but certainly not translate) the original into the other language. Even though finished, the book feels unfinished if it does not exist in the other language. Often I begin such an alternate version, but quickly abandon it, out of boredom, I suppose, fatigue or disgust, or perhaps because of what you call "the horror of self-translation," the fear of betraying myself and my own work.

It is curious, however, that when I write something shorter than a novel, a short story and especially a poem, I immediately do a version in the other language. Most of my poems and short stories exist bilingually. My feeling here is that the original text is not complete until there is an equivalent version in French or in English. Perhaps the same need for completeness, for finishedness into the other language is there too for the novels, but laziness, fear, apprehension, and of course time prevent me from doing the work. I am aware also that translating one's work into another language often reveals the poverty, the semantic but also the metaphorical poverty of certain words in the other language. There is no doubt that the process of self-translating often results in a loss, in a betrayal and weakening of the original work. But then, on the other hand, there is always the possibility, the chance of a gain. Yes, the possibility that certain words or expressions in the other language may have the advantage of metaphorical richness not present in the first language. So that even though the self-translator always confronts this possibility of loss, he also hopes for a chance of gain. It seems to me that the translation, or rather the self-translation often augments, enriches and even embellishes the original text—enriches, it, not only in terms of meaning, but in its music, its rhythm, its metaphoric thickness, and even in its syntactical complexity. This is so because the self-translator can take liberties with his own work since it belongs to him.

However, this matter of loss or gain in the process of self-translation raises a crucial question: whether the translation is merely a substitute for the original or if, in fact, it becomes a continuation, an amplification of the work? We always admire the faithfulness of a translation in relation to the original, and quickly deplore and criticize the liberties a translator takes with the original work of a writer. A case in point: the marvelous though greatly unfaithful translations which Richard Howard recently did of Baudelaire's *Les Fleurs du Mal*, which were bitterly criticized.

Yes, we rarely forgive such liberties, and consequently expect the bilingual writer who translates himself to remain faithful to his own texts. On the contrary, one should allow the writer-as-self-translator some freedom, some room for play within his own work, if only for the sake of enriching that work. And of course, I allow myself such playfulness—often simply for the sake of playfulness, but also in an effort to make sense out of my own writing. But there is also a more important reason for wanting to translate one's work: since we know that language is what gets us where we want to go but at the same time prevents us from getting there (I am paraphrasing Samuel Beckett here), then by using another language, the other language in us, we may have a better chance of getting where we want to go, a better chance of saying what we wanted to say, or at least we have a second chance of succeeding. That is to say, we have the possibility of correcting the errors of the original text.

The original creative act, as we all know, always proceeds in the DARK—in the dark, in ignorance, and in error. Though the act of translating (and especially self-translating) is also a creative act, nevertheless it is performed in the LIGHT (in the light of the original text), it is performed in KNOWLEDGE (in the knowledge of the existing text), and therefore it is performed without error, at least at the start. As such the act of self-translation enlightens the original, but it also reassures, reasserts the knowledge already present in the original text. Sometimes it also corrects the initial errors of that text. As a result, the self-translation is no longer an approximation of the original, nor a duplication, nor a substitute, but truly a continuation of the work—of the working of the text.

Basically that is how I understand my work as a self-translator and as a bilingual writer. Sometimes the translation I do of my own work amplifies the original, sometimes it diminishes it, corrects it, explains it even (no, not to the reader, the potential reader of the text, but to the author, to myself, who knows very well that the language he uses, whether French or English, is always an obstacle that must be overcome again and again).

That is what I think it means to be a bilingual writer, to be a writer/self-translator. It means that one is constantly displaced from one language (and one culture) into the other. And yet, at the same time, it means that one can never step outside of the languages inside of us, whatever these languages may be. The bilingual writer allows his readers (if he has any) to listen to the dialogue which he entertains within himself in two languages, even though in most cases the readers (who are usually not bilingual) only hear half of this internal (one should almost say infernal) dialogue.

I feel a sense of incompleteness with my work when the texts I have written exist only in one language. This need, this anxiety rather, I have to see my work exist in both French and English . . . (and I should insist, in my own voice—I have read translations of some of my work into French or into English, translations of poems, stories, essays, and even one of my novels done by someone other than myself, and these always feel totally alien to me) . . . this need I have to speak and write in two languages, almost simultaneously, also affects my reading process. Often when I read a book, either in French or in English, a book I am particularly enjoying, a book which gives me, as Roland Barthes put it, *Le Plaisir du Texte*, I find myself translating the text mentally into the other language while reading.

What often troubles me when I am working on a novel in English (and this because in most of my novels so far, the protagonist remains a Frenchman in exile) is the realization that perhaps it would be easier, and certainly more logical, to write the book in French, or at least to let the protagonist speak French whenever he feels like it. But then, the question can be asked: to whom is the book speaking? My fiction always has an implied reader, or rather an implicit, active interlocutor/listener present in the text, and I believe that this "potential reader" (as I call him) is of the English and not the French language. In other words, my books always seem to be speaking to English reading people, and therefore, even though the central character and even the material are of French origin, they demand to be written in English.

I write more, and have always written more in English than in French, even though English is not my first language. Somehow the French language scares me. It seems to dictate to me how I should write and therefore prevents me from challenging its rules of grammar, whereas English, irrational as it may be in its grammar and syntax, gives me the freedom to experiment with grammar and syntax. Though I did not start learning English until I was twenty years old, I feel that my French is somewhat ancient, perhaps even fossilized, that it is no longer up-to-date, that it is a language of another time in my life. That does not mean that I write badly or poorly in French, I don't think so, nor does it mean that I have rejected the French language, but that when I write in French I become conscious, over-conscious of using a language which is distant from me. And this, not because there have been periods when I did not use French (I use my French all the time), but simply because French is somewhat foreign and restrictive to me now. To put it differently, I feel like a prisoner in the French language, perhaps because it made me, because it captured me originally, and I feel free in English because it liberated me, because it took me out of the French language and the French culture.

"Is there a desire in me to lose, to abandon French?" Elizabeth asked.

No, I do not think so. You must understand that I do not feel afflicted with bilingualism, I feel enriched by it. At the same time, however, I do not feel that I want to preserve the purity of my native tongue, as so many of my French friends and colleagues, who have been living and working in the U.S. for many years, often do or claim to do. On the contrary, I want to corrupt the French language in me, I want the two languages in me to corrupt one another.

I have often contemplated writing a book—a book which would probably be unreadable to most people—in which the two languages would come together in the same sentences. There are a few such pages in some of my novels, but I would like to do a entire book using both languages simultaneously. Here allow me to give you a short example of what I mean. It's a passage from my novel *Take It or Leave It* [1976]. The French protagonist marvels at what he sees when he arrives in New York:

> . . . because me too like a jerk j'attendis une bonne heure or more after the phone call à la même place and then de cette pénombre in this gray rain de cette foule en route discon-tinuous morne surgit around 10:00 p.m une brusque avalanche quite unexpected de femmes absolument belles gorgeous stunning out of nowhere quelle découverte quelle Amérique quel ravissement was I lucky to be here je touchais au vif de mon pélerinage and if je n'avais pas souffert en même temps des continuels rappels the loud gurgling in my stomach de mon appétit wow was I hungry je me serais cru suddenly parvenu à l'un de ces moments de surnaturelle and of surrealistic révélation esthétique les beautés that I découvrais just like that incessantes m'eussent avec un peu de confiance and de confort and a bit more self-confidence ravi à ma condition trivialement humaine. . . .

Yes, I have often considered writing a book in which the two languages would merge into one another. On the cover of this book (if such a book were ever to be published), it would say, translated by the author, but without specifying from which language.

There is, quite clearly, an element of playfulness at work in my bilingualism. The two languages play with one another, and I am using the term *play* in its fullest sense— not only in the sense of game, but also in the sense of looseness, as in the expression, there is looseness in the door. My French and my English play with one another as two children do in a playground, or rather as two lovers (loose lovers) play with one another in order to possess and even abolish one another. Perhaps my French and English play in me in order to abolish my own origin. In the totally bilingual book I would like to write, there would be no original language, no original source, no original text—only two languages that would exist, or rather co-exist outside of their origin, in the space of their own playfulness.

At this point my reply to my friend Elizabeth stopped abruptly, either because I had nothing more to say, nothing else to invent on the subject of my bilingualism, or simply because I had run out of space. Whatever the case, in the process of reflecting about bilingualism, I think I had managed to explain (especially to myself) how the struggle, the love affair, and the playful intercourse of the two languages in me have determined and informed my work over the years.

No, I do not feel afflicted by my bilingualism. I feel enriched by it, as I hope the following bilingual poem will demonstrate:

OLD SKIN	VIEILLE PEAU
sixty already	soixante ans déjà
and still not a word	et pas encore un mot
mumbling like a fool	balbutiant comme un con
at best	au plus
two or three groans	deux out trois cris
that's about all	voilà c'est tout
lots of qua qua	beaucoup de qua qua
that's how it is	voilà comment c'est
in the bubble of the skull	dans la bulle du crâne
dragging yourself in verbal mud	te traînant dans la boue verbale
looking for a word	cherchant un mot
the first word	le premier mot
a noun perhaps	un nom peut-être
a verb	un verbe
yes	oui
an imperative	un impératif

* * * * * *

* * * *

* * *

*

21

Challenges to Normal Bilingualism
Down's Syndrome, Deafness, and Dyslexia

Tracey Tokuhama-Espinosa

Can a child who has Down's syndrome, one who is deaf, or one who has dyslexia become a successful bilingual?

Learning a second language can be a difficult task. Raising a bilingual child from birth takes constant vigilance and commitment from both parent and child. To ensure success, I believe parents must evaluate each child against the ten key factors in raising multilingual children (Tokuhama-Espinosa 2001) in order to have a full picture of the situation's potential. The factors are (1) *timing*, or the *windows of opportunity*; (2) the person's *aptitude* for foreign languages; (3) the *motivation* to learn the target language(s); (4) the family's *consistency* with a given choice of (5) *strategy*; (6) determining whether or not the target languages are *linguistically related*; (7) the *opportunity* the child has to use her languages in meaningful situations on a daily basis; (8) the influences of *siblings*; (9) *gender*; and (10) *hand use* as it reflects cerebral dominance.

When considering children with learning challenges, including Down's syndrome, deafness, or dyslexia, in addition to these ten factors, the additional factors of (11) *physical impediments*, such as oversized tongue or malformations in the face and (12) *different cerebral (brain) structure* must be considered. These last two factors are what lead many people to believe that children with the aforementioned problems cannot become successful bilinguals. Another doubt is raised when parents (and many well-meaning doctors) question whether a child who faces challenges developing just one language can harness the mental fortitude to master a second. While much depends on individual cases and complications, happily the answer seems to be that in most cases, Down's syndrome, deaf, and dyslexic children can indeed become successful bilinguals.

Down's syndrome, deafness, and dyslexia are all challenges to individual learning, and each has its own peculiarities. Let us turn to research in each area separately.

DOWN'S SYNDROME AND BILINGUALISM

Down's syndrome, also known as mongolism or trisomy 21, is a chromosome abnormality resulting in mental retardation and other abnormalities. In most cases, an extra chromosome 21 causes Down's syndrome.

Physical Impediments to Normal Language Learning

Some of the characteristics of Down's syndrome children generally include an abnormally shaped, smaller than average head. There are at least seven structural and functional disorders creating challenges to speaking: high, narrow palatal vaults; tongue protrusion; mild to moderate conductive hearing loss; chronic upper respiratory infections; mouth breathing; habitual open mouth posture; and the impression that the person's tongue is too big for his or her mouth (www.downs-syndrome.info). There is an increased susceptibility to visual problems and hearing loss, and increased chances of ear infections. In addition to these physical challenges, mental retardation is synonymous with Down's syndrome; the average mental age achieved is eight years old. Despite these symptoms, and while "there is no research literature of systematic study of bilingualism in people with Down's Syndrome . . . extensive practical experience and many parental testimonies state that it is indeed possible" (Buckley 1998: 30). Buckley "encourages the bilingual family to expose a baby with Down's syndrome to both languages, but suggests that specific language teaching activities, including reading activities focus on the language the child will use in school" (1998: 30).

There is still debate as to whether a second language can serve as a therapy adjunct to speech development, however. Many families have reported that a second language serves as stimulation for overall language development, while others argue in favor of emphasizing the school language, on the assumption that children will quickly learn the translated counterpart naturally. Dr. B. J. Freeman of the Autism Society of America believes that there should be no reason that autistic or Down's syndrome children could not learn and use a second language; in fact, she believes it would be a terrible disservice to the child to deny him that tool so essential to bonding with other members of his family or the society around him.

What Needs to Be Done Differently from Other Bilinguals?

An additional effort must be made to allow children with Down's syndrome to express themselves at their own pace. While this is advisable for any child, Down's syndrome or not, the Down's syndrome child needs to be allowed to lead (Manolson and Buck 1992), and parents must learn to adapt to their child's pace. Problems of oral-motor difficulties (getting the message from the brain to the mouth) can cause many speech delays. In *Becoming Partners with Chil-*

dren (1989), Dr. James MacDonaldson discusses what children need before they can speak and how parents and other adults play and communicate with children to help them speak, and offers specific programs that parents have used in the past to help children with Down's syndrome speak in order to become enjoyable and social members of society. MacDonaldson writes that Down's syndrome children often have too little interaction and limited numbers of verbal exchanges in the day; and most of the conversations they have are one-sided, forcing the child to listen as opposed to managing the conversation.

Due to the abnormalities in hand size, the physical manipulation of writing instruments can be difficult for a Down's syndrome child, making literacy activities tiresome. However, many people who work with Down's syndrome students attest that their verbal skills may indeed be very good, and, given proper stimulation, these students can be good in several different languages. Laura Felzer writes of a multisensory program for teaching reading to people with Down's syndrome, in which they learn to read by seeing, hearing, saying, and signing printed words and phonetic sounds: "The signing component of this program also helps the children increase and develop their speech, and sight words and simple sentences are taught before phonics . . . the students not only see, hear and say the words they're learning but also see and handle corresponding objects. . . . The second and even more significant feature is that the students learn signs for their words" (Felzer 1998). Though multisensory teaching methods have their roots in aiding children with language problems, they are very popular among children in mainstream schools as well. The whole sensory approach to learning, researchers are finding, speaks to the needs of a variety of children and learning styles. Some researchers suggest teaching literacy skills in the more phonetic language only. For example, new research shows that there are far fewer dyslexics in Italian, which is highly phonetic (sound-to-letter correlation), than in English.

It is worth noting that while American and United Kingdom experts in Down's syndrome note a great dearth in the information available about bilingualism, in the Philippines and Singapore, where bilingualism is more common, Down's syndrome children are educated in institutions with all the languages of the normal schooling system.

Conclusions

A reminder about general language development of both Down's syndrome children and bilingualism is worth reiterating. Bilinguals tend to speak slightly later than monolinguals, and Down's syndrome children also are developmentally delayed in their speech acquisition; therefore it should come as no surprise that the process of becoming a bilingual Down's syndrome child is not as fast as for a monolingual child. This requires parents to be even more patient and allow the bilingual Down's child to develop language skills at his or her own pace. The ten key factors are vital to a normal child's upbringing, and families facing the challenge of Down's syndrome must be even more vigilant in addressing and taking advantage of as many of the factors as possible.

DEAF CHILDREN GROWING UP BILINGUAL

While there is relatively little research on Down's syndrome children and bilingualism, there is a host of information about the deaf child acquiring more than one language. This can be accounted for in some part by the concept that the deaf child is already "bilingual" in that he or she participates in both the deaf and the hearing worlds.

Every child, whatever the level of his/her hearing loss, should have the right to grow up bilingual. By knowing and using both a sign language and an oral language (in its written, and when possible, spoken modality), the child will attain his/her full cognitive, linguistic and social capabilities. (Grosjean 1997: 1)

Grosjean (1997) writes that a deaf child has to accomplish at least five things with language. First, communicate with parents and family members as soon as possible. A hearing child will acquire language within the first year of life; this should be so for deaf children as well. Second, develop cognitive abilities in infancy through language input. Third, acquire world knowledge through language. Fourth, communicate fully with the surrounding world, especially within the social systems where he or she lives. Fifth, acculturate into two worlds. The first four points could be applied to hearing children as well; the last point emphasizes the deaf culture. To meet these five needs, a deaf child must learn to function in both the deaf and the hearing language.

By learning the deaf language, which can be in the form of sign language or lip reading, and by learning to work within the hearing world, sharing the written language of the culture that surrounds him or her (and in some cases through speaking), the deaf child is already bilingual. Can a deaf child learn an additional language? Most certainly, say researchers.

As with other bilinguals, the deaf child's "first language," or one of his native languages, must be sign language. "It is a natural, full-fledged language that ensures full and complete communication" (Grosjean 1997). It is well established that, if acquired naturally, a firm grounding in one's native language (to facilitate deep thinking skills, reflections about the world, etc.) aids in the development of future languages. Being able to sign well will aid the deaf child in acquiring the language of society and family, and even a third language. In order to become a "balanced bilingual," the child must have constant input from both languages, a motivation to use his or her language skills, and the opportunity for use.

Just as some bilinguals go on to learn a third language, so deaf people can advance in their linguistic prowess. In families in which there are two parents of different language backgrounds, the most natural course is for each parent to speak his or her own language with the child. This is complicated by the need for two different sign languages, making the situation one of four languages. For example, Tom is the son of Marie and James. Marie speaks German, James speaks English, and they live in the United States, though they frequently visit family in Germany. Tom will have to become a balanced bilingual in English sign and oral language, and a balanced bilingual in German sign and oral language. Is this too much to ask?

Biculturalism and Bilingualism in the Deaf World(s)

Just as it may seem counterintuitive to think that a Down's syndrome child could learn to be a bilingual, somehow we feel it is unfair to tax the brains of deaf children in a bilingual situation. This is a type of reverse discrimination. Why do we believe hearing children can become multilingual and deaf children cannot? Though it is a challenge, requires a great deal of dedication by parents and other family members, and utilizes a good deal of brain power, it is within the grasp of deaf children of normal intelligence, just as it is within the grasp of hearing children, to learn multiple languages. Some would even argue that it is a necessity, in order to enable the deaf child of a mixed marriage to enjoy his or her cultural heritage. Without access to one parent's language, the child will have little insight into his or her roots. Dr. David G. Mason of the Deaf Education Program at York University in Canada feels strongly that the bicultural aspect of deaf bilingualism has been overlooked, and needs more attention if we are to integrate the deaf into society with the acceptance of their own culture (Mason 1995). There is a rich deaf culture that exists within each community. By being taught to communicate in both parents' languages, the deaf child can enjoy the cultural benefits of four cultures, for example, the deaf Spanish culture, the hearing Spanish culture, the deaf English culture, and the hearing English culture.

A communication in a bilingual chat line had a discussion about the challenge of deafness to bilingualism. One very insightful contributor said, " . . . you are lucky (this may sound weird, I know, but it's true) to have a younger son who will pick up sign as his third language and act as an 'interpreter' between [your son] and people who don't know how to sign" (Bilingual Family Helpline, January 2001). Another woman noted that raising a deaf bilingual child "would be a challenge, it was not a tragedy"; she herself was doing it. Another noted the high level of education achieved by many deaf people, some of whom become successful bilinguals in oral languages.

Gallaudet University, in Washington, D.C., is a highly rated, all-deaf university. Like other U.S. institutions, it offers English as a Second Language courses combined with American Sign Language for international students who wish to attend an institution of higher education but do not have high enough scores on the TOEFL (Test of English as a Foreign Language). This program, and the international student orientation program, look very similar to the program I worked on at Boston University when I was an orientation leader for international students, except that students were required to master reading writing and signing skills, whereas the Center for English Language and Orientation Program at Boston University required reading, writing, and speaking proficiency. Gallaudet also has a foreign language requirement for graduation, meaning there are no lowered expectations on this campus compared to hearing universities in the nation.

The Brain

While it would seem that there is a great difference in how the deaf process language, this is not entirely true. In the case of deaf children learning sign language, the motor cortex and visual cortex are far more active than with nonsigning children; the other areas of the brain activated by language are the same. As the hearing child needs to process the intake from the auditory cortex, so the deaf child sees the word as signed in the visual cortex, then both pass the information to Wernicke's area to "dissect" its meaning.

Conclusions

A deaf child, by the nature of his or her hearing difference, will become a bilingual in the sign and the oral language of the culture he or she lives in. When the family situation is also bilingual, there is the challenge of acquiring an additional language. While the task seems great, evidence about the brain's ability to take on this challenge, and testimonials of bilingual deaf people themselves, confirm that it is a worthwhile quest.

DYSLEXIA AND BILINGUALISM

There is more information about the subject of dyslexia than on the other two topic areas combined; perhaps because it has brought to light so many of our school failings, perhaps because it touches the very heart of literacy and how we measure "intelligence," perhaps because it affects an estimated 8.5 percent of all schoolchildren in the United States (thus, an average classroom would have three or four pupils demanding special attention). But there is relatively little information related to bilingualism and dyslexia, though the unification of Europe, higher literacy rates in developing countries in Asia with large bilingual populations, and our understanding of the brain's functioning have all played host to new research in this field.

There is convincing evidence that dyslexia is largely inherited, involving four different chromosomes, including chromosome 6. There are different forms of dyslexia, including ones that are related to one or more of the following: visual-motor, audiophonological, and short-term memory processing. Dyslexia is found three times more often in boys than in girls, and usually becomes evident in the early school years. Albert Galaburda of Harvard University has done brain research on dyslexics and believes that dyslexics should not be regarded as having a learning difficulty, rather a different kind of learning ability.

Signs

All forms of dyslexia affect the speed of information processing. All forms of dyslexia make it very difficult to read and write. "Dyslexic children are noticeably forgetful, and this significantly affects their learning everyday skills," said Chasty at the Action for Dyslexia conference before the European Parliament (November 1994). This situation in turn is reflected in a poor self-image because in typical school systems, success requires a good memory.

The Brain and Dyslexia

Dr. Dirk Bakker of the Free University in Amsterdam has reviewed much of the pioneering work of Norman Gerschwind at Harvard University and has further defined what is known to date about the dyslexic brain. Bakker notes that the cells of the cortex in the brain move from deeper areas of the cortex prior to birth. When the cells fail to reach their final destination, they may collect into clusters along the way. These "misplaced" groups of cells are called ectopias. When examining dyslexics' brains, it was found that ectopic cells were highly evident in the left frontal and temporal lobes, which have been identified as key for language processing in normal individuals (Bakker 2002). There also appears to be a uniform absence of left-right asymmetry in the language area of the brain (affecting the planum temporale). Children who fail to develop appropriate asymmetry of function in the brain may use either their right visual hemispheres or their left auditory cortexes in inflexible strategies that are ineffective in reading. Dr. Galaburda at Harvard University also noted neuroanatomical abnormalities in the pathways linking the eye to the visual cortex that slow the speed at which information is received and processed.

What does this mean for the young bilingual child who happens to be dyslexic? Most researchers involved with dyslexic studies agree that bilingualism is beneficial, and not only for children of superior intelligence (Cooreman 1994).

Dyslexia and Bilingualism

"Dyslexic children have more difficulty coming up with the right word, especially under pressure" said Anny Cooreman in Brussels (November 1994), meaning that a simple one-person, one-language strategy is recommended in order to offer the child the additional clue that "when Mommy is speaking, I must search for the word in English." Problems of word retrieval will occur in all of the child's languages, written and spoken. It may appear that dyslexics go beyond the normal mixing stage because of this problem in word recall. The bilingual dyslexic will often search for a word, and use its equivalent in the wrong language, when he or she feels pressured to respond within a certain timeframe.

Only a minority of dyslexics remain nonreaders into adulthood, but many dyslexics continue to read and spell poorly throughout their lifetime. Dyslexics frequently perform above average on nonverbal tests of intelligence, however. Dyslexia is best treated by a sustained course of proper instruction in reading.

The creative aspect of dyslexics noted by many researchers comes to their rescue in connection with short-term memory. Dyslexics, by the nature of their brain structure, seek out nontraditional strategies to help them remember words. They must invent new strategies for what comes automatically to others (Cooreman 1994). However, new research is offering strategies that appear to give dyslexics the tools they need in order to achieve. Sally Shaywitz of Yale University states that MRI (magnetic resonance imaging) scans show how language is processed in dyslexic brains, and much of the difference from normal subjects seems to lie in the ability to dissect words into their respective phonemes, or smallest parts of speech. For example, the word "cat" has three phonemes: the sounds "kuh," "ahh," and "tuh." Dyslexics apparently see and hear only one sound, "cat." Brain scans show that the rear visual cortex is underused when reading, and the frontal cortex, the seat of higher thinking, is overactivated (Kantrowitz and Underwood 1999: 16). This implied to researchers like Richards (1999) that dyslexics are seeking to devise a new way to remember the word, because the normal audio or visual "pull-apart into-the-smallest-pieces" method does not seem to work for them. Dyslexics perform poorly on rhyming exercises because they have difficulty breaking the "start" of the word away from its "body." People without dyslexia know that "cat," "hat," and "bat" rhyme because they can separate the "c" from the "at" and then the "h" from the "at," and so on. Dyslexics, who understand the word only as a whole, have a very hard time doing this.

The solution? One method has been devised to utilize a different area of the brain to aid dyslexics in their quest for a better strategy. The Lindmood Phoneme Sequencing program, for example, helps students identify how their mouths feel when pronouncing a letter's sound. "For example, 'P' is a 'lip popper' because the lips start together and then come apart" (Kantrowitz and Underwood, 1999: 17). Dyslexics need very intense and concentrated help in the area of phoneme awareness. In the case of bilinguals, this task is indeed possible, but like the other challenges mentioned in this essay, requires additional dedication on the part of child and parents.

Bilingualism and dyslexia can mix. However, parents will need to devote a great deal of time to improving phoneme awareness in both languages. This can be easier in some language pairs than in others. Research by Eraldo Paulesu (2001) of the University of Milan at Biococca has found that "the complexity of the English and French written languages stems from historical events that have introduced spellings from other languages, while, in comparison, Italian has remained quite pure"—and quite phonetic. Most Italian words are spelled as they sound, unlike the many exceptions in English. Whereas English requires combining twenty-six letters in more than 1,100 combinations to produce forty-four sounds, Italian has only with thirty-three letter combinations to make twenty-five sounds.

Such studies should be viewed in context, however. A generalization about the complexities of language structures and their relationship to dyslexia is hard to make, given that statistics on dyslexia do not seem to show a correspondence between "phonetically easy" languages (such as suggested above) and phonetically complex ones. The *International Book of Dyslexia* presents dyslexia rates including those found in table 21.1. It is hard to argue that the fluctuation in dyslexia rates can be related to the language when countries using the same language have such differing rates. For example, the dyslexia rate in English-speaking countries such as the United Kingdom (4 percent), the United States (8.5 percent), and Nigeria (11 percent) are very different. Some have suggested that this study reflects the lack of diagnosis in Italy, for example, rather than the higher rates of dyslexia in English. Only further research will clarify this point. I would venture a guess, though, that just as children brought up bilingual from birth do not find any one language more difficult to learn than any other, neither would the dyslexic bilingual, if he or she was able to develop successful strategies for short-term memory reference.

In the scenario where research such as Paulesu's is correct, then people bringing up their children in "simple" phonetic language pairs (e.g., Italian and Spanish) may have an easier time compared to those with difficult language

Table 21.1
Percentage of Dyslexics by Country

Country	Language	Percentage of Dyslexics
Belgium	French	5%
Britain	English	4%
Czech Republic	Czech	2-3%
Finland	Finnish	10%
Greece	Greek	5%
Italy	Italian	1.5-5%
Japan	Japanese	6%
Nigeria	English	11%
Norway	Norwegian	3%
USA	English	8.5%

pairs (e.g., English and Russian). If the choice of language does come into play, further evidence of dyslexia being far less on Chinese character recognition should hearten those using pictorial or character-based systems. In 1971 a study was conducted at the University of Pennsylvania on a small group of American children who had trouble reading in English. They found that the children could learn to read English represented by Chinese characters. This can be attributed to the fact that pictorial images are a function of the right hemisphere, whereas the Phoenician alphabet as symbols is deciphered in the left hemisphere (Butterworth and Wengang 1991).

Other factors that can affect the bilingual dyslexic arise from the new mobility the world is experiencing. "Children with learning difficulties function best when they are in a stable and secure environment. . . . But when moving abroad, it is not always possible to maintain familiar routines. . . . Children with specific learning difficulties need both special teaching methods and more time to learn things than other children. Above all, they need continuity if they are to be able to carry out the task in hand," said Kirsten Thogersen at the Action for Dyslexia Conference in Brussels (November 1994). Additionally, many international schools pride themselves on high academic standards, and often have a strong sense of competition that can be a problem for dyslexics due to their slower processing of language information. The beneficial side to an international school is that many large international schools also pride themselves on good learning support programs that can be a haven for the dyslexic child. "Moving can be a positive and stimulating experience; it can teach children and young people to be expressive and aware of their strengths and how to cope with their weaknesses. This is especially true if the child with learning difficulties has been labeled and overprotected before moving; and has not had enough stimulation over a period of time. . . . Ironically, what in the first instance appears to be a pressuring educational environment can also be the very catalyst which eventually uncovers the child's potential" (Thogersen 1994).

FINAL WORDS ON LANGUAGE CHALLENGES

While the traditional concepts of Down's syndrome, deafness and dyslexia generally steered parents away from bilingualism, new research gives pause for reflection. Given a more individualized approach to each of these language development problem areas, and given the highly individualistic nature of bilingualism and varying family situations, it becomes evident that families not only must reflect on the ten key factors influencing successful multilingualism but also consider many additional factors. The *physical impediments* that Down's syndrome, deafness, and dyslexia bring with them, and *different brain structures* involved are both extremely important. The individual's family structure, whether living abroad temporarily or in one language environment for the long term, the school options available, and the child's abilities must all be considered before a decision about bilingualism can take place. On balance, however, there is reason for optimism in each of these situations, for individuals have become proficient bilinguals despite challenges to their normal language development.

REFERENCES

Ahlgren, I., and K. Hyltenstam (1995). *Bilingualism in Deaf Education: International Studies on Sign Language and the Communication of the Deaf*. Hamburg, Germany: Signum Verlag.

Bakker, Dirk (2002). "The Brain Makes Waves." *Dyslexia International—Tools and Technologies*, no. 7, Spring: 3.

Bialystok, E. (1987). "Influences of Bilingualism on Metalinguistic Development." *Second Language Research* 3, no. 2: 54–166.

Birsh, J.R. (ed.) (1999). *Multisensory Teaching of Basic Language Skills*. Baltimore, MD: Paul H. Brooks.

Buckley, S. (1998). "Bilingual Children with Down's Syndrome." *Down's Syndrome News and Updates* 1, no. 1: 29–30.

Butterworth, B., and W. Yin (1991). "Universal and Language Specific Features of Reading: Evidence from Dyslexia in Chinese Readers." *Proceedings from the Royal Society Series B* 245: 91–95.

Chasty, H.D. (1994). "What Is Dyslexia." Paper presented at Action for Dyslexia Conference. Brussels, Belgium: Dyslexia International—Tools & Technology, November.

Cooreman, A.G.M.P. (1994). "Bilingualism and Dyslexia—A Practitioner's View." Paper presented at Action for Dyslexia Conference. Brussels, November.

Elliott, D., and D. J. Weeks (1993) "Cerebral Specialization for Speech Perception and Movement Organization in Adults with Down's Syndrome." *Cortex* 29, no. 1: 103–113.

Felzer, L. (1998). "Signing based multisensory reading and language program." Paper presented at the 26th Annual NDSC Convention. Dallas, TX, 7–9 August.

Freeman, B.J. (2002). Options to Meet the Challenges of Autism. Available: www.autism-society.org/packages/options.pdf.

Galaburda, A.M., M. Menard, and G.D. Rosen (1994). "Evidence for aberrant auditory anatomy in developmental dyslexia." *National Academy of Science* 19, no. 17: 8010–8013.

Gregory, S., A. Wells, and S. Smith (1997). *Bilingual Education with Deaf Children*. Clevedon, UK: Multilingual Matters.

Grosjean, F. (1982). *Life with Two Languages: An Introduction to Bilingualism*. Cambridge, MA: Harvard University Press.

Grosjean, F. (1997). "The Right of the Deaf Child to Grow Up Bilingually." University of Neuchâtel, Internet document. Available: www.unine.ch/ltlp/pub/rightdeaf child_en.html.

Herbert, R.K. (1982). "Cerebral Asymmetry in Bilinguals and the Deaf." *Journal of Multilingual and Multicultural Development* 3, no. 1: 47–60.

Johnson, S. (1997). "Preventing oral-motor problems in down syndrome." *Advance* (4 August): 20.

Kantrowitz, B., and A. Underwood (1999). "Dyslexia and the new science of reading. *Newsweek*, 22 November, 72–78.

MacDonaldson, J. (1989). *Becoming Partners with Children: From Play to Conversation*. Chicago: Riverside.

Mahon, M. (1996). "Conversational Interactions Between Young Deaf Children and Their Families in Homes Where English Is Not the First Language." Ph.D. diss., Department of Human Communication, University College, London.

Manolson, A., and H. Buck (1992). *It Takes Two to Talk*. Toronto, Ontario, Canada: The Hanen Centre.

Mason, D.G. (1995). "Why bilingualism/biculturalism is appropriate in deaf education." *Deaf Children's Society Newsletter*, September/October. Available: www.dww.deafworldweb.org/pub/b/bibi.mason.html

Panou, L., and D.F. Sewell (1981). "Cerebral Lateralisation in the Deaf: A Deaf Bilingual Pattern?" *Journal of Multilingual and Multicultural Development* 2: 45–51.

Papagno, C., and G. Vallar. (1995). "Language and non-linguistic memory." *Quarterly Journal of Experimental Psychology* 48A, no. 1: 98–107.

Paulesu, E. (2001). "Dyslexia and Cultural Diversity and Biological Unity." *Science* 291: 2165.

Reagan, T. (1985). "The Deaf as a Linguistic Minority: Educational Considerations." *Harvard Educational Review* 53, no. 3: 399–415.

Richards, T., S.R. Dager, D. Corina, S. Serafini, A.C. Heide, K. Steury, W. Strauss, C.E. Hayes, R.D. Abbolt, S. Craft, D. Shaw, S. Posse, and V. Berninger (1999). "Dyslexic Children Have Abnormal Brain Lactate Response to Reading-Related Language Tasks." *American Journal of Neuroradiology* 20, no. 9: 1393–1398.

Thogersen, K.H. (1994). "Children on the Move—Culture Shock." Paper presented at Action for Dyslexia Conference. Brussels, Belgium: Dyslexia International—Tools & Technology, November.

Tokuhama-Espinosa, T. (2001). *Raising Multilingual Children: Foreign Language Acquisition and Children*. Westport, CT: Bergin & Garvey.

Vallar, G., and C. Papagno (1993). "Preserved Vocabulary Acquisition in Down's Syndrome: The Role of Phonological Short-term Memory." *Cortex* 29, no. 3: 467–483.

Down's syndrome issues and information: www.down-syndrome.info/

Conclusion

Tracey Tokuhama-Espinosa

The beauty of essays like those in this volume is that each question gives birth to new ones. In considering what language multilinguals do math in, one is immediately stirred to hypothesize why, neurologically, this is possible. When investigating how the sense of smell could enhance learning of foreign languages, one is impelled to ask whether other types of memory application could also be enhanced by odors. If we realize that children begin their exposure to languages while in the womb, then we are encouraged to investigate the idea of further learning in the prenatal state.

As socially inquisitive creatures, we pose questions related to learning, memory, language, and interaction. This leads to some of the queries here on linguistic hegemony, the phenomenon of global nomads, the identification of greater numbers of families raising their children trilingually, and the development of the relationship between multilingualism and cosmopolitanism. On an individual level, we question how our minds work, philosophically as well as neurologically. Humans are the only creatures who can think about thinking, and who can can study their own brains. How does it work? Why does it sometimes fail? How can it be further stimulated? What part of the brain is responsible for which skill? How can a person with a different kind of brain still survive given the social limitations we place on him?

My hope is that this book has raised more questions than it has answered. Research into the multilingual mind is in its infancy. As communication between people around the world improves, benefits of multilingualism are beginning to be recognized on a global scale. These essays were gathered primarily through the Internet, which, as one of the essays points out, is the fastest-growing means of global communication today. This tool has contributed to the variety of material that is included in these pages. In this book we have been able to share experiences of an Italian-German third culture kid growing up in Brazil, Belgium, Colombia, and Peru; Turkish immigrants in Germany and questions of foreign adoption; Japanese technology in aromatherapy applied to a Vermont setting; a California two-way immersion model that could become a world standard; a French poet's work as an English author; a Romanian/German polyglot lawyer's perspective on multilingualism and cosmopolitanism; a Spanish linguist's challenge bringing up her daughter in America; and an Australian linguist with a Japanese language background's look at how bilinguals learn math in French-speaking Switzerland. Though the variety of authors and their perspectives in this book is great, questions still remain.

For example, what about social graces and languages? Is it impolite to speak to your child in one language when everyone else in the room is speaking another? How about language extinction? Which languages are in danger of dying out? Should they be saved? Do we have a cultural obligation to preserve them? How? What about the rapidly expanding area of brain research and languages? Can the area of the brain used to learn a foreign language be precisely identified in relation to when the language was learned and what linguistic relationship the first language has to the second? If so, how can it be stimulated? Is there a gene for foreign language ability? Has this been indisputably proven? Which one is it? Can it be cloned or stimulated somehow? What about sibling differences in language acquisition, and the questions of enhanced creativity in relation to multilingualism? How can a school system influence a child's success with languages, or hinder it? Last but not least, is multilingual competency restricted to people with socially privileged backgrounds, or do social and economic factors have just a small influence on the development of a multilingual mind if a certain basic type of intelligence is apparent? Each of these areas merits further investigation.

I remember hearing the dictum "The more you know, the more you know you don't know," sometime in high school. Later in my life, when working on the theory of knowledge curriculum for the international baccalaureate, I remember reinforcing the idea that learning *how* to think, not *what* to think, was of greatest importance. I still find this is true in our search to better understand the workings of the multilingual mind. We need to identify the questions, but not remain satisfied with the answers, and it is clear that the field is wide open for greater research in a great number of areas in cognitive science. My hope is that each answer here breeds a new series of questions, which will in turn bring further attention to the rich depths of the multilingual mind.

Bibliography

Abunuwara, E. (1992). "The Structure of the Trilingual Lexicon." *European Journal of Cognitive Psychology* 4, no. 4: 311–322.

Aciman, A. (1996). *Out of Egypt: A Memoir.* New York: Harvill Press.

Ackerman, B. (1994). "Rooted Cosmopolitanism." *Ethics* 104, no. 3: 516–535.

Acredolo, L., and S. Goodwyn (1996). *Baby Signs: How to Talk to Your Baby Before Your Baby Can Talk.* Chicago, IL: Contemporary Books.

Ada, A.F. (1997). "Mother-tongue Literacy as a Bridge Between Home and School Cultures." In J. Villamil Tinajero and A.F. Ada, *The Power of Two Languages: Literacy and Biliteracy for Spanish Speaking Students.* New York: Macmillan/McGraw-Hill.

Adams, M.J. (1996). *Beginning to Read: Thinking and Learning About Print.* Cambridge, MA: MIT Press.

Ahlgren, I., and K. Hyltenstam (1995). *Bilingualism In Deaf Education.* Hamburg, Germany: Signum Verlag.

Albert, M.L., and L. Obler (1979). *The Bilingual Brain: Neuropsychological and Neurolinguistic Aspects of Bilingualism.* New York: Academic Press.

Allemann-Ghionda, C. (1999). *Schule, Bildung und Pluralität: Sechs Fallstudie im europäischen Vergleich.* Bern: Peter Lang.

Allemann-Ghionda, C. (ed.) (1997). *Multikultur und Bildung in Europa. Multiculture et éducation en Europe.* 2nd ed. Bern: Peter Lang.

Allemann-Ghionda, C., C. de Goumoëns, and C. Perregaux (1999). *Pluralité et culturelle dans la formation des enseignants.* Programme National de Recherche 33. Bern: Presses Universitaires de Fribourg.

Ambert, A.N. (1991). *Bilingual Education and English as a Second Language: A Research Handbook 1988–1990.* New York: Garland.

American Academy of Pediatrics (1997). "Noise: A hazard for the fetus and newborn." *Pediatrics* 100 no. 4: RE9728.

Anderson, A. (1998). "Cosmopolitanism, Universalism, and the Divided Legacies of Modernity." In P. Cheah and B. Robbins (eds.), *Cosmopolitics: Thinking and Feeling Beyond the Nation.* Minneapolis: University of Minnesota Press.

Andersson. U., and S. Andersson (1999). *Growing Up with Two Languages.* London: Routledge.

Andrews, L. (1998). *Language Exploration and Awareness: A Resource Book for Teachers.* 2nd ed. London: Lawrence Erlbaum Associates.

Apeltauer, E. (1993). "Multilingualism in a Society of the Future?" *European Journal of Education* 28, no. 3: 273–294.

Appadurai, A., and C. Breckenridge (1998). "Why Public Culture?" *Public Culture Bulletin* 1, no. 1: 5–9.

Appiah, K.A. (1998). "Cosmopolitan Patriots." In P. Cheah and B. Robbins (eds.), *Cosmopolitics: Thinking and Feeling Beyond the Nation.* Minneapolis: University of Minnesota Press.

Armstrong, T. (1998). *Awakening the Genius in the Classroom.* Alexandria, VA: Association for Supervision and Curriculum Development.

Armstrong, T. (2000). *Multiple Intelligences in the Classroom.* 2nd ed. Alexandria, VA: Association for Supervision and Curriculum Development.

Arnberg, L. (1987). *Raising Children Bilingually: The Pre-school Years.* Clevedon, UK: Multilingual Matters.

Asher, J. (1979). *Learning Another Language Through Actions: The Complete Teacher's Guidebook.* Los Gatos, CA: Sky Oaks Productions.

Baetens-Beardsmore, H. (1982). *Bilingualism: Basic Principles.* Clevedon, UK: Multilingual Matters.

Baetens-Beardsmore, H.B. (ed.) (1993). *European Models of Bilingual Education.* Clevedon, UK: Multilingual Matters.

Baker, C. (1992). *Attitudes and Language.* Clevedon, UK: Multilingual Matters.

Baker, C. (1996). *Foundations of Bilingual Education.* 2nd ed. Clevedon, UK: Multilingual Matters.

Baker, C. (2000). *A Parent's and Teacher's Guide to Bilingualism.* Clevedon, UK: Multilingual Matters.

Baker, C., and S. Prys Jones (eds.) (1999). *Encyclopedia of Bilingualism and Bilingual Education.* Clevedon, UK: Multilingual Matters.

Bakker, Dirk (2002). "The Brain Makes Waves." *Dyslexia International—Tools and Technologies,* no. 7, Spring: 3.

Bassnett, S. (2000). "Language and Identity." *The Linguist* 39, no. 3: 66–71.

Baumann, Z. (1996). "From Pilgrim to Tourist—or a Short History of Identity." In S. Hall and P. du Gay (eds.), *Questions of Cultural Identity.* London: Sage.

Bell, L.G. (1997). *Hidden Immigrants: Legacies of Growing Up Abroad.* Yarmouth, ME: Intercultural Press.

Benziger, K. (2000). *Thriving in Mind: The Art and Science of Using Your Whole Brain.* Dillon, CO: KBA.

Berger, K., and R. Thompson (1995). *The Developing Person: Through Childhood and Adolescence.* 4th ed. New York: Worth.

Bernstein, L. (1962). *The Infinite Variety of Music.* London: Weidenfeld and Nicolson.

Bernstein, M.L., and J. Brannen (eds.) (1996). *Children, Research and Policy.* London: Taylor and Francis.

Bialystok, E. (1987). "Influences of Bilingualism on Metalinguistic Development." *Second Language Research* 3, no. 2: 54–166.

Bialystok, E. (1997). "Effects of Bilingualism and Biliteracy on Children's Emerging Concepts of Print." *Developmented Psychology Journal* 33, no. 3.

Bilingual Education Handbook (1986). *Learning English in California.* Sacramento, CA: Assembly Office of Research.

Bilingual Education Handbook (1990). *Designing Instruction for Limited English Proficiency Students.* Sacramento: California Department of Education.

Bird, J., et al. (1993). *Mapping the Futures: Local Cultures, Global Change*. London: Routledge.

Birsh, J.R. (ed.) (1999). *Multisensory Teaching of Basic Language Skills*. Baltimore, MD: Paul H. Brooks.

Bloomfield, L. (1933). *Language*. New York: Holt, Rinehart and Winston.

Borman, K.M. (1998). *Ethnic Diversity in Communities and Schools*. Greenwich, CT: Ablex.

Brannon, E.M. (2002). "The Development of Ordinal Numerical Knowledge in Infancy." *Cognition* 83: 223–240.

Bransford, J., A.L. Brown, and R.R. Cocking (eds.) (2000). *How People Learn: Brain, Mind, Experience and School*. Enl. ed. Washington, DC: National Academy Press.

Brennan, T. (1997). *At Home in the World: Cosmopolitanism Now*. Cambridge, MA: Harvard University Press.

Brennan, T. (2001). "Cosmopolitanism and Internationalism." *New Left Review* 2, no. 7: 19, 75–84.

Brenneis, D. (1990). "Ecology and Culture." In M.A. Runco and R.S. Albert (eds.), *Theories of Creativity*. London: Sage.

Brown, K.S. (1999). "Striking the Right Note." *New Scientist Magazine* 164, no. 2215: 38–41.

Bruckner, P. (1996). "The Edge of Babel." *Partisan Review* 63, no. 2: 242–254.

Bruer, J. (1999). "Neural Connections, Some You Use, Some You Lose." *Phi Delta Kappan* (December): 264–277.

Bruner, J. (1996). *The Culture of Education*. Cambridge, MA: Harvard University Press.

Buckley, S. (1998). "Bilingual Children with Down's Syndrome." *Down's Syndrome News and Updates* 1, no. 1: 29–30.

Butterworth, B., and W. Yin (1991). "Universal and Language-Specific Features of Reading: Evidence from Dyslexia in Chinese Readers." *Proceedings from the Royal Society Series B* 245: 91–95.

Buttjes, D. (1991). "Mediating Languages and Cultures: The Social and Intercultural Dimension Restored." In D. Buttjes and M. Byram (eds.), *Mediating Languages and Cultures: Towards an Intercultural Theory of Foreign Language Education*. Clevedon, UK: Multilingual Matters.

Buttjes, D., and M. Byram (eds.) (1991). *Mediating Languages and Cultures: Towards an Intercultural Theory of Foreign Language Education*. Clevedon, UK: Multilingual Matters.

Byram, M. (1997). *Teaching and Assessing Intercultural Communicative Competence*. Clevedon, UK: Multilingual Matters.

Byram, M., and M. Fleming (eds.) (1998). *Language Learning in Intercultural Perspective: Approaches Through Drama and Ethnography*. Cambridge: Cambridge University Press.

Byram, M., and J. Leman (eds.) (1990). *Bicultural and Tricultural Education*. Clevedon, UK: Multilingual Matters.

Byram, M., C. Morgan, et al. (1994). *Teaching-and-Learning Language-and-Culture*. Clevedon, UK: Multilingual Matters.

Byram, M., and K. Risager (1999). *Language Teachers, Politics and Cultures*. Clevedon, UK: Multilingual Matters.

Campbell, D. (1997). *The Mozart Effect*. New York: Avon Books.

Canetti, Elias (1977, 1999). *Die gerettete Zunge*. Munich: Hanser. Translated as *The Tongue Set Free: Remembrance of a European Childhood*. New York: Farrar, Straus and Giroux.

Celce-Murcia, M., D.M. Brinton, and J.M. Goodwin (1996). *Teaching Pronunciation. A Reference for Teachers of English to Speakers of Other Languages*. Cambridge, UK: Cambridge University Press.

Cenoz, J., and F. Genesee (eds.) (1998). *Beyond Bilingualism: Multilingualism and Multilingual Education*. Philadelphia: Multilingual Matters.

Cenoz, J., B. Hufeisen, and U. Jessner (2001). "Towards Trilingual Education." *International Journal of Bilingual Education and Bilingualism* 4, no. 1: 1–10.

Centre for Linguistics, University of Western Australia (1998). "Diglossia and Multilingualism." Language, Brain and Culture, Linguistics 102. Index to L-102 notes. October.

Chasty, H.D. (1994). "What Is Dyslexia." Paper presented at Action for Dyslexia Conference. Brussels, Belgium: Dyslexia International—Tools & Technology, November.

Cheah, P. (1998). "Given Culture: Rethinking Cosmopolitical Freedom in Transnationalism." In P. Cheah and B. Robbins (eds.), *Cosmopolitics: Thinking and Feeling Beyond the Nation*. Minneapolis: University of Minnesota Press.

Cheah, P., and B. Robbins (eds.) (1998). *Cosmopolitics: Thinking and Feeling Beyond the Nation*. Minneapolis: University of Minnesota Press.

Chick, K. (1999, August). "Teaching English in Multiethnic Schools in the Durban Area: The Promotion of Multilingualism or Monolingualism?" Paper presented at Annual Conference for Language Teachers, University of Natal, Durban.

Child, I.L. (1943). *Italian or American? The Second Generation in Conflict*. New York: Russell and Russell.

Chomsky, N. (1988). *Creating Curriculum Music*. New York: Prentice Hall.

Christ, H. (1996). "Tests de plurilinguisme." In H. Goebl et al. (eds.), *Contact Linguistics: An International Handbook of Contemporary Research*. Vol. 1. Berlin and New York: Walter de Gruyter.

Classen, C., D. Howes, and A. Synnott (1994). *Aroma: The Cultural History of Smell*. London: Routledge.

Clavet, L.J. (ed.) (1987). *La Guerre des langues*. Paris: Payot.

Clifford, J. (1992). "Travelling Cultures." In L. Grossberg, C. Nelson, and P.A. Treichler (eds.), *Cultural Studies*. New York: Routledge.

Clyne, M. (1982). *Multilingual Australia*. Melbourne: River Seine Publications.

Clyne, M. (1997). "Some of the Things Trilinguals Do." *International Journal of Bilingualism* 1, no. 2: 95–116.

Cockett, M. (1988). "Neuro-linguistic What?" *Mainichi Daily News* (Tokyo), 25 November, p. 9.

Cohen, J. (ed.) (1996). *For Love of Country: Debating the Limits of Patriotism*. Boston: Beacon Press.

Coleman, J.A. (1996). *Studying Languages: A Survey of British and European Students. The Proficiency, Background, Attitudes and Motivations of Students of Foreign Languages in the United Kingdom and Europe*. London: Centre for Information on Language Teaching and Research.

Coleman, J.A. (1998). "Evolving Intercultural Perceptions Among University Language Learners in Europe." In M. Byram and M. Fleming (eds.), *Language Learning in Intercultural Perspective: Approaches Through Drama and Ethnography.* Cambridge: Cambridge University Press.

Cooreman, A.G.M.P. (1994). "Bilingualism and Dyslexia—A Practitioner's View." Paper presented at Action for Dyslexia Conference. Brussels, November.

Coste, D. (1997). "Multilingual and Multicultural Competence and the Role of School." *Language Teaching* 30, no. 2: 90–93.

Council of Europe (1998). *Modern Languages: Learning, Teaching, Assessment. A Common European Framework of Reference* Strasbourg: Council of Europe. Council for Cultural Co-operation, Education Committee.

Crawford, J. (1991). *Bilingual Education: History, Politics, Theory, and Practice.* 2nd ed. Los Angeles: Bilingual Educational Services.

Cromie, W.J. (1997). "How your brain listens to music." *Harvard Gazette,* 13 November. Available: www.news.harvard.edn/guzette/1997/11.13/HowYourBrainLis .html.

Cropley, A.J. (1992). *More Ways Than One: Fostering Creativity.* Norwood, NJ: Ablex.

Crowder, R.C. (1993). "Auditory Memory." In S. McAdams and E. Bigand (eds.), *Thinking in Sound: The Cognitive Psychology of Human Audition.* Oxford: Clarendon Press.

Crystal, D. (2000). *Language Death.* Cambridge: Cambridge University Press.

Csikszentmihályi, Mihály (1988). "Creativity and Problem Finding." In F.H. Farley and R.W. Neperud (eds.), *The Foundation of Aesthetics, Art, and Art Education.* New York: Praeger.

Csikszentmihályi, Mihály (1990). "The Domain of Creativity." In M.A. Runco and R.S. Albert (eds.), *Theories of Creativity.* London: Sage.

Cumming, A.H. (ed.) (1994). *Bilingual Performance in Reading and Writing.* Ann Arbor, MI: John Benjamin's Publishing Co.

Cummins, J. (2001). "Instructional Conditions for Trilingual Development." *International Journal of Bilingual Education and Bilingualism* 4, no. 1: 61–75.

Cummins, J.P., and M. Swain (1979). "Linguistic Interdependence and Educational Development of Bilingual Children." *Review of Educational Research* 49: 222–251.

Cummins, R. (1994). "Interpretational Semantics: Representations, Target and Attitude." In S.P. Stich and T.A. Warfield (eds.), *Mental Representations.* Oxford: Blackwell.

Daley, Suzanne (2001). "In Europe, Some Fear National Languages Are Endangered." *New York Times,* 16 April, A1.

Dalton, C., and B. Seidlhofer (1994). *Pronunciation.* Oxford: Oxford University Press.

De Cos, P.L. (1999). *Educating California's Immigrant Children: An Overview of Bilingual Education.* Sacramento: California Research Bureau.

De Houver, A. (1998). "By Way of Introduction: Methods in Studies of Bilingual First Language Acquisition." *International Journal of Bilingualism* 2, no. 3: 249–263.

De Jong, E. (1986). *The Bilingual Experience.* Cambridge: Cambridge University Press.

Delanty, G. (2000). *Citizenship in a Global Age: Society, Culture, Politics.* Buckingham: Open University Press.

Disability Services, University of Minnesota (1995). *Guidelines Regarding Multiple Chemical Sensitivity/Environmental Illness (MCS/EI).* Minneapolis: University of Minnesota.

Dissanayake, E. (1990, August). *Music as a Human Behavior: A Hypothesis of Evolutionary Origin and Function*. Paper presented at the Human Behavior and Evolution Society meeting, Los Angeles, CA.

Döpke, S. (1992). "A Bilingual Child's Struggle to Comply with the 'One Parent-One Language' Rule." *Journal of Multilingual and Multicultural Development* 13, no. 6: 467–485.

Dranov, P. (1995). "Making Sense of Scents (a Surprisingly Scary Update)." *Cosmopolitan*, August, p. 204.

Draper, T.W., and C. Gayle (1987). "An Analysis of Historical Reasons for Teaching Music to Young Children: Is It the Same Old Song?" In J.C. Peery, I.W. Peery, and T.W. Draper (eds.), *Music and Child Development*. New York: Springer-Verlag.

Dunn, R.S. (1996). *How to Implement and Supervise a Learning Style Program*. Alexandria, VA: Association for Supervision and Curriculum Development.

Early, R. (1999). "Double trouble, and three is a crowd: Languages in education and official languages in Vanuatu." *Journal of Multilingual and Multicultural Development* 20, no. 1: 13–33.

Edwards, C., L. Gandini, and G. Froman (eds.) (1998). *The Hundred Languages of Children: The Reggio Emilia Approach—Advanced Reflections*. 2nd ed. Greenwich, CT: Ablex.

Edwards, J. (1994). *Multilingualism*. London: Routledge.

Eilers, R.E., W. Gavin, and W.R. Wilson (1979). "Linguistic Experience and Phonemic Perception in Infancy: A Cross-Linguistic Study." *Child Development* no. 50: 14–18.

Eilers, R., D.K. Oller, and C. Benito-Garcia (1984). "The Acquisition of Voicing Contrast in Spanish and English Learning Infants and Children: A Longitudinal Study." *Journal of Child Language* 2: 313–336.

Eimas, P. (1985). "The Perception of Speech in Early Infancy." *Scientific American* 252, 1: 46–61.

Einstein, A., and L. Infeld (1938). *The Evolution of Physics*. New York: Simon and Schuster.

Elkonin, D.B. (1993). *Comparative Reading*. New York: Macmillan.

Elliott, D., and D.J. Weeks (1993). "Cerebral Specialization for Speech Perception and Movement Organization in Adults with Down's Syndrome." *Cortex* 29, no. 1: 103–113.

Ellis, A. (1994). *Reading, Writing and Dyslexia: A Cognitive Analysis*. 2nd ed. Hillsdale, NJ: Lawrence Erlbaum Associates.

Ellis, R. (1985). *Understanding Second Language Acquisition*. Oxford: Oxford University Press.

Elson, A. (1927). *The Book of Musical Knowledge: The History, Technique, and Appreciation of Music, Together with Lives of the Great Composers*. Boston: Houghton Mifflin.

Elwert, W.T. (1959). *Das zweisprachige Individuum: Ein Selbstzeugnis*. Wiesbaden: Franz Steiner-Verlag.

Engen, T. (1991). *Odor Sensation and Memory*. New York: Praeger.

Erb, R.C. (1968). *The Common Scents of Smell: How the Nose Knows and What It All Shows!* Cleveland, OH: World Publishing Co.

ESEA Title VII Directory: Bilingual Education Basic and Demonstration Projects (1985). Sacramento: Bilingual Education Office, California State Department of Public Education.

European Commission (1996). *White Paper on Education and Training. Teaching and Learning: Towards the Learning Society.* Brussels: European Commission.

Fantini, A.E. (1985). *Language Acquisition of a Bilingual Child.* Clevedon, UK: Multilingual Matters.

Farley, F.H., and R.W. Neperud (eds.) (1988). *The Foundation of Aesthetics, Art, and Art Education.* New York: Praeger.

Featherstone, M. (1993). "Global and Local Cultures." In J. Bird et al., *Mapping the Futures: Local Cultures, Global Change.* London: Routledge.

Featherstone, M. (ed.) (1990). *Global Culture: Nationalism, Globalization and Modernity.* London: Sage.

Featherstone, M., S. Lash, and R. Robertson (eds.) (1995). *Global Modernities.* London: Sage.

Felzer, L. (1998). "Signing based multisensory reading and language program." Paper presented at the 26th Annual NDSC Convention. Dallas, TX, 7–9 August.

Ferguson, J. (1999). *Expectations of Modernity: Myths and Meanings of Urban Life on the Zambian Copperbelt.* Berkeley: University of California Press.

Fishman, J.A. (ed.) (1968). *Readings in the Sociology of Language.* The Hague: Mouton.

Flege, J.M. (1981). "The Phonological Basis of Foreign Accent: A Hypothesis." *TESOL Quarterly* 15: 443–453.

Flesch, R. (1986). *Why Johnny Can't Read.* 2nd ed. New York: Harper & Row.

Fodor, J.A. (1975). *The Language of Thought.* New York: Crowell.

Freeman, B.J. (2002). Options to Meet the Challenges of Autism. Available: www.autism-society.org/packages/options.pdf.

Friedman, J. (1995). "Global Systems, Globalization and the Parameters of Modernity." In M. Featherstone, S. Lash, and R. Robertson (eds.), *Global Modernities.* London: Sage.

Fuller, R. (1995). "Parabola: Myth, Tradition and the Search for Meaning." *Language and Meaning* 20, no. 3: 33–38.

Galaburda, A.M., M. Menard, and G.D. Rosen (1994). "Evidence for aberrant auditory anatomy in developmental dyslexia." *National Academy Journal* 19, no. 17: 8010–8013.

Galindo, R. (1997). "Language wars: The ideological dimensions of the debates on bilingual education." *Bilingual Research Journal* 21, no. 2–3: 163–201.

Gallistel, C.R., and R. Gelman (1992). "Preverbal and Verbal Counting and Computation." *Cognition* 44: 43–74.

Garcia-Vasquez, E., et al. (1997). "Language proficiency and academic success: Relationships between proficiency in two languages and achievement among Mexican-American students." *Bilingual Research Journal* 21 no. 4: 395–408.

Gardner, H. (1976). *The Shattered Mind.* New York: Knopf/Vintage.

Gardner, H. (1983). *Frames of Mind: The Theory of Multiple Intelligences.* New York: Basic Books.

Gardner, H. (1988). "Creative Lives and Creative Works: A Synthetic Scientific Approach." In R.J. Sternberg, (ed.), *The Nature of Creativity: Contemporary Psychological Perspectives.* New York: Cambridge University Press.

Gardner, H. (1993). *Multiple Intelligences: The Theory in Practice*. New York: Basic Books.

Gardner-Chloros, P. (1991). *Language Selection and Switching in Strasbourg*. Oxford, UK: Clarendon Press.

Gaudinier, K. (October 1995). Personal conversation with author.

Geller, E. (1994). *Encounters with Nationalism*. Oxford and Cambridge, MA: Blackwell.

Gelman, R., and K. Brenneman (1994). "First Principles Can Support Both Universal and Culture-specific Learning About Number and Music." In L.A. Hirschfield S.A. Gelman (eds.), *Mapping the Mind: Domain Specificity in Cognition and Culture*. Cambridge: Cambridge University Press.

Genesee, F.H. (1982). "Experimental neuropsychological research on second language processing." *TESOL Quarterly* 6, No. 3: 315–322.

Genesee, F., W.E. Lambert, L. Mononen, M. Seitz, and R. Starch (1979). "Language processing in bilinguals." *Brain and Language* 5, no. 5: 1–12.

Gerritsen, J. (1996). *How the Tomatis Method Accelerates Learning Foreign Languages*. Paris, France: Tomatis Listening and Learning Center.

Gnutzmann, C. (1997). "Multilingualism and Language Teaching: Some Pedagogical Implications with Reference to Language Awareness." *Fremdsprachen Lehren und Lernen* 26: 156–166.

Goddard, V.A., J.R. Llobera, and C. Shore (1994). "Introduction: The Anthropology of Europe." In V.A. Goddard, J. Llobera, and C. Shore (eds.), *The Anthropology of Europe: Identities and Boundaries in Conflict*. Oxford and Providence, RI: Berg.

Goddard, V.A., J. Llobera, and C. Shore (eds.) (1994). *The Anthropology of Europe: Identities and Boundaries in Conflict*. Oxford and Providence, RI: Berg.

Goebl, H., et al. (eds.) (1996). *Contact Linguistics: An International Handbook of Contemporary Research*. Vol. 1. Berlin and New York: Walter de Gruyter.

Goetschy, H., and A.-L. Sanguin (1995). *Languages régionales et relations transfrontalières en Europe*. Paris: L'Harmattan.

Gordon, A.I. (1966). *Intermarriage*. London: Beacon Press.

Graddol, D. (1998). "What's the Future for Languages?" *The Linguist* 37, no. 5: 144–146.

Graddol, D., and S. Thomas (eds.) (1995). *Language in a Changing Europe: Papers from the Annual Meeting of the British Association for Applied Linguistics, Held at the University of Salford, September 1993*. Clevedon, UK: Multilingual Matters.

Green, A., and C. Warren (1995). *Perfume*. Advertising Supplement. New York Times, October: 24.

Gregory, S., A. Wells, and S. Smith (1997). *Bilingual Education with Deaf Children*. Clevedon, UK: Multilingual Matters.

Griessler, M. (2001). "The Effects of Third Language Learning on Second Language Proficiency: An Austrian Example." *International Journal of Bilingual Education and Bilingualism* 4, no. 1: 50–60.

Griffin, K. (1992). "A whiff of things to come." *Health*, November/December, pp. 34–36.

Grillo, R.D. (1989). *Dominant Languages: Language and Hierarchy in Britain and France*. Cambridge: Cambridge University Press.

Grosjean, F. (1982). *Life with Two Languages: An Introduction to Bilingualism*. Cambridge, MA: Harvard University Press.

Grosjean, F. (1997). "The Right of the Deaf Child to Grow Up Bilingually." University of Neuchâtel, Internet document. Available: www.unine.ch/ltlp/pub/rightdeaf child_en.html.

Grossberg, L., C. Nelson, and P.A. Treichler (eds.) (1992). *Cultural Studies*. New York: Routledge.

Gutmann, A. "Democratic Citizenship." In J. Cohen (ed.), *For Love of Country: Debating the Limits of Patriotism*. Boston: Beacon Press.

Hagège, C. (1996). *L'Enfant aux deux langues*. Paris: Editions Odile Jacob.

Hakuta, K. (1986). *Mirror of Language: The Debate on Bilingualism*. New York: Basic Books.

Halemariam, C., S. Kroon, and J. Walters (1999). "Multilingualism and nation building: Language and education in Eritrea." *Journal of Multilingual and Multicultural Development* 20, no. 6.

Hall, S., and P. du Gay (eds.) (1996). *Questions of Cultural Identity*. London: Sage.

Hammarberg, B. (2001). "Roles of L1 and L2 in L3 Production and Acquisition." In J. Cenoz, B. Hufeison, and U. Jessner (eds.), *Crosslinguistic Influences in Third Language Acquisition: Psycholinguistic Perspective*. Clevedon, UK: Multilingual Matters.

Hannerz, U. (1990). "Cosmopolitans and Locals in World Culture." In M. Featherstone (ed.), *Global Culture: Nationalism, Globalization and Modernity*. London: Sage.

Hannerz, U. (1992). *Cultural Complexity: Studies in the Social Organization of Meaning*. New York: Columbia University Press.

Hannerz, U. (1996). *Transnational Connections: Culture, People, Places*. London: Routledge.

Harding, E., and P. Riley (1996). *The Bilingual Family: A Handbook for Parents*. 9th printing. Cambridge: Cambridge University Press.

Harley, B. (1986). *Age in Second Language Acquisition*. Clevedon, UK: Multilingual Matters.

Harley, B., P. Allen, J. Cummins, and M. Swain (eds.) (1990). "The development of second language proficiency." In M.H. Long and J.C. Richards (eds.), *Cambridge Applied Linguistics Series*. Cambridge, UK: Cambridge University Press.

Harris, J.R. (1998). *The Nurture Assumption*. New York: The Free Press.

Held, D., et al. (1999). *Global Transformations: Politics, Economics and Culture*. Cambridge: Polity Press.

Hepper, P.G. (1996). "Fetal Memory: Does It Exist? What Does It Do?" *Acta Paediatrica* supp. 416. 16–20.

Herbert, R.K. (1982). "Cerebral Asymmetry in Bilinguals and the Deaf." *Journal of Multilingual and Multicultural Development* 3, no. 1: 47–60.

Hinkel, E. (1999a). *Culture in Second Language Teaching and Learning*. Cambridge: Cambridge University Press.

Hinkel, E. (1999b). "Introduction: Culture in Research and Second Language Pedagogy." In Eli Hinkel, *Culture in Second Language Teaching and Learning*. Cambridge: Cambridge University Press.

Hirschfield, L.A., and S.A. Gelman (1994). "Towards a Topography of the Mind: An Introduction to Domain Specificity." In L. Hirschfield and S.A. Gelman (eds.), *Mapping the Mind: Domain Specificity in Cognition and Culture*. Cambridge: Cambridge University Press.

Hirschfield, L., and S.A. Gelman (eds.) (1994). *Mapping the Mind: Domain Specificity in Cognition and Culture*. Cambridge: Cambridge University Press.

Hoffmann, C. (1985). "Language Acquisition in Two Trilingual Children." *Journal of Multilingual and Multicultural Development* 6, no. 6: 479–495.

Hopson, J. (1998). "Fetal psychology." *Psychology Today* 31, no. 5: 44.

Horgan, T. (1994). "Computation and Mental Representation." In S.P. Stich and T.A. Warfield (eds.), *Mental Representations: A Reader*. Cambridge, MA: Blackwell.

Hornby, P. (ed.) (1977). *Bilingualism: Psychological, Social and Educational Implications*. New York: Academic Press.

Horowitz, E.K., D.J. Young, and J.A. Cope (1991). "Foreign Language Classroom Anxiety." In E.K. Horowitz and D.J. Young (eds.), *Language Anxiety: From Theory and Research to Classroom Implications*. Englewood Cliffs, NJ: Prentice Hall.

Howieson, N. (1984). "Is Western Australia Neglecting the Creative Potential of Its Youth?" Paper presented at the Annual Conference of the Australian Psychological Society, Perth. August.

Hunter, B.T. (1995). "The Sales Appeal of Scents." *Consumer's Research*, October, pp. 8–9.

Hurwitz, I., P.H. Wolff, B.D. Bortnick, and K. Kokas (1975). "Nonmusical Effects of the Kodaly Music Curriculum in Primary Grade Children." *Journal of Learning Disabilities* 8: 45–51.

Imhoff, G. (ed.) (1990). *Learning in Two Languages: From Conflict to Consensus in the Reorganization of Schools*. New Brunswick, NJ: Transaction.

Johnson, S. (1997). "Preventing oral-motor problems in down's syndrome." *Advance* (4 August): 20.

Johnson, W., with R. Leutenegger (1967). *Stuttering in Children and Adults: Thirty Years of Research at the University of Iowa*. Minneapolis: University of Minnesota Press.

Joseph, R. (1993). *The Naked Neuron: Evolution and the Languages of the Body and Brain*. New York: Plenum Press.

Jourdain, R. (1997). *Music, the Brain and Ecstasy: How Music Captures Our Imagination*. New York: William Morrow.

Jusczyk, P. (1997). *The Discovery of Spoken Language*. Cambridge, MA: MIT Press.

Kamwangamalu, N.K. (ed.) (1998). *Aspects of Multilingualism in Post-Apartheid South Africa*. Berlin: Mouton de Gruyter.

Kantrowitz, B., and A. Underwood (1999). "Dyslexia and the new science of reading." *Newsweek*, 22 November, 72–78.

Kellman, S.G. (2000). *The Translingual Imagination*. Lincoln: University of Nebraska Press.

Kenrick, D.T., S.L. Neuberg, and R.B. Cialdini (eds.) (1999). *Social Psychology: Unraveling the Mystery*. Needham Heights, MA: Allyn & Bacon.

Kessler, C. (1984). *Language Acquisition Processes in Bilingual Children*. Los Angeles: Evaluation, Dissemination, and Assessment Center.

King, A. (ed.) (2000). *Languages and the Transfer of Skills: The Relevance of Language Learning for 21st Century Graduates in the World of Work*. London: Centre for Information on Language Teaching and Research.

Klein, E.C. (1995). "Second Versus Third Language Acquisition: Is There a Difference?" *Language Learning* 45, no. 3: 419–465.

Klein, R. (1995). "Get a whiff of this: Breaking the smell barrier." *The New Republic*, February, pp. 18–23.

Krashen, S. (1982). *Principles and Practices in Second Language Acquisition*. Oxford: Pergamon Press.

Kravin, H. (1992). "Erosion of Language in Bilingual Development." *Journal of Multilingual and Multicultural Development* 13, no. 4: 307–325.

Kymlicka, W. (2001). *Politics in the Vernacular: Nationalism, Multiculturalism, and Citizenship*. Oxford: Oxford University Press.

Lamb, S.J., and A.H. Gregory (1993). "The Relationship Between Music and Reading in Beginning Readers." *Educational Psychology* 13, 19–27.

Lamb, S.M. (1999). *Pathways to the Brain: The Neurocognitive Basis of Language*. Amsterdam: John Benjamin's Publisher.

Lambert, R.D. (1993). "International Education and International Competence in the United States." *European Journal of Education* 28, no. 3: 309–325.

Lambert, W.E. (1977). "The Effects of Bilingualism on the Individual: Cognitive and Sociocultural Consequences." In P. Hornby (ed.), *Bilingualism: Psychological, Social and Educational Implications*. New York: Academic Press.

Lambret, N.M., and B.L. McCombs (eds.) (1997). *How Students Learn: Reforming Schools Through Learner-Centered Education*. Washington, DC: American Psychological Association.

Lantolf, J.P., and G. Sunderman (2001). "The Struggle for a Place in the Sun: Rationalising Foreign Language Study in the Twentieth Century." *Modern Language Journal* 85, no. 1: 5–25.

Larson, A. (1997). *Dads at a Distance: An Activities Handbook for Strengthening Long Distance Relationships*. Provo, UT: A&E Family Publishing.

Lawrence, R. (2002). *How the Tomatis Method Affected My Violin Playing*. Available: www.tomatis.com/English/Stories/violin_playing.htm.

Lee, J.F., and B. Van Patten (1995). *Making Communicative Language Teaching Happen*. New York: McGraw-Hill.

Le Guerer, A. (1992). *Scent: The Mysterious and Essential Powers of Smell*. New York: Turtle Bay Books.

Leighton, M.S., A. Hightower, and P. Wrigley (1995). *Model Strategies in Bilingual Education: Professional Development*. Washington, DC: U.S. Department of Education.

Lenneberg, E.H. (1967). *Biological Foundations of Language*. New York: John Wiley & Sons.

Leopold, W. (1949). "Speech Development of a Bilingual Child, a Linguist's Record." In *Vocabulary Growth in the First Two Years*. New York: AMS Press.

Liberman, I.Y., D. Shankweiler, B. Blachman, L. Camp, and M. Wefelman (1980). "Steps Towards Literacy: A Linguistic Approach." In P. Levinson and C. Sloan (eds.), *Auditory Processing and Language: Clinical and Research Perspectives*. New York: Grune and Stratton.

Literacy and Culture: The Problems and Promises of Bilingual Education (1996). Sacramento, CA: The LegiSchool Project.

Love, P.G., and A.G. Love (1995). *Enhancing Student Learning: Intellectual, Social, and Emotional Integration*. ASHE-ERIC Higher Education Report no. 4. Washington, DC: Graduate School of Education and Human Development, George Washington University.

Lüdi, G. (1996). "Mehrsprachigkeit." In H. Goebl et al. (eds.), *Contact Linguistics: An International Handbook of Contemporary Research*. Vol. 1. Berlin and New York: Walter de Gruyter.

Lundber, I., J. Frost, and O.-P. Peterson (1988). "Effects of an Extensive Program Stimulating Phonological Awareness in Preschool Children." *Reading Research Quarterly* 23: 264–284.

Lvovich, N. (1997). *Multilingual Self*. Mahwah, NJ: Lawrence Erlbaum.

MacDonaldson, J. (1989). *Becoming Partners with Children: From Play to Conversation*. Chicago: Riverside.

Mackay, W.F. (1968). "The description of bilingualism." In J.A. Fishman (ed.), *Readings in the Sociology of Language*. The Hague: Mouton.

Magiste, E. (1986). "Selected Issues in Second and Third Language Learning." In Y. Vaid (ed.), *Language Processing in Bilinguals: Psycholinguistics and Neuropsychological Perspectives*. Hillsdale, NJ: Lawrence Erlbaum.

Mahon, M. (1996). "Conversational Interactions Between Young Deaf Children and Their Families in Homes Where English Is Not the First Language." Ph.D. diss., Department of Human Communication, University College, London.

Mai, J.K., J.K. Assheuer, and G. Paxinos (1998). *Atlas of the Human Brain*. New York: Academic Press.

Malcomson, S.L. (1998). "The Varieties of Cosmopolitan Experience." In P. Cheah and B. Robbins (eds.), *Cosmopolitics: Thinking and Feeling Beyond the Nation*. Minneapolis: University of Minnesota Press.

Manolson, A., and H. Buck (1992). *It Takes Two to Talk*. Toronto, Ontario, Canada: The Hanen Centre.

Mason, D.G. (1995). "Why Bilingualism/Biculturalism Is Appropriate in Deaf Education." *Deaf Children's Society Newsletter*, September/October. Available: www.dww.deafworldweb.org/pub/b/bibl.mason.html.

May, S. (1994). "Making Multicultural Education Work." In *The Language and Education Library*. Vol. 7. London, UK: Taylor & Francis.

McAdams, S., and E. Bigand (eds.) (1993). *Thinking in Sound: The Cognitive Psychology of Human Audition*. Oxford: Clarendon Press.

McCarthy, T., and Watahomigie (1999). "Indigenous Community-Based Education in the U.S.A." In S. May (ed.) *Indigenous Community-Based Education*. Clevedon, U.K.: Multilingual Matters.

McConnell, M.W. (1996). "Don't Neglect the Little Platoons." In J. Cohen (ed.), *For Love of Country: Debating the Limits of Patriotism*. Boston: Beacon Press.

McCullough, C. (1977). *The Thorn Birds*. London: Warner Books.

McKenna, M., and J.D. Williams (1998). "Co-operation Between Families and Schools: 'What Works in Canada.'" *Research Papers in Education: Policy and Practice* 13, no. 1: 19–41.

McLaughlin, B. (1985). *Second-Language Acquisition in Childhood* Vol. 2, *School Age Children*. 2nd ed. Hillsdale, NJ: Lawrence Erlbaum.

McLaughlin, B., and R. Nation (1986). "Experts and Novices: An Information-processing Approach to the 'Good Language Learner' Problem." *Applied Psycholinguistics* 7: 41–56.

McLynn, F. (1990). *Burton: Snow upon the Desert*. London: John Murray.

Miller, N.E., and J. Dollard (1941). *Social Learning and Imitation*. New Haven, CT: Yale University Press.

Milroy, L., and P. Muysken (eds.) (1995). *One Speaker, Two Languages*. Cambridge: Cambridge University Press.

Molony, C. (ed.) (1977). *Deutsch im Kontakt mit andern Sprachen*. Kronberg, Germany: Scriptor Verlag.

Montague, N.S. (1997). "Critical Components for Two-Way Immersion Programs." *Bilingual Research Journal* 21 no. 4: 409–417.

Morgan, C. (2001). "Multilingualism and Multilingual Language Learning." In W. Wei-dinger (ed.) *Bilingualität und Schule? Ausbildung, wissenschaftliche Perspek-tiven und empirische Befunde.* Vienna: Öbv & Hpt (Österreichischer Bundesverlag & Verlag Hölder-Pichler-Tempsic).

Morley, J. (ed.) (1992). *Perspectives on Pronunciation, Learning and Teaching.* Alexandria, VA: TESOL.

Myhill, J. (1999). "Identity, Territoriality and Minority Language Survival." *Journal of Multilingualism and Multicultural Development* 20, no. 1: 34–50.

Naiman, N., et al. (1996). *The Good Language Learner.* 2nd ed. Clevedon, UK: Multilingual Matters.

Nanz, P. (2000). "L'Europa a più voci: Una concezione dialogica della sfera pubblica." *Il Mulino* 4, no. 390: 641–652.

National Research Council, Committee on Hearing, Bioacoustics, and Biomechanics, Assembly of Behavioral and Social Sciences (1982). *Prenatal Effects of Exposure to High-level Noise.* Report of Working Group 85. Washington, DC: National Academy Press.

Neumann, P.G. (1992). "Russian computer productivity in ascent in de scent exposure." *The Risks Digest* 13, no. 4: Available: www.catless.nel.ac.uk/Risks/13.04.html.

Ngugi, T. (1981). *Decolonizing the Mind: The Politics of Language in African Culture.* London: James Carey.

Nieto, S. (1996). *Affirming Diversity: The Sociopolitical Context of Multicultural Education.* New York: Longman.

Nullis, C. (2001). "Swiss-based Family Speaks in Many Tongues. Lessons for Learning?" AP news article. 7 January.

Nunberg, G. (2000). "Will the Internet Always Speak English." *The American Prospect* 11, no. 10. Available: www.prospect.org/VII/10/nunberg-g.html.

Nussbaum, M.C. (1996). "Patriotism and Cosmopolitanism." In J. Cohen (ed.), *For Love of Country: Debating the Limits of Patriotism.* Boston: Beacon Press.

Odent, M. (1992). *The Nature of Birth and Breastfeeding.* Westport, CT: Bergin & Garvey.

Ojemann, G.A., and H.A. Whitaker (1978). "The Bilingual Brain." *Archives of Neurology* 35: 409–412.

Oksaar, E. (1977). "On Being Trilingual." In C. Molony (ed.), *Deutsch im Kontakt mit andern Sprachen.* Kronberg, Germany: Scriptor Verlag.

Oller, D.K., R. Eilers, R. Urbano, and A.B. Cobo-Lewis (1997). "Development of Precursors to Speech in Infants Exposed to Two Languages." *Journal of Child Language* 24: 407–425.

Ondaatje, M. (1992). *The English Patient.* London: Macmillan.

Osborn, T.A. (2000). *Critical Reflection and the Foreign Language Classroom.* Westport, CT: Bergin & Garvey.

Osherson, D. (ed.) (1997). *An Invitation to Cognitive Science.* Vol. 1, *Language.* Vol. ed. L.R. Gleitman and M. Liberman. 2nd ed. Cambridge, MA: MIT Press.

Oxford, R.L. (1990). *Language Learning Strategies: What Every Teacher Should Know.* New York: Newbury House.

Panou, L., and D.F. Sewell (1981). "Cerebral Lateralisation in the Deaf: A Deaf Bilingual Pattern?" *Journal of Multilingual and Multicultural Development* 2: 45–51.

Papagno, C., and G. Vallar (1995). "Language and non-linguistic memory." *Quarterly Journal of Experimental Psychology* 48A, no. 1: 98–107.

Paradis, M. (1995). *Aspects of Bilingual Aphasia*. New York: Elsevier.

Paradis, M. (ed.) (1983). *Readings on Aphasia in Bilinguals and Polyglots*. Montreal, Canada: Didier.

Paulesu, E. (2001). "Dyslexia and Cultural Diversity and Biological Unity." *Science* 291: 2165.

Peery, J.C., I.W. Peery, and T.W. Draper (eds.) (1987). *Music and Child Development*. New York: Springer-Verlag.

Pennington, M.C. (1992). "Recent Research in Second Language Phonology: Implications for Practice." In J. Morley (ed.), *Perspectives on Pronunciation, Learning and Teaching*. Alexandria, VA: TESOL.

Perkins, D.N. (1981). *The Mind's Best Work*. Cambridge, MA: Harvard University Press.

Pinker, S. (1994). *The Language Instinct: How the Mind Creates Language*. New York: William Morrow.

Pinsky, R. (1996). "Eros Against Esperanto." In J. Cohen (ed.), *For Love of Country: Debating the Limits of Patriotism*. Boston: Beacon Press.

Polan, D. (1996). "Globalism's Localism." In R. Wilson and W. Dissanayake (eds.), *Global/Local: Cultural Production and the Transnational Imaginary*. Durham, NC: Duke University Press.

Pollock, D.C., and R.E. Van Reken (1999). *The Third Culture Kid Experience: Growing Up Among Worlds*. Yarmouth, ME: Intercultural Press.

Porter, R.P. (1996). *Forked Tongue: The Politics of Bilingual Education*. New Brunswick, NJ: Transaction.

Putnam, H. (1996). "Must We Choose Between Patriotism and Universal Reason?" In J. Cohen (ed.), *For Love of Country: Debating the Limits of Patriotism*. Boston: Beacon Press.

Quist, G. (2000). "Language Teaching at University: A Clash of Cultures." *Language and Education* 14, no. 2: 123–139.

Ramirez, J.D., S. Yuen, and D. Ramey (1991). *Final Report: Longitudinal Study of Structured English Immersion Strategy, Early-Exit and Late-Exit Transitional Bilingual Education Programs for Language-Minority Children*. San Mates, CA: Aguirre International.

Rayner, R.R., and S.R. Rayner (1998). *Cognitive Styles and Learning Strategies: Understanding Style Differences in Learning and Behaviour*. London: David Fulton.

Reagan, T. (1985). "The Deaf as a Linguistic Minority: Educational Considerations." *Harvard Educational Review* 53, no. 3: 399–415.

Rée, J. (1998). "Cosmopolitanism and the Experience of Nationality." In P. Cheah and B. Robbins (eds.), *Cosmopolitics: Thinking and Feeling Beyond the Nation*. Minneapolis: University of Minnesota Press.

Reid, J.M. (1995). *Learning Styles in the ESL/EFL Classroom*. Boston: Heinle & Heinle.

Ribbens, J. (1994). *Mothers and Their Children. A Feminist Sociology of Childrearing*. London: Sage.

Ricciardelli, L.A. (1992). "Creativity and Bilingualism." *Journal of Creative Behaviour* 26, no. 4: 242–254.

Rice, E. (1990). *Captain Sir Richard Francis Burton*. New York: Scribner's.

Rice, M.L. (ed.) (1996). *Towards a Genetics of Language*. Mahwah, NJ: Lawrence Erlbaum Associates.

Richards, T., S.R. Dager, D. Corina, S. Serafini, A.C. Heide, K. Steury, W. Strauss, C.E. Hayes, R.D. Abbott, S. Craft, D. Shaw, S. Possee, and V. Berniniger (1999). "Dyslexic Children Have Abnormal Brain Lactate Response to Reading-Related Language Tasks." *American Journal of Neuroradiology* 20, no. 9: 1393–1398.

Riess, M., and W. Yee (1993). "Attending to Auditory Events: The Role of Temporal Organization." In S. McAdams and E. Bigand (eds.), *Thinking in Sound: The Cognitive Psychology of Human Audition*. Oxford: Clarendon Press.

Roach, M. (1992). "Scents and Science." *Vogue*, (November), p. 208.

Robbins, B. (1995). "The Weird Heights: On Cosmopolitanism, Feeling, and Power." *Differences* 7, no. 1: 165–187.

Robbins, B. (1998). "Comparative Cosmopolitanisms." In P. Cheah and B. Robbins (eds.), *Cosmopolitics: Thinking and Feeling Beyond the Nation*. Minneapolis: University of Minnesota Press.

Robbins, B. (1999). *Feeling Global: Internationalism in Distress*. New York: New York University Press.

Romaine, S. (1995). *Bilingualism*. 2nd ed. Oxford: Blackwell.

Roman, B.D. (1999). *Let's Move Overseas: The International Edition of Let's Make a Move!* Wilmington, NC: BR Anchor.

Ronjat, J. (1913). *Le development du langage observe chez un enfant bilingüe*. Paris: Librarie Ancienne H. Champion.

Rooney, K., et al. (eds.) (1999). *Encarta World English Dictionary*. London: Bloomsbury.

Runco, M.A., and R.S. Albert (1990). *Theories of Creativity*. Newbury Park, CA: Sage.

Ryman, D. (1993). *Aromatherapy: The Complete Guide to Plant and Flower Essences for Health and Beauty*. New York: Bantam Books.

Sarup, M. (1996). *Identity, Culture and the Postmodern World*. Edinburgh: Edinburgh University Press.

Schaetti, B.F. (1995). "Families on the Move: Working Together to Meet the Challenge." In B.F. Schaetti (ed.), *Moving On: Strategies for the Homeward Bound*. London: FOCUS.

Schaetti, B.F. (1996). "Phoenix Rising: A Question of Cultural Identity." *Perspectives*. Available: www.transition-dynamics.com.

Scherer, H.S. (1992). "Heinrich Schliemanns Sprachlernmethode und Möglichkeiten ihrer Nutzung in der modernen Sprachdidaktik." *Neusprachliche Mitteilungen aus Wissenschaft und Praxis* 45, no. 3: 151–158.

Schneider, A. (2001). "A University Plans to Promote Languages by Killing Its Language Department." *Chronicle of Higher Education* 9 March.

Segal, W. (1995). "Parabola: Myth, tradition and the search for meaning." In *Language and Meaning* (August), 8.

Seidl, M. (1998). "Language and Culture: Towards a Transcultural Competence in Language Learning." *Forum for Modern Language Studies* 34, no. 2: 101–113.

Serafine, M.L. (1988). *Music as Cognition: The Development of Thought in Sound*. New York: Columbia University Press.

Shepard, S. (1997). *Managing Cross-cultural Transition: A Handbook for Corporations, Employees, and Their Families*. New York: Aletheia.

Shore, C. (2000). *Building Europe: The Cultural Politics of European Integration*. London: Routledge.

Siegal, M. (1997). *Knowing Children: Experiments in Conversation and Cognition*. 2nd ed. East Essex: Psychology Press.

Siegler, R.S., and E. Jenkins (1989). *How Children Discover New Strategies*. Hillsdale, NJ: Lawrence Erlbaum.

Silver, H., F. Richard, W. Strong, and M.J. Perini (2000). *So Each May Learn: Integrating Learning Styles and Multiple Intelligences*. Alexandria, VA: Association for Supervision and Curriculum Development.

Sims, R.R., and S. Sims (eds.) (1995). *The Importance of Learning Styles: Understanding the Implications for Learning, Course Design, and Education*. Westport, CT: Greenwood.

Skutnabb-Kangas, T. (1976). *Teaching Migrant Children's Mother Tongue and Learning the Language of the Host Country in the Context of the Socio-cultural Situation of the Migrant Family*. Tampere, Finland: Tutkimuksia Research Reports.

Slobin, D.I. (ed.) (1985–1992). *The Cross-linguistic Study of Language Acquisition*. 3 vols. Hillsdale, NJ: Lawrence Erlbaum.

Sloboda, J.A. (1985). *The Musical Mind: The Cognitive Psychology of Music*. London: Oxford University Press.

Smith, C.D. (1996). *Strangers at Home: Essays on the Effects of Living Overseas and Coming "Home" to a Strange Land*. New York: Aletheia.

Smith, G.A. (ed.) (1993). *Public Schools That Work: Creating Community*. New York: Routledge.

Smith, L.E. (ed.) (1987). *Discourse Across Cultures: Strategies in World Englishes*. London and New York: Prentice-Hall.

Snow, C.E., and M. Hoefnagel-Höhle (1978). "The Critical Period for Language Acquisition: Evidence from Second Language Learning." *Child Development* 49: 114–128.

Springer, S., and G. Deutsch (1997). *Left Brain/Right Brain: Perspective from Cognitive Neuroscience*. New York: Worth.

Steel, D., and C.J. Alderson (1995). "Metalinguistic Knowledge, Language Aptitude and Language Proficiency." In D. Graddol and S. Thomas (eds.), *Language in a Changing Europe: Papers from the Annual Meeting of the British Association for Applied Linguistics, Held at the University of Salford, September 1993*. Clevedon, UK: Multilingual Matters.

Stein, C.B. (1986). *Sink or Swim: The Politics of Bilingual Education*. New York: Praeger.

Steiner, G. (1998). *After Babel: Aspects of Language and Translation*. 3rd ed. Oxford: Oxford University Press.

Sternberg, R.J. (1990). *Metaphors of Mind: Conceptions of the Nature of Intelligence*. Cambridge: Cambridge University Press.

Sternberg, R.J. (ed.) (1988). *The Nature of Creativity: Contemporary Psychological Perspectives*. New York: Cambridge University Press.

Stich, S.P., and T.A. Warfield (eds.) (1994). *Mental Representation: A Reader*. Cambridge, MA: Blackwell. 1994.

Storr, A. (1992). *Music, Brain and Body*. New York: Free Press.

Storti, C. (1997). *The Art of Crossing Cultures*. Yarmouth, ME: Intercultural Press.

Strevens, P. (1987). "Cultural Barriers to Language Learning." In L.E. Smith (ed.), *Discourse Across Cultures: Strategies in World Englishes*. London and New York: Prentice-Hall.

Tagore, R. (1921). *The Home and the World*. London: Macmillan.

Therborn, G. (1995). *European Modernity and Beyond: The Trajectory of European Societies 1945–2000*. London: Sage.

Theroux, P. (1986). *Sunrise with Seamonsters*. Harmondsworth, UK: Penguin.

Thogersen, K.H. (1994). "Children on the Move—Culture Shock." Paper presented at Action for Dyslexia Conference. Brussels, Belgium: Dyslexia International—Tools & Technology, November.

Tileston, D.W. (2000). *10 Best Teaching Practices: How Brain Research, Learning Styles and Standards Define Teaching Competencies*. London: Corwin Press.

Tishman, S., D.N. Perkins, and E. Jay (1995). *The Thinking Classroom*. Boston: Allyn and Bacon.

Titon, J.T., D.P. McAllester, M. Slobin, and D. Lock (eds.) (1996). *Worlds of Music: An Introduction to the Music of the World's Peoples*. New York: Shirmer Books.

Todorov, T. (1982). *La Conquête de l'Amérique: La Question de l'autre*. Paris: Seuil.

Tokuhama-Espinosa, T. (2001). *Raising Multilingual Children: Foreign Language Acquisition and Children*. Westport, CT: Bergin & Garvey.

Tomatis, A. (1996). *The Ear and Language*. Trans. B.M. Thompson. Norval, Ontario: Moulin.

Tomatis, A.A. (1960). "Conditionnement Audio-Vocal." *Bulletin de l'Academie National de Medicine*, 144, no. 11 et 12: 197–200.

Tomatis, A.A. (1981). *La Nuit uterine*. Paris Editions Stock.

Tomlinson, J. (1999). *Globalisation and Culture*. Cambridge: Polity Press.

Tosi, A., and C. Leung (eds.) (1999). *Rethinking Language Education: From a Monolingual to a Multilingual Perspective*. London: Centre for Information on Language Teaching and Research.

Treanor, P. (2000). *Making Europe Multilingual*. Hanover: Verlag Heinz Heise.

Trehub, S.E., and L.J. Trainor (1993). "Listening Strategies in Infancy." In S. McAdams and E. Bigand (eds.), *Thinking in Sound: The Cognitive Psychology of Human Audition*. Oxford: Clarendon Press.

Trudgill, P. (1975). *Accent, Dialect and the School*. London, UK: Open University Press.

Trudgill, P. (1992). "Sociolinguistics." In T. McArthur (ed.), *The Oxford Companion to the English Language*. Oxford, UK: Oxford University Press.

Tsuda, Y. (1994). "The Diffusion of English: Its Impact on Culture and Communication." *Keio Communication Review* 16, 48–61.

Tsuda, Y. (1996). *Shinryaku-suru Eigo, Hangeki-suru Nihongo* (The Invading English, the Counterattacking Japanese). Tokyo: PHP. 1996.

Tucker, R.G. (1995). "Some Thoughts Concerning Innovative Language Education Programs." *Journal of Multilingual and Multicultural Development* 17, no. 24: 315–320.

Turkle, S. (1995). *Life on the Screen*. New York: Simon and Schuster.

United States Committee on Education and the Workforce (1998). *Head Start Reauthorization*. Washington, DC: U.S. Government Printing Office.

Vaid, Y. (ed.) (1986). *Language Processing in Bilinguals: Psycholinguistics and Neuropsychological Perspectives*. Hillsdale, NJ: Laurence Erlbaum.

Vallar, G., and C. Papagno (1993). "Preserved Vocabulary Acquisition in Down's Syndrome: The Role of Phonological Sort-term Memory." *Cortex* 29, no. 3: 467–483.

Van Heteeren, C.F., P.F. Boekkooi, H.W. Jongsma, and J.G. Nijhuis (2000). "Fetal learning and memory." *The Lancet* 356, no. 9236: 1169–1170.

Villamil Tinajero, J., and A.F. Ada (1997). *The Power of Two Languages: Literacy and Biliteracy for Spanish Speaking Student.* New York: Macmillan/McGraw-Hill.

Visser, J. (1997). *Multilingualism in a Pervasive Learning Environment.* New York: UNESCO.

Vygotsky, L.S. (1962). *Thought and Language.* Ed. and trans. E. Hanfmann and G. Vakar. Cambridge, MA, and New York: MIT Press and John Wiley & Sons.

Wakefield, J. (1992). *Creative Thinking: Problem Solving Skills and the Arts Orientation.* Norwood, NJ: Ablex.

Wallraff, B. (2000). "What global language?" *The Atlantic Monthly*, November. Available: www.theatlantic.com/issues/2000/11/wallraff.htm.

Walzer, M. (1996). "Spheres of Affection." In J. Cohen (ed.), *For Love of Country: Debating the Limits of Patriotism.* Boston: Beacon Press.

Watson, I. (1991). "Phonological Processes in Two Languages." In E. Bialystok (ed.), *Language Processing in Bilingual Children.* Cambridge, UK: Cambridge University Press.

Watts, R.J., and J.J. Smolicz (eds.) (1997). *Cultural Democracy and Ethnic Pluralism: Multicultural and Multilingual Policies in Education.* New York and Frankfurt: Peter Lang.

Wei, L. (1998). "Language Maintenance and Loss of Ethnic Communities in Britain: What Schools Can and Cannot Do." Paper presented the Children and Multilingualism conference. University of North London.

Wei, L., N. Miller, and B. Dodd (1997). "Distinguishing Communicative Difference from Language Disorder in Bilingual Children." *Bilingual Family Newsletter* 14, no. 1: 1–3.

Weinrich, U. (1953). *Languages in Contact.* New York: Linguistic Circle of New York.

Weisberg, R.W. (1993). *Creativity: Beyond the Myth of Genius.* New York: W.H. Freeman.

Werker, J.F. (1997). "Exploring Developmental Changes in Cross-language Speech Perception." In D. Osherson (ed.), *An Invitation to Cognitive Science.* Vol. 1, *Language.* Vol. ed. L.R. Gleitman and M. Liberman. 2nd ed., Cambridge, MA: MIT Press.

Werker, J., and R.C. Tees (1984). "Cross-Language Speech Perception: Evidence for Perceptual Reorganization during the First Years of Life." Infant Behavior and Development 7: 49–63.

Werlen, I. (1997). "Mehrsprachigkeit und Europa." In C. Allemann-Ghionda (ed.), *Multikultur und Bildung in Europa. Multiculture et éducation en Europe.* 2nd ed. Bern: Peter Lang.

West, M.L. (1991). *The Ringmaster.* London and Melbourne: William Heinemann.

Whitaker, H.A., D. Bub, and S. Leventer (1981). "Neurolinguistic Aspects of Language Acquisition and Bilingualism." In H. Winitz, (ed.), *Native Language and Foreign Language Acquisition.* New York: New York Academy of Sciences.

Widdicombe, S. (1997). "Code-switching, Coining and Interference in Trilingual First Language Acquisition: A Case Study." M.Sc. thesis, Aston University, Birmingham, UK.

Wierzbicka, A. (1986). "Does Language Reflect Culture? Evidence from Australian English." *Language in Society* 15: 349–374.

Wierzbicka, A. (1997). *Understanding Cultures Through Their Key Words: English, Russian, Polish, German, and Japanese.* Oxford: Oxford University Press.

Wild, R. (2000). *Raising Curious, Creative, Confident Kids: The Pestalozzi Experiment in Child-based Education*. Boston: Shambhala.

Wilke, M. (1995). *Scent of a Market*. Riverton, NJ: American Demographics.

Willis, M., and V. Kindle-Hodson (1999). *Discover Your Child's Learning Style: Children Learn in Unique Ways—Here's the Key to Every Child's Learning Success*. Indianapolis, IN: Prima.

Wilson, R., and W. Dissanayake (eds.) (1996). *Global/Local: Cultural Production and the Transnational Imaginary*. Durham, NC: Duke University Press.

Winitz, H. (ed.) (1981). *Native Language and Foreign Language Acquisition*. New York: New York Academy of Sciences.

Wodak, R. (ed.) (1989). *Language, Power and Ideology: Studies in Political Discourse*. Amsterdam: John Benjamin's Publishing Co.

Wong Fillmore, L. (1991). "When learning a second language means losing the first." *Early Childhood Research Quarterly* 6, no. 3: 323–346.

Woods, P. (1999). *Bilingual Education and Bilingualism*, no. 16. Clevedon, UK: Multilingual Matters.

Worringer, W. (1963). *Abstraction and Empathy*. Trans. Michael Bullock. Munich: FUNDUS.

Ziegler, E. (1986). "Why Our Children Aren't Reading." Foreword to R. Flesch, *Why Johnny Can't Read*. 2nd ed. New York: Harper & Row.

WEB REFERENCES

Annenberg CPB, Project. "The Universal Language: Math." www.learner.org/exhibits/dailymath/language.html

AsiaWeek.com magazine editorial. (2000). "English imperialism: The Japanese Have More to Gain Than Lose by Learning the Language." *Asia Week* 26, no. 13 (7 April). www.asiaweek.com.asiaweek/magazine/2000/0407/ed.english.html

Babies and speech perception. www.jhu.edu/njhumag/02 98web/baby.html

Campbell Union School District Bilingual Program, Santa Clara County, California. www.sccoe.k12.ca.us/future10.htm

Damico, J.S. (1995). "Language Difficulties in Multicultural Children: Are semilinguals Different or Disordered?" www.ucs.usl.edu/~jsd6498/damico/ottawa-notes. html

Directory of two-way bilingual immersion programs. http://www.cal.org/twi/directory/

Down's Syndrome. (1998). "Bilingual children with Down's syndrome." In *People with Special Needs: Down's Syndrome Report*. Autumn. http://www.he.net/~alton web/ec/downsyndrome/pwsnfall98.html

Down's syndrome issues information. *www.down-syndrome.info/*

Educational Demographics Office, State of California. www.cde.ca.gov/demographics Escuela Montessori de Montopolis, Austin, TX. "Learning in two languages: Escuela's dual-language program." www.main.org/escuela/dual.htm

Family.go.com. *Widening Horizons: Parent Advice for Bilinguals*. www.family.go.com/Features/family_1999_08/penn/penn891language/penn89language3.htm

Gold, D. (1988). "Two Languages, One Aim: 'Two-way' Learning." *Education Week on the Web*. 20 January. www.edweek.org/ew/1988/07410009.h07

Grosjean, Francois. "The Right of the Deaf Child to Grow Up Bilingual." www.unine.ch/itlp/pub/rightdeafchild-en.html

Hauser, M. (2001). Department of Psychology, Program in Neurosciences, Mind, Brain and Behavior, Speech and Hearing Sciences Faculty, MIT-Harvard-MGH. www.wjh.harvard/edu//~mnkylab/LabPersonnel.html

Henderson, A. (2001). "Has Internet Spelt the End of the English Language?" 9 April. www.smh.com.au/news/0104/09/features/features2.html

Hendricks, M. (1998). "Origins of Babble." *John Hopkins Magazine*. February. http://www.jhu.edu/~jhumag/0298web/baby.html

Linguasphere. (2000). "What Languages Are Most Spoken in the World." 25 February. www.linguasphere.org/language.html

Mason, D.G. "Why Bilingualism/Biculturalism Is Appropriate in Deaf Education." Deaf Education Program, York University. www.deafworldweb.org/pub/b/bibi.mason.html

Miner, B. (1999). "Bilingual Education: New Visions for a New Era." *Rethinking Schools*, 13, no. 4. www.rethinkingschool.org/Archives/13_04/newera.htm

Multilingual Brain. "Current research on the multilingual brain." University of Basel. www.unibas.ch/the multilingualbrain/

MuSICA Research Notes. (1997). "The Musical Infant and the Roots Roots of Consonance." *Music and Science Data Base* 4, no. 1 (Spring). www.musica.cnlm.uci.edu/index.html

National Clearinghouse for Bilingual Education. www.ncbe.gwu.edu/

Nunberg, G. (2000). "Will the Internet Always Speak English?" www.prospect.org/vii/10/nunberg-g.html

Sancar, F. (1999). "Music and the Brain: Processing and Responding." Response to Biology 202 at Bryn Mawr University. http://serendip.brynmawr.edu/bb/neuro99/web1/Sancar.html

Tramo, M., as quoted in W.J. Cromie. (1997). "How your brain listens to music." *Harvard Gazette*, 13 November. www.hno.harvard.edu/science/archives/biology/brain_music_13.Nov.97.html

Treanor, P. (2000). *Making Europe multilingual*. Hanover: Verlag Heinz Heise. www.heise.de/tp/english/inhalt/te/1155/1.html University of California. Two-Way Immersion Studies. www.cal.org/cal/ab/2way

Visser, J. (1997). *Multilingualism in a Pervasive Learning Environment*. New York: UNESCO. www.unesco.org/education/educprog/lwf/doc/multi.html

Authors' Home Pages

Dr. Cristina Allemann-Ghionda www.allemann-ghionda.ch www.uni-koeln.dc/philfak
Andrea Bader-Rusch www.thenewstorktimes.com
Suzanne Barron-Hauwaert www.ualberta.ca/~german/ejournal/barron.htm
Raymond Federman www.federman.com
Maria Johnson www.multilingualmunchkins.com
Tracey Tokuhama-Espinosa www.Multi-Faceta.com

Subject Index

Name Index

This index is designed to facilitate research by indicating all of the authors who may have contributed to a cited work. As authors listed here may not be the main or first named author of a given work, you may not find all of the names here cited on the page referenced.

About the Editor and Contributors

TRACEY TOKUHAMA-ESPINOSA is the author of *Raising Multilingual Children: Foreign Language Acquisition and Children* (Bergin & Garvey, 2001). She has been a teacher, counselor, and researcher since 1990 in South America, Asia, and Europe and is on the Editorial Board of the *Bilingual Family Newsletter*. She received her Master's of Education with distinction from Harvard University (for work in philanthropy and education), and undergraduate degrees in international relations (B.A.) and mass communications (B.S.) from Boston University (magna cum laude). A native Californian, Tracey currently lives with her three multilingual children and Ecuadorian diplomat husband in Geneva, Switzerland, where she conducts workshops on foreign language development and learning for schools, businesses, and the diplomatic community. She is the founder and project director for Geneva's first interactive children's museum on themes of the environment, Planète Exploration (www.planete exploration.com).

CRISTINA ALLEMANN-GHIONDA is a full professor of education at the University of Cologne, Germany. Her teaching and publications focus on intercultural and comparative education, as well as multilingual issues. From 1990 until 2000, she was a lecturer and researcher at the universities of Zurich, Bern, and Geneva (Switzerland), and Münster (Germany). Before undertaking her university career, she worked for several years as a teacher, then as an organizer of adult education programs for migrants, and finally as a freelance researcher and education consultant. Born in Rome, she was raised as a multilingual child and studied in seven Latin American and European countries, She presently lives in Cologne and Basel Switzerland. She can be contacted at Cristina.Allemann-Ghiondn@uni_koeln.de.

SARA ACKERMAN AOYAMA was a graduate student in TESOL at the School of International Training in 1994. Previous to this, she spent twelve years in Japan and was an instructor at Tokyo Tanki Daigaku in Tokyo. She currently is a freelance Japanese–English translator, and resides in Brattleboro, Vermont, where she is raising two bilingual children.

ANDREA BADER-RUSCH is founder of *The New Stork Times* in Zurich, Switzerland. Ms. Bader-Rusch has been working with children and investigating the "human potential" since 1967, when she began her career as a teacher and founding member of the Film-Media Center for the School District of Philadelphia in the United States. She continued weaving this "red thread" through her life as director of a foundation supporting educational and health projects for women and children worldwide. Since 1995 she has managed her own family support service, The Stork Knows, where she works with expectant parents as childbirth educator and doula, and offers a variety of courses facilitated by professionals that support parents and children. Ms. Bader-Rusch is also the editor of *The New Stork Times, Parenting Source for Switzerland*, a monthly publication in English. She is the mother of two daughters, and lives in Zurich, Switzerland.

SUZANNE BARRON-HAUWAERT is a teacher of English as a foreign language who has taught adults in Japan, primary school children in Poland, and at the Central European University in Budapest. In 1999 she completed her master's degree in education with Sheffield University, England, and her final dissertation allowed Suzanne to study an area of personal interest—families using three languages. She is English, married to a Frenchman, and they have lived with their two young children as expatriates in Hungary, Egypt, and Switzerland. Suzanne plans to do further research in this field, particularly on families living with two or more languages, and is on the educational board of *The Bilingual Family Newsletter*. She is currently writing a book on parental strategies within multilingual families. Contact Suzanne at opol_uk@yahoo .co.uk.

RAYMOND FEDERMAN, born in France, is a novelist, poet, essayist, and translator who writes in both French and English. He also translates his work from one language to another—or rather, as he prefers to call the rendering of his work into the other language, he transacts it. He has published some two dozen books in both languages.

JENNIFER FRENGEL was born and raised in northern California. She received her interdisciplinary studies (education, sociology, psychology) degree at the University of California at Berkeley in 2000. Her studies included one year at the University of Padua in Italy. Her work on new curricular structures for bilingual education in the United States is at the heart of her essay on two-way immersion programs. After spending time in Switzerland, Ms. Frengel has returned to California to continue her research.

MANUELA GONZÁLEZ-BUENO is an assistant professor of foreign language education at the University of Kansas. She was born in Seville, Spain, where she earned her undergraduate degree in Spanish philology. After teaching English as a foreign language in a private secondary school, she moved to the United States to pursue doctoral studies in applied linguistics. She has taught Spanish as a foreign language and methodology of foreign language teaching at the College of William and Mary, Penn State University, and the University of Louisiana at Lafayette, and is currently teaching courses in foreign language education and TESOL at the University of Kansas. She and her husband, Michael Marksberry, have one daughter, Alicia, who is growing up bilingual. Manuela's work is focused on drawing connections between foreign language acquisition theories and theories of bilingualism. She can be contacted at mgbueno@ukans.edu or at mmarksberry@mindspring.com.

KONRAD GUNESCH, born in Romania, has a law degree from the University of Bonn (Germany) and a master's degree in contemporary European cultures from the universities of Bath and Paris. He has studied and worked in seven European countries and in Canada, and is currently a doctoral student in education at the University of Bath. His Ph.D. thesis, "The Relationship Between Multilingualism and Cosmopolitanism," forms the basis of his essay in this volume. Mr. Gunesch is fluent in ten languages—German, English, French, Spanish, Italian, Swedish, Portuguese, Dutch, Catalan, and Norwegian—and is currently learning Greek. He can be contacted at edpkg@bath.ac.uk.

MARIA JOHNSON was born to an American military family, and grew up in Florida, Italy, Hawaii, and California, where she was exposed to many cultures and languages. She received her interdisciplinary studies (Russian and Italian) degree at the University of California, Riverside, in 1992. Her program included one term at the University of Perugia in Italy. She is the mother of three children, whom she and her husband are bringing up to speak English, Italian, and Korean. She is the founder of Multilingual Munchkins, both an Internet and and an interperson group that helps parents who are raising their children with more than one language, or who are considering introducing another language. Besides promoting and expanding her Internet presence, she manages a language center for children in her local area.

NICOLA KÜPELIKILINÇ is a psychologist who works with numerous multilingual children and youths in Offenbach/Main, Germany. Nicola is English, her husband is Turkish, and they have two trilingual children. Nicola can be contacted via E-mail: kuepelikilinc@t-online.de.

MARIE PETRAITIS has a B.A. in linguistics and Japanese from the Australian National University, Canberra. She currently lives in Switzerland with her husband and two children, and has been working with bilingual children on their English language skills for several years.